Arthur Rau
11-3-92

D1164056

Experience, Reason and God

**STUDIES IN PHILOSOPHY
AND THE HISTORY OF PHILOSOPHY**

Founding editor: John K. Ryan (1960-1978)
General editor: Jude P. Dougherty

Studies in Philosophy
and the History of Philosophy   Volume 8

Experience,
Reason
and God

edited by Eugene Thomas Long

THE CATHOLIC UNIVERSITY OF AMERICA PRESS
Washington, D.C.

"Religious Experience" by Hywel Lewis is printed with permission of the International Society for Metaphysics. This paper was delivered at the August, 1977 meeting of the International Society for Metaphysics held in Jerusalem.

Library of Congress Cataloging in Publication Data
Main entry under title:

Experience, reason, and God.

(Studies in philosophy and the history of philosophy; v. 8)
Includes index.
1. Experience (Religion)—Addresses, essays, lectures. 3. God—Proof—Addresses, essays, lectures. I. Long, Eugene Thomas. II. Series. B21.S78 vol. 8 [BL53]   200'.1   80-11334
ISBN 0-8132-0553-0

CONTENTS

94632

INTRODUCTION:
EXPERIENCE, REASON AND GOD

Eugene Thomas Long

There have been two basic approaches to the philosophy of religion in the history of western thought. One places primary emphasis on reason and the other places primary emphasis on experience. The rationalist approach has tended to ignore or treat inadequately the experiential dimension of religious faith, and to think of God as an inferred entity and of religious faith as the acceptance of a theistic hypothesis. Against this those writers who place primary emphasis on experience have argued that experience of God is the indispensable ground for belief in God, that arguments for the existence of God have no compelling force independent of the experiential dimension of religion, and that religious faith is a commitment which differs from the tentative kind of commitment that is associated with the acceptance of an hypothesis.

The "empiricist" approach to the philosophy of religion has a long history in the western tradition but this approach has tended to dominate religious thought since the nineteenth century. Along with this domination, however, has come at times a tendency to separate the experiential from the rational and to the extent that this has happened the rationalist is correct to argue that one is left only with reports of some private mental states which can at best be expressed in ways that lead to fideism.

There are a number of factors which have tended to bring about this separation of the ways of reason and experience and, although I cannot develop them fully in this essay, I do want to give some indications of what they are. Certainly one of the key factors accounting for this separation of reason and experience is to be found in the frequent equation of 'experiences' with 'mental events' or 'feeling states,' where the intent is to distinguish between experiences and references to the external world, the latter being where the question of truth claims is held to be relevant. This limiting of the notion of experience stands in sharp contrast to ordinary notions in which experiences are said to intend or refer to that which is experienced. Thus I may talk of an experience *of* being loved, *of* teaching students and so forth. And it is precisely this intentional characteristic of experience some would argue which permits me to talk about experiences being appropriate or inappropriate to some situation. The tendency to equate experiences with subjective events

1

is most typically associated with positivism where experience is understood as the passive reception of uninterpreted sense data. However, this also forms the background to those contemporary approaches to philosophy of religion which in attempting to speak about God within the limits of the verifiability or falsifiability criteria of meaning have reduced talk of God to the expression of an attitude for which no rational support can be given. And even where some of these philosophers attempt to get beyond these limits by reference to Wittgenstein's claim that language is a form of life and by his analysis of the concept 'seeing-as' there is a tendency in the final analysis to remain within a more subjectivist account of experience thus raising problems in efforts to speak of the justification of religious faith. The tendency to separate experience and reason can also be seen in the works of many existentialists who argue that God is not an object of thought, that there can be no religious *Weltanschauung* and that one can know and speak of God only out of a relation to Him. Although this position has had the value of preserving the element of unconditional commitment considered by many to be essential to religious faith, it comes at a significant cost when one is unable to make a reasonable case for belief in God or even say anything significant about God.

The tendency to divorce experience and reason has resulted at times in what appears to be an impasse, one which Basil Mitchell has summarized quite succinctly in saying "Either God is at best an inferred entity and faith in God is no more than acceptance of a hypothesis; or God is an experienced reality about which rational doubt is, at least for the one who experiences, impossible."[1] The idea for this collection of essays originated with the belief that a more adequate theory of experience is needed if one is to get beyond this impasse in which argument and language are separated from experience, and from the observation that philosophers and theologians from various traditions are showing a renewed interest in theories of experience at a time when the various forms of fideism represented in contemporary thought are coming under sharp attack. Many recent Thomists, pragmatists, process philosophers, phenomenologists and analytical philosophers have stressed the experiential element in religion but emphasize that experience adequately understood has more to do with such concepts as meeting and encounter than with feeling and undergoing.

It is probably the case that few, if any, persons become religious as a direct result of arguments and perhaps most persons would agree that there is an experiential dimension to religious faith. However it is an error to identify this experiential dimension with mental states or attitudes which are divorced from one's being in the world, one's behavior, thoughts and beliefs.

---

[1] *The Justification of Religious Belief* (London: MacMillan, 1973), p. 112.

Experience in religion, as in other dimensions of life, takes place in a context in which one is related to other persons and things and it cannot be divorced from one's history and tradition. It is the belief that experience is divorced from one's beliefs in the world which accounts in part for the failure of more rationally oriented philosophers of religion to treat adequately the experiential dimension of religion. But if an adequate theory of experience can be developed showing it to be the product of the interaction between persons and things in the world, the rationalist may be more willing to consider its role in religion. It is this understanding of experience in terms of interaction which allows us to judge experiences as appropriate or inappropriate, rational or irrational. I cannot make of experience merely what I will. There is some sense in which it is given. Yet it is not given independently of my conceptual framework. There is a reciprocal relationship between me and what is given requiring an interpretative act on my part and it is in this that my efforts to understand and explain are rooted. Interpreting, understanding and explaining then are not activities contrary to experience but are part and parcel of my efforts to articulate my encounters with persons and things in the world. In this sense experience has a social dimension for it is in interpreting that I encounter others, interact with them and compare judgments. This means that experience is not self-authenticating. It is always subject to error and misinterpretation and I must try to give an account of the data of experience which neither ignores nor distorts it.

If experience is understood in somewhat the way that I have suggested, there should be less reluctance on the part of "empiricists" to look to the role of reason and argument in religion. It may be, probably is the case, that the type of argument that is relevant to religious faith is not of a strictly deductive or inductive kind. But in this religion probably differs little from other humanistic disciplines. I do not intend by this to ignore the differences between the subject matter of philosophy of religion and other humanistic disciplines. The crucial problem after all for philosophers of religion and theologians is that of justifying belief in and speaking significantly of the transcendent dimension within experience. I do want to suggest that in religion, as in other fields, we are faced with presenting and representing patterns of experience which go towards supporting a conclusion. Perhaps another way of putting this point is to say that religious faith in the presence of the transcendent involves beliefs that such and such is the case and this requires the kind of justification that can come only by way of giving an adequate account of the data of experience.

In a related way I would argue that language of religious faith is rooted in experience but looks to the language of metaphysics in an effort to illuminate and justify religious assertions. Metaphysical models suggest patterns for relating the various data of experience including the religious dimension of experience. Such an approach need not, I believe, result in the assimilation of religious faith to metaphysical theory. Ultimately the religious form of life is not merely a matter of making true assertions. The language of faith is a language of commitment, of self-involvement, in which one expresses a new self-understanding in relation to the presence of the divine and a metaphysical theory adequate to this experience must point to the primacy of the practical, to the self-involving language of religious faith which opens up the possibility of experiencing in certain ambiguous events the presence of God.

I am not claiming in these introductory remarks to have provided either a fully developed theory of experience or a justification for this understanding of experience and its place in the philosophy of religion. I am suggesting that an empirical approach to the philosophy of religion somewhat along the lines that I have sketched may provide an avenue beyond the impasse encountered in many contemporary discussions of religion and that this approach does depend on some of the conditions which I have mentioned. I should also say that while the authors of essays in this book were invited to contribute to a volume, the general theme of which is reason, experience, and God, it was intended that contributions come from persons representing different philosophical traditions. It would be misleading to suggest that they are at one on the understanding of experience, its relation to reason and argument in religion, and its relation to the language of religion. However they are at one in their efforts to move beyond the fideistic tendencies of much recent philosophy of religion and in their appreciation of the experiential dimension of religion. It is expected that these essays will contribute to a greater awareness of the role of experience in the several traditions represented by these authors and that some of the foundations for an"empirical" approach to the philosophy of religion will have been clarified.

University of South Carolina

1 EXPERIENCE, ANALOGY AND RELIGIOUS INSIGHT

John E. Smith

It would, I believe, be generally admitted that the present situation in theology and philosophical discussion concerning religion is marked with some confusion and not a little uncertainty. The state of affairs, moreover, is quite paradoxical; there has been widespread erosion of religious concern as the result of an increasing secularization of society, and this erosion is manifest, among other ways, in scepticism about the possibility of any rationality or intelligibility in religion whatsoever. On the other hand, there is side by side with this development an upsurge of interest in finding some purpose in life which is essentially religious, but it expresses itself exclusively in forms of fervent immediacy, a passion to pursue the oneiric, the exotic and the occult. Meditation, mysticism, and fascination with demons have emerged as very powerful concerns. One of the reasons for this turn of events is the neglect of the experiential aspect of religion; a suppressed dimension usually breaks forth anew in ways that are turbulent and frenetic. We shall return to this problem later on; at this point I am concerned primarily with the intellectual climate and some explanation of why we seem to be so much in need of an intellectual orientation in religious thought.

Obviously many factors have been at work, including the great variety of winds of doctrine that blow, the fragmentation of modern life, and the complexity of the religious situation in a pluralistic society. More basic, however, than any of these factors is that we are still experiencing the aftermath of the decline of the metaphysical traditions which had for so many centuries served as the *firmament* or medium for the articulation of religious insight. Our confusion and disorientation are due largely to the lack of a consensus as to where a new firmament can be found.

Let me clarify what is meant by a firmament for theology or a medium of expression for the articulation of religious insight. If we consider the beginnings of the Christian theological tradition we see that no thinker was able to pass directly from the many forms of primary religious expression found in the Bible to theology or the conceptual and systematic formulation of central ideas concerning God, man, the world and the relations holding be-

tween them. Some form of "logos" or medium of expression is required if
one is to develop a body of doctrine from the variety of materials which the
Bible makes available. One must work with parables, exhortations, poems,
stories, chronicles, moral prescriptions and, as seen in the case of St. Paul,
explicit theological interpretation. To arrive from such a multiplicity at a
theological form which expresses the religious meaning of the range of experience behind the biblical writings it is necessary to have a framework of
concepts and principles governed by logical canons. Since God, moreover,
is not a matter of ordinary experience and perception but needs to be apprehended through another, the theologian must have an accessible plane on
which to project the insight he seeks to express about the divine nature. A
framework of concepts and principles together with the projection plane is
what I call a "firmament"; no system of theology is ever without one.

The classical instance of such a firmament is found in the theological
tradition which we associate with Augustine, Anselm and Bonaventura, the
tradition of "faith seeking understanding." For these thinkers the things of
God can be understood in the light of Being, Good and Truth with the help
of similitudes and analogies drawn from experience. With a reflective dialectic reminiscent of Plato as their rational instrument and the three forms
Esse, Verum, Bonum, later to be called the "transcendentals," they sought
to show the intelligibility of faith, eschewing a merely external authority as
a guarantee. Augustine, it is important to note, spoke of understanding but
not of *proof,* and in this sense he did not assume the bolder rationalism of
Anselm who proposed to prove religious doctrine even to those who did not
accept certain Christian assumptions. But common to all three, despite significant differences among them, was the conviction that the mind can be led
to understand religious insight through experience, reflection and an interpreting word. The program of the Augustinian tradition assumed that the
Christian ideas express truths about realities transcending, but also including,
man and that these can be apprehended to some degree with the help of the
theological firmament they had adopted. Augustine's profound attempt to
plumb the depths of the Trinity through reflection on the tripartite being of
the human self, Anselm's meditative experience of Perfection which issued
in his famous argument, and Bonaventura's charting of the soul's journey to
the Uncreated Light by means of traces in nature and God's image in man
as reflected in a mirror, all represent their firmament at work.

Theirs was not, of course, the only firmament invoked for the purpose of
theology in the Middle Ages. The monumental synthesis of Aquinas came
in many ways to supersede the Augustinian approach, but employing a different conception of Being and a logic of a syllogistic kind as compared with
the reflective dialectic of his Augustinian predecessors. He, no less than they,
however, appealed to a metaphysical firmament without which neither of the
Summae would have been possible. The same holds true for both Duns Scotus
and Ockham; despite the profound difference manifest in their respective

writings, they were still sustained by, and could work within, the metaphysical firmament.

Despite an undercurrent of opposition to this involvement of Christianity with philosophy and secular knowledge—criticism of the same sort as that expressed much later and under different circumstances by Kierkegaard and Barth—the ancient program of making religious insight intelligible through a philosophically oriented theology was pursued for almost a millennium, until the metaphysical framework it presupposed began to erode under the impact of new ideas and approaches to the world. Four principle factors contributed to that erosion. First, there was the rise of modern science with its emphasis on fact and inductive generalization. It was not only the adoption of science as the paradigm of knowledge which had an adverse effect on metaphysics, but rather, as Whitehead has so well shown, the anti-rationalistic bias of the new science which stressed fact as superior to reason. Newton's famous *hypothesis non fingo* provides an excellent example. Secondly, there was the attack made by classical Protestantism on philosophical mediation in favor of a return to purely biblical foundations plus a new emphasis on the primacy of the *religious* dimension over all speculative theology. Thirdly, there was the development from within philosophy itself of classical empiricism with its attack on metaphysics and its elevation of sense to the level of an absolute criterion for all thought. Along with this development went also that "reflexive turn" in philosophy which meant the priority of epistemological problems and the postponement of many first-order issues in the belief that the latter cannot be approached until the problems of knowledge, logic and, more recently, language, have first been resolved. Finally, there was the enormous influence of Kant, especially for Protestantism, and his legacy still continues to determine our present situation. Kant accepted the sense-bound conception of knowledge inherited from Aristotle at the same time that he sought to maintain the rights of reason through the doctrine that we can *think* more than we can *know*, *plus* the claim that reason necessarily and validly raises questions about God, freedom and the self which it nevertheless cannot answer in a cognitive way. What cannot be accomodated within the sphere of theoretical knowledge becomes a matter of the practical employment of reason.

As is well known, Kant's position led to two distinct continuations; the gap between them still determines the shape of the contemporary scene, and not only in the sphere of religious thought. First, the positivist standpoint denied Kant's distinction between thinking and knowing and held that all meaning is determined in terms of verification, actual or possible, with the consequence that theological, metaphysical and other philosophical statements must be declared meaningless since they cannot be verified in scientific fashion. At present it is fashionable to declare that this position is dead, and indeed as an avowed position it no longer has the wide support it once enjoyed, largely because of Wittgenstein's influence in establishing the prior-

8 JOHN E. SMITH

ity of use over a monolithic criterion for meaningfulness. But the basic empiricism behind positivism has by no means left the scene. Secondly, there appeared numerous versions of a *fideist* position according to which religion is seen as performing some essential function in human life, but it can make no claim to truth and has to be understood in some non-cognitive way. From this perspective no attempt whatever can be made to relate religious insight to other spiritual pursuits or to the body of culture at large. How great the gap has become can be seen from the suggestion of Wittgenstein that if there were "evidence" in support of some religious utterance, it would cease to be"religious"!

In order to show that the problem of finding a new theological firmament is no minor one, let me briefly indicate some of the attempts that have been made to arrive at a replacement for the classical one. Hegel understood well the consequence of Kant's position for theology and made an attempt to recover the ontological depth of reason and thus provide a new foundation. Unfortunately, for a variety of reasons, it was too late. Too few understood the peculiar nature of his concept of reason which was shaped so largely by the need to overcome the theological antinomies, and saw in his thought no more than an unrestrained and even arrogant rationalism. As a result, thinkers like Kierkegaard sought to destroy the Hegelian system by finding the reality "that thought cannot think," namely, *Existenz*. Despite the element of truth expressed in the existentialist approaches, there is the basic difficulty, at least in Kierkegaard's version, that to claim any sort of intelligibility for Christianity is either to *distort* it, or to *avoid* it by supposedly turning it into something "palatable." Such a view, of course, runs counter to the ancient enterprise of faith seeking understanding. It is as if to get Christianity into your "head" is a sure sign that it cannot be in your "heart." On these grounds all discussion ceases.

In the brief enumeration of other attempts to find a new medium of expression for religious insight, it will become clear that, with a few exceptions, all are determined by the Kantian dichotomy of theoretical and practical and the curious fact is that many have simply accepted the Kantian position as *the* final solution to the problem of theology and speculative philosophy without any serious attempt to re-examine his arguments. I can do no more than indicate the alternatives proposed and offer brief comment.

Following totally in the footsteps of Kant, Ritschl decades ago sought to construe theology as essentially statements of *value* or worth quite apart from any cosmological or ontological connection. Value as a realm of its own was made to serve as a theological firmament. The position has an affinity with Matthew Arnold's well known characterization of religion as "morality tinged with emotion," and with the more recent re-working of this idea in the writings of Braithwaite. Another alternative, developed in different ways by such thinkers as Tillich, Bultmann and Gogarten, is to use the situation of the existing individual—*Existenz*—as the projection plane so that theology becomes the illumination and resolution of the problems encountered by man in existence. The predicament of finite and alienated man drives toward a redemption which cannot come from man alone but only from a source beyond himself. With the exception of Tillich who had an ontological foundation for his theology, this approach tends in a definitely anthropological direction and runs the risk of losing the world of nature and perhaps the social order as well because of the exclusive emphasis on the existing individual.

In view of the biblical stress on history as the medium of divine disclosure, it was to be expected that that dimension which emerged so powerfully in the later nineteenth century would be made to serve as a theological firmament. The alternative has had numerous representatives among the most recent of whom are Moltmann and Pannenberg who interpret theology in terms of *eschatological history*. The enormous difficulty facing that approach stems from the fact that it must flourish in a climate wherein the concept of history has become increasingly positivized so that one has a major problem in explaining what sort of "history" it is upon which theological doctrine can be projected and religious insight expressed.

One alternative which certainly cannot be understood as within the grip of the Kantian tradition is that of the *process philosophy* derivative from Whitehead and others. This position represents one of the few speculative schemes of thought on the current scene which might stand to religious insight in something like the relation in which the classical metaphysical position stood. Process philosophy is distinguished by its reinterpretation of the cosmos in the light of modern scientific developments, by its refusal to be encapsulated in critical or epistemological issues and by its persistent attempt to frame a set of metaphysical notions which are, in the words of Whitehead, "relevant to the interpretation of everything that happens." As a candidate for the theological firmament, this outlook is not to be taken lightly and all the more so because it allows for that ancient dialogue between theology and philosophy which is not possible when philosophy is represented by a purely critical stance. My one reservation in connection with this way of thinking, and I regard it as a substantial difficulty, has to do with the viability of the fundamental category of Becoming to do justice to the substantiality of all individuals, including the individuality of God.

Another alternative and one which deserves more attention than it has received on the American scene where it has largely been developed, is that of personalitic idealism. This position, set forth in the early decades of this century by Brightman who was following in the steps of Bowne, has been pursued in a very able way by Bertocci more recently. Here the projection plane is the person and the distinguishing marks of personality taken as an ultimate category. This category provides the key for the articulation of religious insight, starting with the Person God is, passing through the essentially teleological manifestation of that Person in nature and extending to the level of individual and social life where the development of creative and responsible personality stands as a moral and religious ideal. This position has great merit especially in its recognition of the need for an ontological firmament capable of doing justice to the concept of a living God. If there is any basic shortcoming in this approach it is the tendency towards individualism and a subordination of the social dimension so well symbolized by classical Trinitarianism wherein God is a community of *personae*, but not a fourth "Person" as Personalism seems to suggest.

Some other alternatives can be reviewed more rapidly. I need not dwell at length on the many forms of the view that whatever theology is possible must be construed as the elucidation of religious *language* and its modes of use by believers within a religious community. While much has been learned from the representatives of this approach, for example, their pointing out the many different kinds of language (parable, myth, exhortation, poem, etc.) to be found in the Scriptures and theology as "religious" language, I have reservations at the point where it becomes apparent that their presuppositions stem for the most part from classical empiricism and a conception of experience which is far too narrow. There is, moreover, the difficulty that concentration on *expression*, what has already been said, will direct attention away from the *experience* involved and what is to be learned from a second look at that.

More recently, in the wake of some disenchantment with philosophy, it has been proposed that the *social sciences* can serve as a theological firmament and attempts have been made to redirect religious insight toward the social, psychological and even political dimensions of contemporary life and culture. Important as such applications of theological concepts to the problems of our society may be, the approach is derivative in the sense that it must feed on theological resources which it does not itself generate. The subject matters of the social sciences as such are in any case inadequate as a projection plane for theology because they do not concern themselves with human life in the religious dimension.

I pass by the theology of the "death of God" and the religion of "no-religion," not because I fail to appreciate the sorts of problems to which the representatives of this position were seeking to respond, but because the approach has shown itself to be ephemeral and without the possibility of a substantial continuation. But even here, paradoxical as it may seem, the problem of a firmament makes itself felt. This form of radical theology, if such it be, uses as its projection plane the need of man who has "come of age" to exist as if there were no God of the sort which man can encapsulate in his own thought. This position needs to be acted out, rather than thought, as indeed it was by Bonhoeffer who was alone in a position to embody it.

Finally there is the alternative pursued at such length by Barth which proposes to dispense with all external mediation and set forth a purely biblical theology. Although even Barth had to speak of the need to "work up" a theology from the biblical materials and that, plus his own practice, clearly imply that there is no immediate transition from the Bible to theology. In fact, in my view, his firmament consists in projecting the biblical content on a sort of divine space by means of a *logos* derived from the Bible without reliance on either philosophical categories or secular knowledge. I shall not repeat here the reason why I believe that this enterprise cannot succeed; suffice it to say that it does serve as an attempt to resolve the firmament problem and is thus at the same time a recognition of its existence.

Although, as should be clear, I do not regard any of these alternatives as entirely satisfactory, I am not claiming that they represent just so much error. Nor would I place them all on the same level, since those having a metaphysical orientation seem to me superior. Something of value is to be learned from each, even from the Barthian position which serves to focus *the* problem of all theology: the danger of encapsulating the religious content which is in *some* sense "the same yesterday, today and forever," in a framework which is contingent and time-bound. But that possibility is a necessary risk of the theological venture itself and can be avoided only by recourse to the mystical silence—and even that has frequently turned out to be very eloquent!

In the midst of such a variety of alternatives it may well seem futile to propose still another candidate for the theological firmament, but I do so nevertheless with the firm conviction that we have not yet fully realized the resources to be found in *experience* as a medium of expression or firmament, together with a metaphysics of self-hood that is required by a conception of experience taking into account all that happens in actual *experiencing*. I do not here refer to so called "religious experience" because, while the expression itself is well established and difficult to avoid, I have reservations about some of its connotations. I have set these forth elsewhere and would prefer to speak instead of the religious dimension of experience. This expression is admittedly clumsier, but, in my view, more adequate because it does not imply that experience in religion means primarily singular and psychologically specific occasions when one "feels presences," "hears voices," "has visions," etc., in short, all the phenomena with which James has made us so familiar from the *Varieties* and which, in the popular imagination, represent religion *par excellence*. There is, moreover, the difficulty that religious experience taken in the sense just indicated inevitably comes to coincide with mysticism; important, however, as that form of spirituality may be, it by no means exhausts what religion is and means.

In appealing to experience as a firmament, I am pointing to a distinctive level of being which has emerged in the course of a long evolutionary process and is the result of an affinity or congruence between the structure of what there is and the subject or sign-using being capable of grasping and expressing that structure. All meaningful existence takes place within and is undergirded by a world of experience. In this sense it is more concrete than all other firmaments because it encompasses each one and they are all abstractions from it. Experience, moreover, stands as a *prius* to expression and articulation as being the what, the why and the how that is being expressed. As we learn from the history of religion, religious insight exists in an experiential mode before it comes to full articulation in a conceptual system, which is the reason for the crucial role it played for the revelatory persons who have been the Founders of the great religious traditions. In each case it was their *experience* and their being as shaped by and expressed in that experience which has been the primary focus of interpreters seeking to lay hold of the religious insight disclosed through their lives.

As such diverse thinkers as Schleiermacher, Edwards and James have pointed out, religious insight is not to be understood initially as a form of theoretical apprehension aimed at causal explanation and technological control, but is instead a form of experience imbued with a living understanding which affects the being of the person who has it and serves as an orientation for life in the many communities which go to make up the social whole. In making a distinction between the theoretical stance and an affecting experience, however, there is no need or reason for committing the error of opposing the two to each other as has so often been done in the past. Reflecting and knowing represent the articulation of experience, what it means in its many contents and contexts. Of course the articulation is no surrogate for experience, just as the concept of love is not the virtue itself, but without articulation experience becomes an 'I know not what.'

There is yet another consideration, briefly noted at the outset, which shows the need for a recovery of the experiential dimension in religion. It has to do with the somewhat frightening response that is being made on the current scene to its suppression in religions that have become too prosaic and underestimate the role of imagination. The upsurge of the mystical, the exotic and the occult, the interest in the meditative traditions and the myriad forms of sporadic "spirituality" on the contemporary scene, all testify to the need for experiential participation in a Power that transcends merely human and finite concerns. In the absence, however, of a critical theory of experience and a grasp of its proper function as both participation and understanding through an interpreting word, it will be impossible to sift the genuine from the spurious and religion will be engulfed by a frenzy of immediacy, more sensational than religious. We must deplore these distortions as superstition bordering on entertainment and self-indulgence, but the very existence of the beliefs and rituals associated with the so-called "new religions" testifies to the essential connection between religion and experience. If, however, that experience is not to spend itself in mere esthetic enjoyment, its genuinely religious character has to be made clear and it must be brought within a critical community of shared experience with which it can be compared.

In proposing experience as the theological firmament, I am pointing to three distinct though closely related considerations; first, there is the matter of conceiving experience in its full breadth and depth which means rescuing it from its captivity at the hands of classical British empiricism; second, there is the task of making religious insight intelligible by means of particular analogies drawn from experience; and third, there is the need to provide for experience a status as a distinct level of being having an integrity of its own and to show that it involves a metaphysics of self-hood which can serve as a theological firmament for projecting the idea of God.

Each of these considerations is essential. Identifying experience with the materials of the senses is hopelessly inadequate, not only because that doctrine itself is not based on all the facts of actual experiencing, but because it must render dubious or unintelligible so much of familiar experience. It is impossible, for example, to account for the experience one self has of another on the classical view, to say nothing of its inability to give an adequate treatment of either religion or morality. The theory to be given up is the one which says that experience is a tissue of subjectivity of which we are immediately aware, a veil which stands between ourselves and the world so that it is possible to claim that experience is "merely" some inner state which, though it may have some sort of psychic existence, does not disclose any reality beyond it. But that is precisely the conception of experience which has come under attack from the phenomenologists, the pragmatists and the existentialists, not to mention the tradition represented by Bergson and Whitehead. Experience is not a "mental" product lodged in a private mind cut off from the "real" world, but a fund of meaning, including both knowing that and knowing how, which is the intersubjective product of many encounters between intelligent beings and whatever realities there are. Although it always has an individual locus, experience is not an exclusively private affair but has an essentially social character that allows for sharing and comparing for the purpose of discovering what is pervasive as over against the merely idiosyncratic. When St. Paul described his experience in the well-known words, "The good I would, I do not . . ." he was expressing a fact which every reflective person can identify in his or her own experience and it is highly unlikely that this description would have gained the acceptance it has if this were not so.

Let me approach the second consideration which is the use of particular analogies drawn from experience in the above sense taken as the projection plane for understanding religious insight, by means of three illustrations. Two will be drawn from the Judeo-Christian tradition and one from a wider sphere of experience encompassing several of the historical religions. Since we are in no position to express, for example, the nature of God from the "inside," as it were, we must avail ourselves of likenesses and analogies— the reason for the need of a firmament in the first instance. Who will claim to know the relation between divine justice and the divine mercy as expressed in one of the "dark" Parables like that of the Laborers in the Vineyard without recourse to our own available human experience of justice and forgiveness and to an imaginative reconstruction of the experience in Jesus' own life that lay behind that story? The same holds true for any attempt to understand the entire spectrum of theological concepts, sin, atonement, salvation, grace together with those characterisitics expressing the divine nature and the relations between God and man. Consider the concept of atonement as an attempt to show how Christ effects the reconciliation between God and man and between a man and himself made necessary by an alienation which is itself the result of human self-assertiveness against the divine love. If this doctrine is to have any significant relation to human life, it cannot be left in the forensic form which it has assumed in much classical theology wherein God is represented as engaged in a ransom transaction with the forces of evil. Instead it will be necessary to approach the meaning intended through some experiential analogy of a broken or alienated relationship which has been transformed and reinstated on the far side of the brokenness. Royce used for this purpose and with great effect the ancient story of Joseph and his brothers. Consider that, through envy and hurt pride, the brothers banded together against their youngest kin, deprived him of his prized possession and abandoned him to die. The bond of love existing in the primal human community, the family, was thus broken. How is it to be recovered? According to the story, the bond of love was re-established by the forgiving deed; when Joseph later had the opportunity to redress the balance, as, from the standpoint of simple justice he had every right to do, he overcame that temptation, forgave his brothers and brought them again within the compass of a redeeming love, something which a retaliation in kind could not have accomplished.

This illustration is drawn from a particular human situation, but if made to serve as an analogy it helps us to *understand* the concept of atonement in the cosmic dimension required of a theological doctrine. Here we have not Joseph and his brothers but human existence itself in its alienation from God and it then becomes necessary to understand how from within this circle of broken humanity where *all* are separated from God and all are guilty, there can appear a redeeming force capable of breaking through the tragic circle. What or who is able to transcend a tragic situation in which all finite beings are caught? On this point and despite much variety of interpretation, the Christian tradition has always been clear: the redeeming force must partake of humanity, but it must also be *more than* human because man alone is incapable of re-establishing the community of love which he has himself broken. The atoning or self-emptying deed of Jesus in giving himself so that, to use the expression of Royce, "the Beloved Community" can be brought into existence, is what breaks the tragic circle.

Consider as a second illustration of the appeal to experience for analogies that serve to illuminate religious insight, the doctrine of Creation. Who will deny that the concept of a creation out of nothing is among the most opaque of notions, although it is surely ironic that there are those at present who believe that they understand what this means when it concerns man! But suppose that attention were directed not to the category of causality understood primarily as an object-object relationship, but rather to our experience of intentional action, the experience of *meaning* to express this or that idea and of *meaning* to do this or that action. In all intentional situations we experience the presence of a purpose which points beyond itself to a target or a goal to be reached or fulfilled. These situations are clear instances of the much over-worked category of self-transcendence because in the nature of the case an intention must surpass the moment of its coming into being as an intention and it must belong to a centered self moving beyond the present. In short, it demands an issue or anticipated outcome. We are most vividly aware of the meaning of intentionality by way of contrast with what is accidental, what just happens or was not meant. To intend to convey a meaning or to carry out a certain action is to communicate ourselves, to connect ourselves essentially with the idea or deed. If we are fully aware and self-consistent, we acknowledge ourselves as validly expressed in the object of our intention. When, on the other hand, we find ourselves conjoined with a meaning we did not intend or an act not done ''on purpose'' our immediate response is to point up the disconnection between the event and our intentions. If someone takes me to have asserted an idea other than the one I meant, I put this down to a mistake and hasten to disown it. Similarly, if I ''just happen'' to jostle another person in a crowded train, I am quick to make it clear that I was not responsible and did not ''mean'' the impact as a result. The intended is not ''just there'' but is always connected with a self transcending itself. In this sense, intention is the source of creation.

Suppose all this were used as an analogy both for elucidating the idea of the divine Creation and of God's relation to the redeeming Person. God intends the world; it is not ''there'' as just so much brute fact, but was ''meant'' in all its plurality as the expression of the divine purpose and the Transcendent Self. All that exists is therefore a matter of concern. Human experience is, however, only the key to the meaning of creation because, as finite and conditioned, it does not really provide us with the analogue for the ''out of nothing'' feature which is the idea whereby the biblical writers sought to exclude the dualism that would result from an alien ''matter'' co-eval with God but standing over against what is divine. For the intentional creativity is never ''out of nothing,'' whereas for God the world and man are the self expression of a Creator seeking to communicate a Perfection which, as it were, remains unappreciated in the absence of a rational being like man who can appreciate it not only for itself, but also in the measure to which it shines forth in the starry heavens above. Seeing the world as thus intended means that it can never be regarded as mere ''matter,'' as a scene to be denied or escaped from, nor can it be viewed as if it were wholly at man's disposal and without a being of its own to be exploited at his will and for his own selfish purposes. I need not point out the practical consequences for human life following from this way of seeking to understand through an experiential analogy a doctrine which has often seemed remote and unconnected with life in the world.

A similar sort of analogical elucidation is possible in connection with the concept of Incarnation and the historical embodiment of the Word. The experience of intentional expression is once again the key. So viewed, Christ is the concrete embodiment of the divine intention to overcome the alienation manifest in the travail of the whole creation. What more appropriate translation can there be of the central idea that "God was in Christ reconciling the world to Himself," than that of intentional Being? The Jesus of history has his decisive religious significance not in some brute existence, important as his life and thought undoubtedly are, but in his being "meant" by God and in his pointing beyond himself—as he continually did—to the Lord who meant him to be as the total expression of a redeeming will. In neither of these illustrations am I proposing to set forth anything like full-blown doctrines of Creation or Incarnation; I am merely attempting to indicate how a world of experience can serve in an analogical mode for the understanding of religious insight. And, as should be clear, an understanding which is itself couched in terms of experience makes the application of that insight to experience less of a mystery.

Let us now consider a world of experience that goes beyond the confines of any one religious tradition in the hope of discovering pervasive traits which can throw new light on these traditions themselves and on the entire phenomenon of religion in the world's history. Seventy-five years ago, William James in setting forth his "Conclusions" to the *Varieties* proposed a twofold formula expressing what might be called the generic structure of religion. Religion, he said, starts with a felt uneasiness stemming from the perception that there is some ideal fulfillment for man which he is in danger of failing to attain because of some defect in his own natural existence. Coupled with this is the sense of a resolution or deliverance from this danger by becoming related to the religious reality which James referred to generally as "the unseen world." The striking fact is that this two-fold experience manifests itself throughout the fabric of all the world religions. Instead of beginning with the popular conception that religion ignores the brute realities of the actual world in order to claim that "God's in his heaven and all's right with the world," the insight of the great religions focuses instead first on the flaw or defect which inhabits the "natural man" and from which he needs to be saved. In short, prior to the vision of fulfillment is a diagnosis of the actual human predicament aimed at detecting what obstacle is to be overcome. The role of the deliverer in whatever form that may come is thus seen in correlation with the power of that obstacle. This formula, to be sure, remains quite general and indeed must remain so if it is to reflect a generic structure and to allow for the fact that the significant differences between the historic religions are most evident in their different perceptions of what defect is to be found in man's natural existence and what power of salvation is available for delivering us from it. The important point is the universal character of the experience ingredient in religions which are in many other respects quite different from each other.

Some examples will help to establish the point: they can be only briefly developed. Consider, first, that in the tradition of classical Hinduism represented especially by the *Upanishads,* man is seen as essentially caught in a web of ignorance concerning the true nature of himself and the world in which he exists. As a result he misperceives the world and fails to understand who he is and the sort of fulfillment for which he may hope. The first step in the overcoming of his predicament is for man to become aware of it and to acknowledge the need for deliverance. The resolution of the situation comes in the form of a kind of knowledge able to penetrate the deceptive veil through which the unenlightened view the world and reveals the essential identity of the individual soul or Atman with the universal Brahman. We can see here the perfect coordination of the flaw in natural existence which is ignorance and the saving power which is the knowledge or enlightenment of mystical insight.

The same generic cycle of experience is to be found in the quest of the Gotama Buddha, in this case even more sharply focused by the intensity of a singular experience. Not satisfied with the diagnosis and resolution offered by the tradition in which he was brought up, the Buddha sets forth, with self-sacrifice and devotion, to discover the cause of human suffering and the manner in which it might be dispelled. The insight he attains is that man as he naturally exists is controlled by inordinate desire which is inevitably directed toward objects that are transient and of no enduring worth. This is the Buddha's diagnosis of man's predicament, which he needs to be delivered from if he is to realize himself, and it points the way to the resolution which takes the form of a discipline, a regimen, of contemplation and of action, aimed at the transformation and redirection of human desire toward the virtues of right views, right aspirations, right conduct, right mode of living, etc., with the result that the suffering attendant upon misguided desire now comes to an end. Once again, as in the previous case, the path to salvation comes into view only after an examination of man's situation for the purpose of discovering the flaw that infects his being.

The parallel to the two preceding illustrations in the Judeo-Christian tradition is quite obvious and need not be dwelled upon at length. In this case the flaw in human nature is more internalized in the sense that the human self-assertiveness which sets itself over against the divine love and law is seen as stemming from man's own self-consciousness and freedom. The vision of a community of love uniting all men expressed in the New Testament preaching about the Kingdom of God stands in contrast to the actuality of the "natural man" who worships the idols and gives priority to the demands of his own will. The role of the deliverer in this situation is to offer the resource of a forgiving love which transforms the man of "flesh" into the man of "spirit" whose heart is set on God and the love of his neighbor.

The point to be emphasized in connection with this illustration is that it manifests patterns of *pervasive* experience despite vast cultural differences. Such experience is regarded in all areas of empirical inquiry as providing a foundation or warrant for the knowledge claims we make. Why should the case be otherwise with respect to religion? Why should it be said that in the religious context the phenomena to be met with are "merely psychological," or "merely subjective" or "no more than the 'experience' of some individual"? I believe that the answer is quite simple. The view of experience as being "in here" as contrasted with what is the case "out there" is false. Experience is the medium of *disclosure* of reality not a veil which either obscures or falsifies it. Experience is a distinct level of reality which emerges at the interface of encounters between what is there to be met and an intelligent, sign-using creature. The occasions of experiencing and the significance or interpretation thoroughly interpenetrate and this synthesis forms the integrity of all experience. What is required is the development of a metaphysics of experience which will serve to make clear its complex nature and unique status in the scheme of things. That is, of course, a program and not its fulfillment but the central idea behind such a metaphysics can be set forth. Despite all that has been said in criticism of the subject-object distinction, the belief still lingers that all we have before us are things to be known and selves or minds to know them. But that dyadic view leaves out the crucial *fact,* and it is a fact, that there is an *intelligible affinity* between self and world without which no experience would be possible at all. The recovery of the existence of this affinity, well-known to the classical metaphysical tradition but lost through the development of modern "empiricism," is the task of a new metaphysics of experience and of human self-hood. Here I can do no more than indicate the outlines of that metaphysic.

The only reality we know that is rich enough to express the nature of God as love, power and purpose is the self. The self to which we have access in the experience of ourselves and others manifests itself as the togetherness of a one (a center of intention—"I") and a manifold of experience or content. The self both identifies itself with its experiences or autobiography and distinguishes itself from them in standing beyond and interpreting, explaining and evaluating them. Characteristic of self-hood is the capacity for *having* experience which in turn presupposes a being related essentially to the world and other selves, and yet at the same time distinct from both in virtue of a continuing unity and identity. When I refer to experience as a *medium* for disclosing and projecting the nature of God, I am *not* proposing to identify God with human experience, but rather attempting to find the appropriate continuum wherein the Transcending Self and the finite selves become related to each other in a community informed by love, power and purpose. A metaphysics of self-hood consonant with an intentional theory of experience constitutes the theological firmament for the understanding of God.

Yale University

2 RELIGIOUS EXPERIENCE

Hywel Lewis

The notion of religious experience appears to me central to all discussions of major religious issues today. It is however a notion about which there appears to be a great deal of confusion and misunderstanding. There are such terms as 'Nature' and 'Freedom', which admit of such a wide variety of interpretation (some of them sharply contradictory) that their use tends to become almost pointless. 'Religious experience' is apt to fall into this class. It is sometimes used to refer to any religious activity or practice whatsoever, and thus may become quite otiose. This is the use that some have in mind when they say that they have never had a religious experience; they just mean that they are agnostics. For others 'religious experience' means some very peculiar type of experience, like having visions or hearing voices, or having a distinctively mystical experience. For some the term is associated, with some but only very limited justification, with an excessively emotional religious indulgence. In its main use, and in the profound importance ascribed to it by devout persons in all ages, the term stands for none of these things. It is important therefore to indicate just what we should normally understand by 'religious experience.' I shall attempt to do this as fairly as I can within a limited space, and I shall also try to give a brief indication of how this relates to other major concerns.

I shall waste no time over those who think of religious experience primarily, and perhaps exclusively, in terms of paranormal phenomena. Such occurrences need not in fact be properly religious at all. To what extent they may be I have discussed at some length in my *Our Experience of God*.[1] Those who have had paranormal experiences in the context of their religious life, ascribe importance to them only in relation to other aspects of their faith; usually they minimize their importance and treat them as quite peripheral to

---

[1] *Our Experience of God* (London: George Allen and Unwin, 1959), pp. 211-237. Cf. also chapter 3 of my *Persons and Life After Death* (New York: Macmillan, 1978).

19

their essential commitment. This is why it seemed to me so unreasonable for a critic of the standing of Alasdair MacIntyre, in a well-known book some years ago, to make such heavy weather over claims to have had visions of the Virgin Mary etc.[2] Did she "speak Aramaic," did she "remember Galilee?" Questions of this kind seem to me to show a total, indeed obtuse, insensitivity to what religion is essentially like, even in the contexts where visions and voices and other forms of 'the marvellous' are in fact invoked.

But we must be equally careful not to think of religious experience merely in terms of some features of human experience as a whole or some generalizations or deductions from what our situation as human beings is like. Religious experience, in essentials, is not incipient metaphysics, however important it may be for metaphysical reflection. Its peculiar significance derives from its being a distinctive experience which people undergo, as they may have a moral or an aesthetic experience. This does not mean that it is always easy to recognize or delimit, as in the case, for example, of some forms of pain. But it would be quite wrong to identify it with features of experience which all can recognize, or with neutral occurrences to which some further religious significance may be ascribed. Religious experience is essentially religious, a distinct ingredient, to my mind a vital one, in an essentially religious awareness, and identifiable as such.

I go out of my way to stress this because of a prevailing tendency, in current philosophy of religion, to think that so much of religion is initially neutral, even the sense of the numinous according to some. In my view, we cannot produce any proper form of religion out of non-religious elements. There is indeed a place for the interpretation of experience; perception for example looks very different as the philosopher considers some of its extraordinary features. The last thing I wish to do is to discourage reflection on religious awareness, or to present it as a raw datum which some may accept, others not, and no more. We need in fact to think more carefully about it than anything else in religious commitment at present. But we must not, in the process, so dilute it that it is nothing recognizable in and for itself.

The same goes for some fashionable views which equate religious experience with an alleged contentless relation with God sometimes known as an "I-Thou relation." I have a very great regard for Martin Buber, and I wish more heed were paid by those who refer to him to my fairly close discussion, in Chapter XIII of *The Elusive Mind,* of what emerges in a positive way from all that he had to say on this theme. But I make no sense whatsoever, in human or in divine relationships, of a mere relation to which no kind of a

---

[2] A. Flew and A. MacIntyre, eds. *New Essays In Philosophical Theology* (London: S.C.M Press, 1955), Chap. XIV.

[3] *The Elusive Mind* (London: Allen and Unwin, 1969).

distinctive precise significance can be attached. The nearest we get to this is the insight or intuition into the inevitability of there being God, and of this I shall say more shortly. But an encounter which is no particular kind of encounter, a 'meeting' which cannot be characterized in any way, appears to me to be just nothing. To make the invocation of it a way of by-passing all the hard epistemological problems is just an escape from our intellectual responsibility, it plays into the hands of contemptuous agnostics.

For related reasons I dismiss all accounts of religious experience in exclusively emotional terms. Emotion plays its part, but the core of religious experience, I submit, is essentially cognitive. How then should we understand it?

At the centre, it seems to me, is the enlivened sense of the being of God— or, if that at this stage is too theistic a term, of some supreme transcendent reality—as involved in the being of anything at all. This is what lies behind the traditional arguments. We all know their inadequacy as arguments notwithstanding all the refinements attempted in recent times. But they still haunt us, and this seems to me to be because they reflect in different ways the conviction that there can be no ultimate fortuitousness in the being of things. We seek explanations of the way things are, not as a mere psychological compulsion but as rational beings. We do not give up when no sort of explanation is possible, we insist that it must be available somewhere; but no finite explanation is fully adequate, each proceeds in terms of the way we actually find that things cohere, but there remains the question why they should be this way at all, or why anything at all should exist. We can, at least without sheer inconsistency, say that it all just happened, that somehow things began to *be* out of a total void and took the remarkable course which enables us to manipulate and understand our environment, in terms of perfect concomitant variation even to the astonishing vastness and complexities of macroscopic and microscopic science of today. We may not contradict ourselves if we say that all this just came into being out of nothing, but is it credible? Why should anything start up at all, much less take the remarkable intelligible shape it has out of just nothing? On the other hand it is equally unintelligible to suppose that the world has always been, that in no sense has there been any sort of origination. 'Always' in this sense becomes meaningless. Aeons beyond all computation, and certainly beyond imaginative realization, we can at least comprehend, but a strictly infinite past is just not intelligible.

It is these radical antinomies that compel us to recognize some more ultimate reality in which all that we can, in principle, comprehend is rooted, but which is not itself comprehensible beyond this recognition of its inevitability, a mystery, not partial but total, in which everything there is, is invested, but not the mystery of mere bewilderment, the mystery of real transcendent being.

Philosophers put this in fairly sophisticated terms. But the sense of it, however imperfectly expressed, does not require great sophistication. It is elicited in various ways, not least by what Jaspers has called "limit situations," and I have ventured myself elsewhere to indicate in more detail how the sense of the transcendent awakens in the minds of the most naive as well as of sophisticated persons and societies. It can be traced back as far as recorded history goes. Art and practice as well as intellectual reflection involve it. But granted some intimation in this way of a supreme or transcendent reality, how do we go from there?

It is at *this* point that I would wish to invoke the idea of religious experience. I wish to stress very much that I do not appeal to the notion of religious experience as such to establish the existence of God, least of all in the naive form of insisting that there must be God because we experience him. That would clearly not do without indication of the sort of experience this is and how it is warranted. It could be a gigantic begging of the question. Religious experience properly comes in at the point where we ask, how we go further than the sense of some ultimate all-encompassing mystery involved in all that we are or find.

There are of course some who do not seek to go further. They stay at the sense of profound wonderment at the essentially incomprehensible source of all there is, sometimes almost to the point of the repudiation of finite being. In practice actual religion has rarely been able to remain at this rarefied level. Present existence claims its right and our attention. Finite existence cannot be denied any more than the infinite, even if it finds no better place than some mode or articulation of the infinite. At some level there appear, from the remotest times to our own, particular practices, attitudes, obligations, varied and suggestive symbolism, all intimating that the sacred which, in one sense, we cannot approach and whose essential mystery we cannot fathom, is nonetheless peculiarly present, "in thy mouth and in the heart," as one scripture puts it, that it involves a way of life for us, a purpose, a formative influence in personal and social history, a meaning and a presence articulating itself in all manner of ways and leading, in some instances, to highly refined formulations of belief, even to the curiously presumptuous intimacy of petitionary prayer. Men speak of meeting God, of "walking" with him, of hearing his voice, of turning away from him, of encountering his wrath and, in the same awareness almost, finding him a seeking, reconciling God who draws all men to their ultimate fulfilment "in him." They even speak of God incarnate as a living, limited finite creature who died in a scandalously shameful way. How is any of this to be warranted, affirmed or rejected? What meaning can it have?

It is here, in my view, that religious experience is the seminal and vital consideration. I do not, of course, wish to deny, that the "insight" into there having to be God, along the lines indicated, is itself an experience. But it is so in the sense that all cognition is experience. To apprehend that twice two is four, or that the angles of a triangle add up to 180 degrees, is experience.

But no one would claim, in these cases, that we know from experience, on the basis of what we find or observe, that these things are so, as we know that grass is green and fire is hot. "The appeal to religious experience," as it is sometimes called, is not a strictly empirical one, in the sense of empiricism which confines it to presentations of sense, but it has more in common with it than strictly a priori knowledge. Certain things are claimed on the basis of certain things that have happened.

The one qualification of this, and it is a vital one, is the point already noted, namely that at the core of religious experience, is the enlivened insight into the being of God. We do not know this because things happen in any particular way, but, essentially, because they happen at all. The insight involved is peculiar but certainly not quasi-empirical. On the other hand, the enlivening of this insight in peculiar conditions, and the repercussions of it on other crucial aspects of particular experiences, seem to me to be the raw material out of which all other genuine religious awareness is built—and by which it is tested.

At this point there is a very close analogy between the way we know one another and the way we know God. We do not know the existence of other persons generally in any a priori or in any intuitive way, though some philosophers make that strange claim. We know all we know about other persons, I submit, in some mediated way, however close and intimate this may be. Without some evidence we would not know the existence of anyone. But the being of God we know quite differently as indicated. It is in no sense a matter of evidence as this usually goes. But *all the rest is,* and it is along these lines that I, at least, react to the familiar challenge of empiricist critics— what would count for or against your belief? For the existence of God I answer "nothing." It is not that kind of awareness, it is a quite peculiar insight about which nonetheless much may be said, again along the lines indicated. But for all other affirmations, the live particularization of profound devotion, we turn to specific evidence, to what counts for or against, to what can, in some respects at least, be analyzed and set forth, though by no means in exclusively sensible terms.

I make a special point of stressing this, as so many who are concerned about religion, at highpowered professional levels or more simply, fall back before the fashionable challenge on either blind appeals to authority or some vague noncognitive attitude or commitment for which there is no rational justification. Interest in religion may be revived today, in fleeting and transitory ways, by simple-minded appeals to emotion or hysteria or palliatives to those who hunger for spiritual sustenance—or we may make do for a while with attenuations which but thinly disguise the essential secularity of our attitudes. But this will not last. Religion needs justification, most of all in a sophisticated age like our own. No great religion can survive without it.

It is this justification of what is distinctive in the claims of the great religions, and the means of assessment and the basis of dialogue, that is to be found essentially, in my view, in religious experience, rightly understood. The points of convergence as well as the differences can be much better understood in these terms and a means made possible of maintaining our distinctive stances while entering with genuine empathy and appreciation into the religious devotion of others. It will also be a very great gain indeed, in all religions, to show that we are fully equipped to confront the demand for justification and fully take the point of empiricist critics, though by no means entirely on their own terms.

Let us return, then, to the question what a religious experience involves besides the enlivened sense of the being and mystery of God. I want first to add here that, if the transcendent is to function adequately as the ultimate answer to our "why questions," or as explanation in the very special elusive sense indicated, it must be deemed to be complete and adequate in all respects in itself, in other words perfect in the evaluational sense as well as self-sustaining. I do not see how anything less than supreme perfection could meet the case, and in this context I would like to refer you to a quite admirable, but not I suspect sufficiently regarded, book by Professor Sontag entitled *Divine Perfection*.[4] The sense of the holy is essentially evaluational, and does not become so, as is implied in some readings of Otto, by further schematization. This point I must leave as it is for our purpose.

The main point to be stressed now is that the sense of ultimate being, mysterious beyond any fathoming in what it must be in itself other than ultimate perfection, has a distinctive impact on other formative features of the total experience in which it occurs. It corrects the perspective in which we view the world around us, it highlights what is of greatest import for us, it makes us see the familiar anew, as in art and poetry; and it does this under the insistent sense of transcendent being unavoidably having its place in our thought. The transcendent claims what it stimulates for its own, and God, whom no man hath seen, the impenetrably Holy, removed and remote as infinite being from finite, becomes a closely intimate articulate presence in the very core of our own essentially finite awareness.

The substance of what we come to learn about God in this way is finite. It may present difficulties but no difficulties beyond our understanding and resolving in the normal exercise of finite intelligence. *What* we learn is finite and has no irresolvable mystery in it, much is indeed very simple, however astonishing on occasion. The peculiarly divine factor comes in when these exceptional insights into our own situation and its requirements are seen to be induced in a very sharp way, deepened and refined, under the impact of the movingly enlivened sense of the Holy and the transcendent. As I have put it elsewhere God puts his own imprimatur on certain insights and sen-

---

[4] Frederick Sontag, *Divine Perfection* (New York: Harper, 1962).

sitivities, he underlines, as it were, certain things in our experience and writes his own mind into them. They come to carry his authority in addition to their own. They are what he specifically wants us to note. The devout acquire the art of listening and heeding what is communicated thus within our own sensitivity and concentration.

One feature of exceptional importance in the process whereby our understanding is extended in the enlivened sense of the involvement of our lives in a supreme and transcendent reality is the refinement and deepening of moral awareness. It is of great importance that this should be understood aright. The view has often been advanced that we cannot ascribe genuine objectivity to ethical principles unless they are considered to be expressly dependent on some religious reality. This seems to me to be dangerous doctrine. It is plain that persons with no religious awareness or commitment can have profound appreciation of moral ideals and splendid devotion to them. There is no inconsistency or logical impropriety in their being so. The objectivity of morals is autonomous, as I have stressed myself on many occasions, and some of the most notable and persuasive defenders of moral objectivity have been prominent agnostic philosophers such as G. E. Moore and C. D. Broad. Their case, a very convincing one to me, does not rest at all on religion. Ethics has no more direct dependence on religion than mathematics or science. But this does not preclude morality from being, as most persons would take it to be, at the very heart of religion.

It is so not just because the ultimate is also supreme perfection, and commitment to it is also therefore commitment to what is surpassingly good, but also because it is in the refinement of ethical understanding, in the sharpening of conscience as it may more popularly be put, that the peculiar disclosure of divine intention for us takes place. It is in the voice of our own conscience that the voice of God is most distinctly and significantly heard. This does not make conscience an essentially religious faculty, but it does make it the preeminent medium within which the articulation of the mind of God to us takes place. It is here above all that we find our exceptional clue to what God is like and what is our own involvement and special relation to him.

None of this means that devout people are morally infallible or have a monopoly of all good sense and advance in ethical understanding. There are perversions of religion and profound misunderstandings of its nature that have been very gravely detrimental to ethical good sense and which have from time to time brought religion itself into serious discredit. The refinement of moral understanding involves moreover a great deal besides the sharpening of ethical insight as such; it requires sound appreciation of the facts and circumstances in various situations and the over-all consequences of various policies. On these matters the devout may not always be the best authorities, and religion certainly confers no immunity from error on matters of fact. Nor does it always carry with it the guarantee of the finest ethical insight as such. The agnostic may sometimes excel in both regards.

What we can say however is that, other things being equal, the enlivened sense of the transcendent carries with it essentially a refinement of moral sensitivity and that it is moreover to this source that the most impressive advances in ethical principles over the years have been due. This is not the place to justify the latter submission in detail. My concern at the moment is more with the general contention that, while it is inherently impossible for us to rise beyond our finite nature and comprehend the being and mind of God as it is for him, we find the incursion of the divine into specific human experience, and thereby a preeminent clue into what our relation to it should be, in the peculiarly religious toning and refining of moral experience.

This is not the only example, far from it. We may speak in similar terms of our appreciation of the world around us and its significance, and of the impetus this has given, among other things, to the advance of science. The artistic attitude is in the same way close to religion here, and each has immensely fructified the other for that reason. But it is not primarily a matter of general affinity as of moments of profound religious awareness in which the deepening of religious insight as such takes its course in the blending of itself with perceptions and sensitivity in other secular regards which thereby afford distinctive matter, apprehensible in the normal secular way by us, out of which the fullness and the richness and the intimacy of genuine religious existence is shaped, and by which it is also corrected and criticized.

Correction and criticism are indeed of very great importance here. For the distinctively religious factor, in a total religious experience, operates upon and within the other secular features of our situation. These often have faults of their own, and this is how it comes about that we sometimes sincerely ascribe to the voice of God items which are only too grievously marked by our own limitations and failings. It would be fine in some ways if the mind of God were disclosed to us in some indelible and wholly unmistakable way, written in the sky or on tablets of stone or of gold in some inscription which is indisputably divine. Dispute, and presumably doubt, would be at an end. But it does not happen that way. Short of being God ourselves what sanction could we invoke, what are the credentials of a message so conveyed? There is indeed no such way for the voice of God to be heard by finite beings. He speaks in the ways we can understand in his peculiar obtrusion into the normal exercise of the faculties with which he has endowed us. But it is not the mere exercise of finite powers that is involved. There is the peculiar transformation of them which we have the reasons indicated for ascribing to divine intervention in the enlivened sense of the transcendent already described.

A genuine prophet can, for these reasons, be sincerely mistaken, and devout persons have always to be searching out their own minds and hearts to be as sure as they can that what they take to be the voice of God is not the voice of their own errors and failings, or at least tinged by these. That does not preclude firmness of conviction and deliverance. The prophet may speak with authority, but he must be mindful also that he is but a medium, a vessel that is often cracked and broken.

One particular feature of the fallibility of genuine prophetic awareness is the involvement of all of us in the particular circumstances of our age and society. When, as in societies at a relatively low level of moral development, the sense of the divine impinges upon their attitudes, the progress they make will be correspondingly limited and sometimes distorted. If the ethical understanding of a community has not advanced beyond the level of crude retribution and collective guilt, there may well be a genuinely religious ingredient in the perpetuation of ideas which a more enlightened age would find morally abhorrent. What we have to be constantly heeding is the intertwining of genuine religious disclosure and insight with other all too fallible aptitudes and interests of finite creatures. Much in the sacred scriptures of various religions will become more intelligible to us and can be viewed judiciously in their proper setting if we think as indicated, of divine disclosure as a leaven in the totality of our own aptitudes and aspirations. At the same time the distinctiveness of the transcendent influence must not be lost or wholly merged in the finite media on which it operates.

The precise moment of genuine religious awareness, operating within the functions it claims for its own operation, may not always be easily delimited. It may be sharp as in sudden conversion, but even in these cases there is often a period of subtle maturing in which truly religious elements come to their open and more explicit formulation. More commonly, although religious awareness and sensitivity may be clear and explicit, it has its own ebb and flow, it merges itself in other concentrations of attention, it may be gentle and unobtrusive, in acts of worship or meditation, much as aesthetic awareness is not always easily delimited and isolated from the observations and attentiveness which it takes up into itself. It is for these reasons that some may even fail to detect the moment of live religious awareness or allow it in retrospection to be lost in the media which it embraces. This, in particular is where very careful thought is needed in our times to detect and uphold the element of genuine religious awareness against crude and bogus travesties of it.

This is all the more the case because the live religious awareness lives on in other experiences and practices and also perpetuates itself dispositionally in our way of living as a whole. Its occurrence may be known obliquely and indirectly, and this in notable cases is no mean assurance of its presence. It may well become apparent by its fruits. But we can never rely on that alone. The enlivened individual awareness is the indispensable religious factor, and it is out of it preeminently that the distinctively religious shape of any faith is formed.

In my fuller discussion of these matters, in my book *Our Experience of God,* I also ascribed particular importance to what I described as the patterning of religious experience. There are significant recurrences and variations which I sought to describe. It has often been found, for example, that the enlivened awareness of transcendent being often comes about in situations where we have least justification for expecting it, for example in states of an overwhelming sense of guilt. The latter, especially a sense of grievous wrong-doing, comes between us and one another and between us and God, it drives us on our own inner resources which dry up without the sustaining sense of the world around us and of other persons. It is in this debility that we find the real penalty of sin. But, surprisingly, it is often in just this situation of despair and desperation that men have found the onset of the renewed aware-ness, sometimes gently, sometimes disturbing, of infinite being as the end and sustainer of their own existence, and life as a whole becomes renewed again and transformed. The recurrence of this, its variations and the extension of it into the religious consciousness of various societies, builds itself up over the ages into the sense of God, not as mere remote sustainer or "Unmoved Mover," but as a seeking reconciling God peculiarly involved in what we are and in our relationship with him. This is, to my mind, a very important aspect of the emergence of the more theistic forms of religion.

The same may be said of other situations of desperation, whether we bring them on ourselves or not. It does not follow that distressing circumstances and evil are straightway resolved. Appalling evil is still with us and presents the severest tension and strain for religious commitment. It is not a problem I can lightly deviate into now. But in these situations also men have found the sustaining and recurring sense of God invading their attitudes as a whole and giving them renewal of strength. God comes to be known as "an ever present help in trouble."

My submission, without pursuing any of these illustrations in further detail here, is that it is in the substance and the patterning, which I would also much stress, of the moulding and refining of otherwise neutral sensitivities and attitudes by the insistent impact of the transcendent rather than in a priori and essentially empty attempts to determine abstract properties of God, that we find the vindication and shaping, as well as the appropriate critique, of the more particular affirmations and practices of actual living religions. The parallel with "other minds" is here very close. We do not, as I have per-sistently maintained elsewhere, know the minds of other persons as we know our own; however close our relationships may be, however intimate, there is an essential element of mediation. The relation we have with God is no less intimate and close because it comes in the mediation of the peculiar modification of our own experience, it is as close as finite-infinite relation-ships can be, and to those who experience it profoundly there is no barrier that matters.

For many who persist in an agnostic or sceptical view of religion I suspect that a major determinant of their attitude is the expectation that religion must vindicate itself for them, if at all, in some form of supernatural experience of which finite beings are not capable at all. This is the sophisticated version of the expectation that the astronauts may discover God for us. What we need is to know better where and how to look, and to persevere more in the demanding discipline of looking in the right way. Far too often we take it all to be a matter of a few formal considerations one way or the other when in fact it is a matter of living committed lives in the closest association with the witness of profound experience over the ages.

Closely related to the same mistake is the supposition that religious experience is essentially and wholly a private matter. It has to be initially and in itself private, but what matters most is not the intimations of God that we may chance to have in our more exclusively private existence, but rather the absorption into our individual awareness of the wealth and significance of the sustained and developing religious awareness of men down the ages. It is not in a void that we encounter God but in all the rich diversities of our cultures and the formative part of religion within them. This is what must come alive for us in our individual experience.

This is what is sustained for us in various ritual and symbolic practice. How these function, and where they are genuine and healthy, is a subject in itself. There can clearly be perversions and parasitic imitations, just as there can be over-intellectualized treatments of practices where the true significance is closely bound up with the figurative and symbolic expression. Symbolism is not a thing apart, a decorative superimposition, it is a major, and often indispensable way of articulating what is profoundly perceived and felt and finds its appropriate depth in the fertilization and sustaining of one another's experience within a continuing social unit. At the same time the symbol is not final, and the ritual must not become an end in itself, much less be exploited for purposes extrinsic to its proper motivation, indeed as has sometimes happened for evil purposes.

All the same, in the last resort, the symbol is not final and it does not exist for itself. It derives its proper power from the continuity of the experience it expresses. The same is true in art. Poetry, or other forms of art, which depend entirely on lively image or emotional overtones, is not the finest. It palls unless it high-lights or exhibits something distinctive and notable, however impossible it may be to distil the meaning from its figurative expression. The symbol must not, in religion, take wing on its own, it must be anchored in experience.

The same is true of the more formally credal expressions of religious truth. There is a place for sophisticated formulation, acutely difficult though it is and full of pitfalls, but it is not, alas as has too often been assumed, an *a priori* intellectual exercise. It proceeds on the basis of what is taken to be conveyed in the medium of live experiences enriching and extending one another in a variety of social contexts. This means that the theologian has a peculiarly difficult task and requires a greater variety of skills and aptitudes than is usually realized, least of all by the practitioners themselves - a point which I much stressed elsewhere.[5] It is particularly hard because one has to be responsive to the symbolism, and the appropriate artistry, and also to the critical assessment of all which these convey.

A very serious pitfall, most of all for Western theologians and religious thinkers, is to take some striking religious symbol or story out of its context in the total themes of the scriptures in which it appears. This has happened, for example, when juristic metaphors in the New Testament have been made the basis of doctrines of retributive punishment and vicarious suffering in ways appalling to any moral or intellectual sensitivity. Credal affirmations do have their important place, most of all in religions in which the historical factor is important. They help to concentrate attention in the right way. But they must proceed on the basis of what is initially made evident in the formative disclosures in experience.

In Semitic religion there is usually accorded an exceptionally important place to a distinctive form which divine disclosure in human experience is alleged to have taken in a particular stretch of history. This is not the place to assess that claim or the even more astounding claim that the one transcendent reality was able, in some way which baffles all comprehension, to so limit itself as to enter into a fully human limited form in the culmination of the process which had been taking shape in Hebrew history. This remains the central Christian affirmation and I myself make very little sense of recent attempts to retain the formulae and ritual practices of the Christian faith if these central themes, as they seem to me, of the New Testament and traditional Christian understanding are so eroded as to bear little relation to the sources from which they came and the meaning they would normally be given. Far better, it would seem to me to abandon them altogether, though that is far from what I myself commend.

At the moment the question is not the soundness of the distinctive claims of the Christian faith or any other. But there is one point I do want to stress, namely that the assessment of these and like affirmations must, in the last analysis, go back to the profoundest appreciation of the subtle interlacing of normal sensitivity with divine intimation. If this adds up, in the available evidence about Jesus and his background, to the central affirmations of the New Testament and traditional Christian thought, so be it - it is what I myself think. But if the central claims are not to be sustained along those lines I know of no way in which they can be so sustained that they can stand in the light of open reflection and criticism today.

It remains most important however to recognize that, which ever way the evidence points in respect to the distinctive stances of various religions, this is no bar to the profound recognition of one another's insights and achieve-

---

[5] *Freedom and History* (London: Allen and Unwin, 1962), Chap. XVII.

ments. We have learnt much better today how much of mutual enrichment of one another's experience and insight is possible in this way. The differences, where they remain, must not be blurred, any more than they must be hardened by misunderstanding. We can reach across to one another's practices and histories to the great deepening and enlivening of our own experience, and the gain in this way to the West today is much too evident for me to need to underline it now. We have learnt enormously from varieties of experience that were new to us, and the range of our sensitivity has been much extended. Meditation has acquired a new depth for us, and flights of religious imagination opened up that were little known before. My contention is that the major clue for understanding and assessment, when expertise and scholarship has done its work, is the religious toning and directing of religious experience along the lines indicated.

There is one point of considerable substance which I would like to add. It refers to what I was saying at the beginning about the initial awareness of the transcendent. In my understanding, the transcendent is altogether beyond and other than finite being. Creaturely existence, though wholly dependent, is not any part or mode of ultimate being. This is however much in dispute, not only in extensive features of Eastern thought but in Western philosophies from Plotinus to Hegel and contemporary mystical philosophers like W. T. Stace. This again is a vast issue in itself and the opposition of view varies a great deal in its sharpness. I maintain, however, that this is the crucial issue for today in religious thought. It is not an easy one, and we all have our attachments to entrenched positions which we find hard to surrender. My own allegiance has been made plain in one publication after another. I strongly insist on the distinct reality of finite existences and especially on the peculiar distinctness of persons. On the line we take on this issue will turn, more than on anything else at present, the ultimate understanding we have, and even the sensitivity to genuine religious reality as such. It is an issue we must firmly face, though the last thing we must fall into is the temptation to settle the question lightly out of hand to ensure easy accommodation and good will. The right sort of good will does not call for that sort of price, and is contaminated by it. But we must have this central issue steadily before us, and it is on our success in coping with it, I maintain, that the best eventual progress will be made with all our other major problems and our power to share the wealth of one another's insights and experience.

I have spoken mainly of communication and assessment of truth. No space is left to consider the part which our own responsiveness plays in the process as a whole. The wind may blow "where it listeth" but "prayer and fasting" has its place too. An age committed to exclusively secular pursuits, and those not always the most elevated, can hardly expect to be well appraised of things that have to be "spiritually discerned." What Simone Weil and others have reminded us about heeding and "waiting on God" is immensely relevant, and this means more than being religiously attentive in a general way, it means also the continual response, in practice as in thought, of individuals in the ebb and flow of the illumination they have in their own religious experience and what they assimilate from the religious life of their community. It is in these terms, in the exchanges of genuine response, in the part we play ourselves in the formulation of our own religious awareness, that we come again, if I may again reflect my personal allegiance, to our understanding of the more theistic approach to religion and our proper participation in it.

Religious experience, so conceived, is not passive, and it does not underrate the essential mutuality of living, personal relationship as involved centrally in it. The language of prayer and devotion, of struggle and surrender, as well as the essential serenity, bring us to the vitally personal character of religious existence which we are also apt to overlook, even though some like myself may be inclined to over-stress it. The "God of the living," even of the wayward and rebellious, the relentlessly seeking God, is the God I have encountered in my own experience.

I hope such an element of personal testimony is not out of place. What matters for us here is that, in discussion and amity, we should enter into one another's views and sensitivity with as much imaginative insight and empathy as we can. Where the gaps can be closed let us hasten to do so, but our main concern is with the truth and "the wind of the argument whithersoever it takes us." We must understand as much as we can across the boundaries, with humility as much as with firmness. There is no place in true religion for confrontation or rancour, there is all the place in the world for empathy and humility.

King's College, London

3

GOD IN EXPERIENCE AND ARGUMENT
John Macquarrie

Philosophies of religion can be classified in many ways, but one of the most basic distinctions is between those which appeal to experience and those which base themselves on argument. Although I am going to maintain that finally each type needs the other, this is not obvious and there is no simple way of showing how the two types can be brought into relation with one another. To begin with, one is more aware of the differences between them. Philosophers who embrace the first type are often impatient of the second. They say that the philosophy of religion which proceeds by reasoning and argument has strayed far from the life of religion itself, that it deals in abstractions rather than with the concrete reality known in religion, and that it is in any case superfluous, for what proofs are needed by the person who has had firsthand experience of the religious reality and has known God face to face? Attempts to prove the validity of the experience (it is said) can lead only to bewilderment and uncertainty. On the other hand, philosophers who embrace the second type of theory may hold that theirs is the only correct approach *for philosophers*. Perhaps the religious person can get by on the basis of his religious experience alone, but the philosopher is committed to asking questions, seeking reasons, entertaining and discriminating among competing explanations. He knows that experience is sometimes deceptive, and he may think that the experiences of the religious person are so subjective that no truth claims can be established upon them. So he finds the appeal to experience unconvincing, and holds that if there is indeed a reality called God who is known in religion, this can be established only by a logical procedure which would develop a coherent concept of God and would then show that this concept refers to something real.

It is the second type of philosophy of religion that has the longer history. It was used in classical times, flourished in the middle ages and the enlightenment, and has persisted down to modern times. In that long history, there have been many arguments and counter-arguments, and ever more subtle refinements of the opposing points of view. The first type of philosophy of religion, the type which appeals to experience, has been more typical of the

modern age. Its rise may be due in part to the high value which we moderns
accord to experience, since we all share something of the empirical temper-
ament. On the other hand, it may be due in part to the fact that from the
time of Hume and Kant the older arguments have been seen to have serious
weaknesses, so that if one continues to practice religion and to believe in
God, and if one is not content to do this simply on the authority of Bible,
Church or tradition, one looks for another ground than that provided by the
classic theistic proofs. But it may be due in part also to the rise of modern
individualism and to the demand for what is called 'personal' religion. Pascal
is a good illustration of the shift from the rational argumentative type of
philosophy of religion to the experiential type. Descartes is the philosopher
whom Pascal has in mind in his criticisms, and Descartes is indeed a case
where the philosophical approach to the problem of God seems at its most
abstract. The existence of God is established by the most thoroughly rational
of all the traditional arguments, the ontological argument, and the function
of God in Cartesian philosophy seems to be chiefly that of guaranteeing the
veracity of our knowledge of the external world. It is against such a background that we are to understand Pascal's famous words, "God of Abraham,
God of Isaac, God of Jacob, not of the philosophers and scholars."[1] In
another passage, he declares that "the metaphysical proofs of God are so
remote and complicated that they make little impression; and even when they
are useful to some people, they are so only in that moment when their
demonstrative force is perceived, but an hour later, the same people fear that
they have been deceived."[2] The separation of the God of faith from the God
of metaphysics, the distrust of argument and the appeal to experience continue, though in different forms, in Schleiermacher, Kierkegaard, Ritschl and
many other religious thinkers down to the present time.

Let us consider more closely the type of philosophy of religion that bases
itself on an appeal to experience. It includes a variety of subtypes. In one
form, the appeal is to distinctively religious experience, though this again is
very diverse and includes worship, conversion, mysticism, spirit possession
and so on. The appeal to distinctively religious experience is basic to the
thought of Schleiermacher and Otto, and is believed by them to give assurance of the presence and reality of God or of the holy. But among more
recent thinkers, the appeal is to a broader spectrum of experience. Perhaps
it is even claimed that there is no distinctive *religious* experience, but that
there is a religious dimension in many of our everyday experiences which
would not be thought of as primarily religious. Here one might mention 1)
self-experience, the basic experience of existing as a human person. This

---

[1] Blaise Pascal, *Pensées* (Paris Garnier-Flammarion, 1973), p. 247.
[2] *Ibid*, p. 136.

carries with it a sense of finitude, which might direct the person thus made aware of his fragmentariness to the search for a reality more stable and enduring than himself; though it also carries the sense of transcendence, the drive inherent in the human being to go beyond every state of himself toward a fuller being. Next one may mention 2) conscience. Though this may not be crudely equated with the voice of God, yet moral experience seems to many people to have a religious significance—as witness the many books that have been written on how the moral life finds its completion in religion. Of course, conscience may be experienced as condemning and as accusing of guilt, or it may be experienced as directing toward some course of action or some state of being, and both types of conscience can have religious significance. 3) Commitment, in its many forms, is still another type of experience that may have religious overtones. Here we are thinking of the more important commitments which a person takes upon himself or herself. They confer identity on the person who accepts them, and form what Tillich felicitously called "ultimate concern." 4) In some persons of an intellectual cast of mind, the experience of order in the world has a religious character. The rationality of the human mind looks for a rationality in the world, and feels a sense of kinship when such rationality is discovered. There are scientists of whom this is true—Einstein, for instance, spoke of 'cosmic religion,' meaning the faith that the universe is rationally ordered. Something similar is found in some philosophers; Bradley wrote that "with certain persons, the intellectual effort to understand the universe is a principal way of thus experiencing the Deity" and that philosophy is "a satisfaction of what may be called the mystical side of our nature."[3] We may add 5) esthetic experience. The beauty and harmony experienced by certain people in nature or in art has something of a religious character. Many of the romantic poets had a religious—albeit somewhat pantheistic—feeling for nature, while in the present secularized atmosphere of our culture, many people seem to get some religious satisfaction from music or the visual arts. 6) Interpersonal relations constitute still another area where some people are sensitive to a religious dimension. In a deep relation to another person, the boundaries of self are transcended and this may have religious significance for some people or in some situations. We recall Buber's familiar words: "Every particular'Thou' is a glimpse through to the eternal 'Thou.'"[4] Finally, 7) even suffering and death can have for some a definitely religious character. If there are those who think of suffering and death as destructive of meaning in human life, there are others who claim that they prevent them from trying

---

[3] F.H. Bradley, *Appearance and Reality* (Oxford: Clarendon Press, Second Edition, 1897), pp. 5-6.

[4] Martin Buber, *I and Thou*, tr. R. Gregor Smith (Edinburgh: T.&T. Clark, Second Edition, 1959), p.75.

to understand themselves within their own narrow individual being, so that they have to see themselves as part of a larger ongoing whole.

I have mentioned here seven areas of experience in which some people might claim to perceive a religious dimension, and no doubt the list could be expanded. We are not to forget, however, that before mentioning those seven areas where the religious element appears in, so to speak, a secondary way, I had already mentioned experiences which are primarily religious—worship, conversion and the like. Perhaps it is only because some people have those primary religious experiences that it is possible to perceive a religious dimension in the other kinds of experience I have mentioned. On the other hand, a person who said that he never had a religious experience and did not know what such an experience was like might be introduced to it if he could be persuaded to focus his attention on what are claimed to be the religious dimensions of, let us say, esthetic or moral or interpersonal experience. Still, in casting the net so widely, we have to be aware of a danger. If religious experience is so widely diffused through many different kinds of experience, does it not lose its distinctiveness and become something so vague and indeterminate that we cannot say anything worthwhile about it? I do not think this is the case, but I do take the point that the so-called religious dimension will have to be specified much more clearly if it is to be taken seriously.

If religious experience (or some other kind of experience having a religious dimension) is held to bring the person having the experience into an encounter with a divine or holy reality, then I do not think that the experience alone guarantees that such an encounter or meeting has taken place. It could reasonably be claimed, of course, that there is a *prima facie* case in religious experience as in any other experience that through the experience there takes place an encounter with a reality beyond the consciousness of the experiencing subject, but the experience cannot be held to be self-authenticating. All experience, even sense experience, is fallible. Sometimes people believe themselves to be seeing or hearing things that just aren't there. Since religious experience is neither as universal as sense experience nor as straightforwardly checkable, its testimony cannot be accepted without further ado. It is true of course that a devoutly religious person may have complete certitude that God has met him or spoken to him, so that anything further would seem to such a person not only superfluous but even verging on the blasphemous. Consider the famous words of John Wesley about his conversion: "I felt my heart strangely warmed, I felt I did trust in Christ . . . and an assurance was given me that he had taken away my sins . . and then I testified openly to all there."[5] No one denies that Wesley had the experience he describes, and

---

[5] As reported by J.R.H. Moorman, *A History of the Church in England* (London: A.&C. Black, Third Edition, 1973), p. 298.

perhaps there is even a *prima facie* case, as I have suggested, for believing that this was an encounter with God in Christ. But if this is challenged, something more is needed than just the testimony of Wesley, irrefutable though it may have seemed to him.

The first move, however, would not be to turn away from the experience and to try to substitute argument for it. It would be to explore the experience more fully. Experience does not come to us in complete rawness. It is more than sensation, though it includes sensation. Our experiences are already clothed in language, so that we can offer a description of the experience. Beyond the description, we often go on to offer an interpretation. In the example quoted, Wesley describes his experience in terms of a sensation of warmth, feeling of trust, assurance and forgiveness. And he interprets or explains the experience in terms of the action of Chirst.

Thus to offer a careful description of an experience must be the first step toward evaluating it. It is such a description too that can enable other people to compare their experiences and ask whether they have known anything comparable to what is described. I think that description either of a primary religious experience or of the religious dimension that is claimed to be present in other kinds of experience would draw attention to two basic characters—intentionality and ultimacy.

I mention first *intentionality*. It is the mark of religion that it draws a person out of himself or herself, that it relates him to a larger reality. It has always been understood, of course, that there is bad religion as well as good, illusory as well as true. No doubt there can be religion in which an experience is enjoyed for its own sake, as one might enjoy, let us say, drug experience. But the aim of religion is to link the life of the devotee with a life that is higher than his own. Religious experience by its very nature stretches out beyond the self of the individual believer. Indeed, to the religious person, what he encounters in faith is more real than anything else. It stands over against him, perhaps judging, perhaps supporting, but always other than himself—indeed, in some forms of religious experience,"wholly other." This intentionality, by which I mean the reference of the experience to a reality beyond the person who has the experience, is a basic characteristic of religious experience. Any interpretation will have to take it into account, and I should think that any interpretation which explained it away would be not so much an interpretation of religion as its abolition. But of this I shall say more in a moment.

Meanwhile I turn to *ultimacy*. By this I mean that in religious experience one strikes against the limits of all experience. This happens directly in such experiences as mysticism or the sense of the presence of God in worship, but it happens also in the various types of experience which I listed as having a religious dimension. Conscience, for instance, in many cases is simply the voice of society, the superego, shot through with the relativism of a particular culture or subculture. But the very fact that conscience can transcend and judge its cultural expressions, pointing beyond them to an ideal of humanity and community, indicates that it cannot be explained only in sociological terms. Or again, the sense of beauty and harmony that arises from some limited scene of nature or work of art points beyond itself to universal form; the discovery of rationality in a limited area of the universe points to a rationality pervading the whole; the relation to another finite person suggests the relation to an "eternal Thou" as the center of a universal community—as Teilhard de Chardin expressed it, the "creatures are not merely so linked together in solidarity that none can exist except all the rest surround it, but all are so dependent on a single central reality that a true life, borne in common among them all, gives them ultimately their consistence and their unity."[6] This, then, is the kind of ultimacy that I have in mind as a basic character of religious experience—a pointing beyond the immediate and the relative to the limits, to the deepest reality which embraces and transcends all finite realities.

Description then yields these two basic characteristics of religious experience—intentionality and ultimacy. Any interpretation that seeks to be plausible must take these characteristics with utmost seriousness. It seems to me that theism is the interpretation that does most justice to the data revealed in the phenomenology of religious experience. A well constructed coherent theism is the most adequate and satisfying way of accounting for those experiences of intentionality and ultimacy which lie at the very foundation of religion.

The alternative, I suppose, is some reductionist explanation of religion, where 'God' is taken to be a veiled and misleading way of referring to society or humanity or something of the sort. It is always possible that the reductionist account is true, and that the elements of intentionality and ultimacy in religious experience are illusory. But here I think one might claim that the theistic explanation is more adequate than the reductionist accounts, not least because it gives a straightforward interpretation of the data and is not involved in ingenious attempts to show that things are other than they seem. But what is probably the least satisfactory account of all in the matter of religious experience is the view that tries to hold on to the value of religion while frankly embracing a reductionist explanation—I have in mind Dewey's "common faith," Maslow's "peak experiences," and the like. For when religion has been deprived of intentionality and ultimacy, the experience has been changed, it is no longer religion but, as I said before, something like a drug experience. For true religion liberates the devotee into a reality larger than himself and is never a sensation to be privately enjoyed. That is why

---

[6] Pierre Teilhard de Chardin, *Hymn of the Universe*, tr. Gerald Vann (London: Collins, 1970), p. 24.

the higher religions have always been closely associated with the life of moral striving and why conversion does not lead to a desire for more experiences but is typically followed by a sense of being called to service in the world.

Up to this point, we have seen that a philosophy of religion that begins from the side of experience can advance quite a long way, whether it begins from specifically religious experience or takes the wider view that "religious experience is ordinary experience controlled by religious selectivity and interpretation."[7] Yet we have also had to acknowledge that in the end it may be illusion. Furthermore, we have passed over the fact that for some people experience points to the absence of God rather than to his presence. While atheism often arises from a logical critique of religion, there is also an atheism that arises from experience. There is therefore a parallel between the two types of philosophy of religion, experiential and argumentative, and two types of atheism, which may be similarly designated. This was made very clear during the debates over the "death of God" in the sixties. Some of the new atheists of that time passionately denied God on the basis of an experience of godlessness. Because their denial had this passionate and experiential quality, we could say that the God whom they denied was the God of Abraham, Isaac and Jacob, the God known in the history of faith. An obvious exemplar of this kind of atheism was Richard Rubenstein, and he made his denial on the basis of the Jewish experience, especially the experience of Auschwitz and the attempted genocide carried out by the Nazis. Very different is the kind of atheism encountered in Paul van Buren's writings of the same period, for what troubled him was the alleged incoherence of God-language. The God whom he denied was primarily the God of the philosophers, the concept of a transcendent being.

We must then acknowledge that experience alone, even though it may seem overwhelmingly convincing to the person who has had some signally revealing experience (whether it has revealed God or the absence of God), and even although it can be refined and made more intelligible through description and interpretation, must still leave us with a question mark. Although the starting point that lies in experiences seems so different from the one that lies in intellectual speculation, the more we explore experience, the more we seem to be driven toward the rational activities of analysis, discrimination, validation. This happens especially when we come to the vital question of interpreting experience and in trying to account for it in terms of realities beyond the experiencing subject. I should add, however, that perhaps this language of an experiencing "subject" is not very happy. Certainly, it is misleading if it suggest that there is an isolated subject who enjoys or

---

[7] Martin Thornton, *My God: A Reappraisal of Normal Religious Experience* (London: Hodder & Stoughton, 1974), p. 91.

undergoes his experiences in himself, and that this subject has somehow to be subsequently related to entities beyond himself. It is only if one sets out from such presuppositions that the claim that religious experience (or some other kind of experience) is "subjective," in the sense that it refers to nothing that exists independently of my own stream of consciousness, comes to be made. On the contrary, it has to be contended that the so-called "subject" of experience is always, in Heidegger's significant expression, a "being-in-the-world." He begins "out there," so to speak, and it is superfluous to attempt to prove the "reality of the external world." Even our most private feelings, such as Wesley's sense of warmth, his trust and assurance, and so on, are registers or indexes of a situation in which he is one item among others,[8] and that is why such feelings are always strongly intentional. Even so, I come back to the point that the description and interpretation of religious experience leads more and more into the area of the exercise of reason and judgment. In spite of the apparently wide gulf separating the way of experience from the way of argument, it begins to be apparent that we could have much more assurance about the results to which the former of these ways leads if the second way were found to provide an independent route to the same destination.

So now we turn to the second of our two types of philosophy of religion, the type that proceeds by way of argument. As with the other type, one may distinguish subtypes. First among these is the purely rational approach, which proceeds simply by considering and analysing concepts already present to the mind, prior to any experience. The most celebrated case is the "ontological proof" of God's existence. If it is acknowledged that the mind has the concept of a being free from the limitations and imperfections that belong to ordinary finite beings, then, it is argued, one is compelled to go on to assert the reality of such a being—"a being than whom no greater can be conceived," in Anselm's language. On the other hand, it may be found impossible to construct a coherent concept of such a being, and in that case the ontological proof would turn to an ontological disproof of God's existence. This purely rational consideration of the concept of God might seem to be at the furthest remove from the God of religious experience—the present writer never came nearer to being persuaded of the absolute disjunction between the God of faith and the God of the philosophers than on the occasion of spending a day with a group of philosophers discussing the ontological argument! Yet however abstract the concept of God might be and however it might be manipulated in argument, the very fact that such a concept is, in the traditional language, "innate" to the human mind is a fact of religious significance. If

---

[8] See my essay,'Feeling and Understanding,' in J. Macquarrie, *Studies in Christian Existentialism* (Montreal: McGill University Press, 1965), pp. 31-42.

this concept can be given a coherent shape, this would not (in my view) prove the reality of God, but it would mean that 'God' has to be taken very seriously, and it would clearly strengthen that interpretation of religious experience which holds that it arises from the impinging of a divine reality upon us. More common, however, than the purely rational arguments are those which introduce an empirical element. The word 'empirical' should not mislead us here, for there is not an appeal to experience in the same way as with philosophies of religion that seek to base themselves on religious experience. In the present case, the arguments have an empirical element only in the sense that they draw upon evidences taken from our observation of the world, and seek to deduce the reality of God from these evidences. Here we have in mind such traditional proofs or arguments as those based on causality and on the alleged evidences of purpose in the universe. Even these arguments might seem once more to be very remote from the religious concern with God. What have a First Cause or an Unmoved Mover or a Supreme Intelligence or a Necessary Being to do with the God of Abraham, Isaac and Jacob or with the God who was incarnate in Christ? But again, these ways of thinking about God may not be at an infinite remove from each other. Is it something like a religious interest, namely the quest to understand man's place in the scheme of things, that motivates inquiries into the nature of reality, however abstract and logically rigorous these may be? While, on the other hand, might it not be claimed that the religious experience of God and the very act of worshipping and adoring him entail that he includes such notions as First Cause, Necessary Being, Supreme Intelligence and the like, though the average worshiper would probably be unaware that such descriptions are implicit in the very act of naming God? Again, just as the way that leads from experience needs confirmation from the independent way that proceeds by argument *(fides quaerens intellectum),* so the abstractions of speculation are fleshed out when the arguments are related to experience. The arguments themselves are inconclusive, but are they not strengthened when people report experiencing a God who is in recognizable relation to the being demanded by the arguments?

We agree with James Richmond that it is a mistake to separate too sharply the God of religion from the God of philosophy. He writes: "When the term 'God' is fully and thoroughly unpacked, vital meanings are discerned which might be overlooked if the unpacking were carried out only in the light of the immediate needs of individual piety and commitment . . . God is indeed the 'being whom we set our heart and trust upon,' but he is that precisely because he is the transcendent and creative ground of the finite world and all that it contains."[9] We could put it in another way by saying that every

---

[9] James Richmond, *Theology and Metaphysics* (London: S.C.M. Press, 1970), p. 151.

belief that we hold, when we subject it to scrutiny, has both a history in our experience and a grounding in our rationality. In the case of religious beliefs, especially the fundamental belief in God, the experience comes first. Then follows the argument, which may either confirm the interpretation of the experience or, in the case of some people, fail to do so. Thus the two ways which in their beginning were so different finally converge.

Oxford University

4 FINDING GOD IN THE TRADITION

Thomas Langan

I. *How God finds Us: On Being Appropriated by the Tradition*

The God who is active in history can reach into a new life through the pervasive formative influences of a highly structured explicit tradition, carrying out its task of transmitting the witness of things unseen through the educational work of several reinforcing institutions—family, Church and religious school. While this highly structured and self-conscious kind of handing down the Good News is obviously only one way God is present to man, it has been, in all those societies seriously influenced by a branch of the great stream of "religion of the Book,"—Judaism, Christianity or Islam—central to their history and remarkably effective in perpetuating and spreading a sense of God's reality. Stretching in unbroken institutional continuity at least to the time of the Davidic kingdom, it constitutes the oldest continuous explicit tradition and remains, in the present epochal situation, one of the massive facts about mankind which all need to try to understand.

In this paper I propose to offer a general outline of one central aspect of this great explicit tradition generated by the religion of the Book. I shall sketch the dimensions of the phenomenon which will require extended study if we are to understand well how one is helped through the life of the Church to come to know God. The phenomenon is separated into two movements, which, while in fact tending to dominate successively as phases of a person's development, are nevertheless both present in later life and thus not as neatly compartmentalized as our outline suggests.

First, I shall outline the way the institution carries out its task of transmitting the tradition, both the explicit, formulated core of it, and the implicit fabric of the actually lived tradition. Then, I shall ask how, with the help of its institutions, one can deepen and become more responsible in his own taking possession of what is graciously offered through this tradition: how through a conscious participation in the living history of the Church, one can come to know and live with God more fully.

My purposes here, appearances to the contrary not withstanding, are ultimately philosophical. I am concerned to understand the mechanisms, as they reveal themselves in the actual situation and through it in the tradition, for transmission of this kind of tradition, the Tradition of Revelation.[1] Such a study is indispensible, I believe, for an adequate evaluation, at a later stage, of the truths transmitted. The media is not the message, but an understanding of it is required if we are to judge the exact and full sense of what is transmitted.

Consider then the ways in which a person "brought up in the Church", as the expression ably puts it, is handed the witness of the tradition and formed to its ways. It is important to keep both aspects in mind. The truth claims handed down in a Christian education, while rich in ontic information (if I may so put it) are not primarily intended for one's theoretical edification but rather are revealed in order to point out to him the Way, that is what he is to do if he is to live meaningfully, as fully as possible. In saying that I do not intend to denigrate in the least the cognitive element. Indeed a Way successful for human beings first of all has to be *known*, to be effective, but more than that it must bring cognitive satisfaction, for we are indeed, as Aristotle insisted, of a nature which has been made to know. *What* there is to know, however, is a reality that can only be appropriately known when embraced by our whole being, it is something which of its nature requires to be put into practice.[2] The Christ expressed these aspects, the cognitive, the normative, and the desire fulfilling in one concise declaration about himself, "I am the Truth, the Way, and the Life!"

This is no small matter we are considering. Indeed, in the practice of the tradition it poses a serious problem. Often truths of the Christian faith are transmitted in the form of cognitive principles divorced from the experiences

---

[1] In my work in progress, *Tradition and Authenticity,* four genera of explicit tradition are distinguished: 1) artistic, 2) associational (such as constitutional government), 3) philosophical-scientific, 4) revelational. The present paper is a very general exploration of some central aspects of this latter kind of explicit tradition.

[2] Francis Cornford, good Enlightenment man that he is, sniffs patronizingly at those mystery religions which, turning away from Olympian detachment and the royal intellectual way of science, sought to involve their adherents in a total knowing, "more emotional than intellectual." But that is precisely what flaws that which is in many ways a great book and a deserved classic, *From Religion to Philosophy,* Cornford's own untenable philosophy of knowledge. He simply fails to consider that there are objects to be known which themselves are not just for the sake of theoretical contemplation. One is avidly interested to know all there is to know about a friend, not in order just to deepen his general understanding of psychology, but in order to love the real person more wholly. One studies the life and the musical development of Bach, not only because they are intrinsically interesting, but in order to increase one's total embrace of what is being performed.

which alone reveal the fullness of their sense; or, conversely, it can happen that cult experiences are enjoyed in the absence of any elaborate cognitive framework. (The most extreme instance is that "evangelism" which seeks to whip up the maximum of enthusiasm with the minimum of theology.) Dogmas without experience are empty, and experiences without dogmas are blind.

The heart of the Christian tradition is *witness*—witness to things unseen by the present generation. The Church is most literally apostolic. Those who have been sent forth (*hoi apostoloi*) tell those who were not present of events they themselves experienced, of things that have happened that are of enormous consequence—consequences for how we are to behave in the light of what they tell us about how it stands with the world.

Now how does the young child, "brought up in the Church," first experience these things? The child, we must remember, knowing nothing, and therefore with no basis from which to mount any criticism, is ready to believe anything. It's just as wonderous to be told that thunder is caused by great discharges of static electricity as it is to learn that God was present in the world in the manger. The fire house is a fascinating presence, the Church an attractive presence, all are parts of one and the same real world. One learns of grandparents one has never seen, of historic heroes, and of Christ Jesus the Lord. It's all the same. It's impressive to see crowds streaming into the cinema, and the rapt attention to what is going on in there adds to its weightiness. Similarly, to see the Church parking lot refilling four times on Sunday, to experience the hush at the moment of consecration, to busy about as an alter boy, to appreciate the daily witness of the nun teaching in her distinctive uniform, all impress the child with the reality of religion. In school one is told that Napoleon invaded Russia, that Moses led the Hebrews out of Egypt, that Columbus discovered America, that gas expands when heated, and that Christ rose from the dead. To the child, it's all the same.

Without meaning to be irreverent and without intending to write satire, I would like to sum up in a few lines some main features of the child's picture of the religious parts of the world as it comes across thanks to the good offices of that redoubtable institution, the parochial school. My reason for doing this is to isolate some of the principal truth claims with a view to examining their nature, especially the form, in which they are transmitted and how they are transformed by experience. The child is told that the world, and he himself individually, were created out of nothing by God. God is presented very much like any historic personage, only even more remote than Lincoln and much more powerful. Yet at the same time He is presented as somehow immediately accessible, as a living presence who may be invoked in prayer and who will answer. The little child learns from experience to expect answers that are extremely discreet, not very definite, not very insistent, except for a rare experience of a remarkably strong movement forming in the heart. And then, he is told, God is present in the Church, through his

Son, in the sacrifice of the Mass. There a people is actually witnessed gathering in expectation, something happens, a community of faith waits in hopeful expectation at the moment of consecration, and proceeds to the altar to participate personally, at the moment of communion. Where God the father is somewhat remote, and the Holy Spirit vague in the extreme, the Son, in his incarnation in Jesus the Christ becomes perhaps the most present of all historic personages and a presence easily summoned up in the prayerful imagination: the Good Shepherd, the Man of Sorrows, the one who was triumphant over death. The child learns of the Church as the continued incarnation of this Christ, assuring His concrete presence in the world, first through the sacraments, then through the corporal and spiritual works of mercy. (''Whenever you do this to the least of my brethren, you do it unto me.'') He witnesses the Church at work in the world. He experiences the Christ-like presence of holy priests and nuns (or conversely he can be shocked by the contradiction of violent or venal clergy and hypocritical church-going parents). He has the example held up before him of the heroes of the Church, down through the centuries, incarnating the ideal in every imaginable kind of situation, in every epoch, a potentially important influence, as I shall explain in a moment.

In all this, a special place should be reserved for the child's encounter with ''the living word'' as he hears it directly from the Bible. Through the medium of scripture, despite the barrier of translation, he is ushered into the very presence of those who recorded the word, the intrinsic power of which remains undiminished.

As one looks back over this list of truth claims, experiences, and encounters with the living word, one is struck by the great differences in kind of reception they represent. Consider the difference between the following, for example:

1) being told God created the world;
2) hearing directly the Word: ''Behold, I will be with you always, even unto the consumation of the world'';
3) experiencing the community's worship at Mass;
4) hearing about St. Francis of Assisi;
5) observing the piety (or lack of it) of the local pastor, and of one's parents;
6) the experience of one's own prayer.

The tradition—the handing down—is at work in all of these, but in such a variety of ways, and not without tensions and perhaps even contradictions. As the child grows towards the critical age of adolescence not only will the contradictions but also the disparity of degrees of impact of these things become crucial. This is what opens a space for critical questioning. He will begin to demand some consistency between what is preached and what is enacted, and he will want arguments—if not formal arguments, at least clarifications—to justify what he has been taught, and to patch over the gaps and tensions.

Within the Church "the power of example" is constantly pointed out. While it would be a mistake to underestimate the ability of the Word to get through with its message despite a mass of mediocre examples—the daily witness to tepid belief offered by everyday Christians—nevertheless, a child traumatized by the hateful example of a sadistic, hypocritical parent or teacher is likely to be insensitized to the Word and unreceptive to what he is told has been or is the case. Nothing as dramatic as trauma is necessary, however, to "turn off" the young. Decent devout parents have seen their children abandon religious practice because they are uninspired, indeed monumentally "bored" by the religious services experienced in the deadening atmosphere of a routine parish. Failure to practise accompanied by rather far-reaching utterances of skepticism and softness on issues like abortion does not preclude the likelihood that nevertheless consciences have been formed and some limits set on egoistic drives. Still, without doubt, the institutions have failed in something the tradition itself considers utterly essential to its task: the passing on of a sense of need for participation in the community, with its sacramental life, and a docility to the magisterium. In an essential way the institutions have failed in their task of appropriating those children of this generation to themselves. Consequently, if things go on as they are, those young people in turn will fail at their appropriative task. They will not address much of the Christian tradition in a spirit of positive, critical appropriation, for they will have rejected much of it without mature, deeply informed consideration. They will never assume in a mature responsible way much of the *possibility* handed down by that tradition. Great opportunities will have been lost to them.

It is not our task here to muster and examine the socio-psychological data needed for understanding the dynamics of this process of handing on—or failing to hand on—the tradition in concrete instances. The actual detailed processes at work as the institutions attempt to appropriate each new generation are obviously very complex and most worthy of serious study.[3] For our properly philosophical task of outlining the structures of the institutions' acculturation of the new generation and then the individual's appropriation of the tradition that has thus been handed him it is sufficient, for now, to survey in a very general fashion the kinds of possibility the institutions hold out to their members.

---

[3] The term "appropriation" is used properly only of the individual making his own the tradition that has been handed him, and is used by extension, analogously, of the institution's acculturating activities. Only a real, not a corporate, fictitious person, can appropriate, properly speaking.

If we look back over the random list of kinds of experiences encountered by the child, we see that in fact quite a variety of *graces* is preferred. I use the term grace here in its basic sense of a gift offered without the recipient's doing anything to merit it, although the acceptance of a grace always entails a commensurate responsibility. What kinds of possibility can we discern?

First, the Word itself: The Bible is kept alive by the Church. Without the active community of believers, it would not reach many ears. Handed down, it offers the vision of the Kingdom as Way to life and truth.

Secondly, the preaching of the Word: Not only is the Bible kept alive and transmitted physically, but attention is called to it, certain passages are drummed home, it is interpreted and explained, and, to some it is even presented with great scholarship and brilliance. Whatever truth is contained in this compilation of reports and prayers covering more than a millenium of religious experience and miraculous events is encouraged to shine forth on many occasions, from Mass, to retreat, to classroom, and the inducement of the community is there to guide and sustain the otherwise wandering attention of the young and to help discipline it to reflection and contemplation.

Thirdly, the opportunity of participating in the sacramental life of the community and in communal prayer: The preaching of the word is of course an integral part of this but the sacramental dimension, which in Catholicism at least has remained strong, offers the opportunity of an entirely different kind of experience from the preaching of the Word and the intoning of canticles, common to all branches of the religion of the Book. Its enemies would say that here Catholicism shows signs of arrested development, of remaining stuck in the magical stage of man's evolution. To the Catholic experiencing it, however, it is proof of the wisdom and generosity of the divine plan in offering man, who is himself incarnate spirit, a truly incarnational religion. The Word became flesh and dwelt among us, and in the sacraments, above all in the Eucharist, that presence of Him who said, "I will be with you all days" is palpable but in a way that calls on the gift of one's own believing spirit in order to reap the benefits of the special sacramental presence of the Spirit in the water or in the bread. Here indeed is an extraordinarily impressive kind of handing on, one which requires a hierarchial, highly institutionalized transmission down through the centuries. From the laying on of hands by the apostles upon the first bishops, and by the bishops to their successors, and by their successors upon the priests, the power is transmitted to convoke in this special intense physical way the divine presence. What was denied Moses when, at Sinai, he asked the divine name so that he might command the presence of this God, was granted by Christ to the ministers of His church, a power that is indeed staggering and like all great delegations, dangerous, subject to sinful exploitation, but also the source of immense life.

To those viewing the mystic assembly from the outside, it may seem that it is the music, the incense, the architecture, the vestments, in short the *mise en scene* which fascinates. These can of course be themselves graces with their own (much more limited) efficacity. But that is of course not the heart of the matter at all. What counts essentially in terms of impact is the holiness of the assembly. The masses which leave the most lasting impression are often those said in little chapels with a handfull of people by a holy priest whose own profound reverence and simplicity opens the eyes and the heart to what is really happening. Then occurs a most memorable and striking ''handing on''. The physical presence of Christ may indeed be convoked only in virtue of the apostolic authority vested in the priest; but only when those present have been led to open their hearts and minds is there an *experience,* of the divine presence.

This very naturally recalls once again the question, so central to traditions, of *example.* It is an essential part of Christian teaching that Christ becomes present to us in other people, who by the example of their lives, serve as a kind of sacramental incarnation. The reverse is also true: the hypocrite becomes an effective block to the divine presence. We have suggested that these incarnations do not have to be actually physically present. The preached about or read about examples of the saints' lives are powerful stimulants to a sense of the divine presence. But nothing can substitute for the Christ-like presence, in flesh and bones, of a good apostle, living out a holy life, and even the example of the faithfulness of an ordinary congregation can be a kind of inspiration.

Finally, but not least important in this list of opportunities to discover the divine which the institutions provide, both systematically and sporadically, is one's own prayer to which one can be led through the disciplined practices of Church, school and home. No more than the most human friend can God be present unless we are. Prayer is nothing more than an exercise in *disponibilté,* to use Gabriel Marcel's term. Without it, we cannot be fully appropriated by tradition and above all by its divine Source; nor without it can we appropriate, for only through prayer can one be in the presence of that which is to be made our own.

II. *How We can Find God: On Appropriating the Tradition*

If the institutions essentially succeed in their work of handing on the tradition, then at that period in life when one begins to examine critically what one has been told and the sense of one's experiences, they will have provided: a) easy access to a fund of information (through Scripture, the works of the Fathers and Doctors [albeit often filtered down and somewhat washed out in popular tracts and catechisms], and general theological teaching); b) a discipline of regular prayer and sacramental life; c) models for one's life; d) a certain basic credibility which will have become a part of the person's natural faith, that is, their basic attitude regarding how it stands with the world. This credibility includes a willingness to consider respectfully the on-going teaching of the Church as a source of truth that is seen to square well with one's global experience; and it involves the experience of the essential respectability of those one sees attempting to live a Christian life.

Each of these has its importance as the critical task of wrestling with tensions and apparent contradictions begins in earnest, and as the task of appropriating the tradition—of responsibly making it one's own—becomes a central concern. Appropriation involves three intimately interconnected aspects: a deepened knowledge of what there is to appropriate; judgment of the genuineness of the handed-down elements; and the fullest participation in the possibilities handed down by the tradition. We could profitably study each of these aspects at length and then investigate their interaction. I propose however here to concentrate on just one important point in the process, because it concerns the question to which the present collection of essays is devoted, the knowledge of God. Supposing then the appropriative process underway according to the best dispositions wished by the tradition, what combination of *information* and *experience* does the tradition offer the person intent on a mature response to the presence of God in the tradition?

I am obliged to reiterate that I am uncomfortable with the term 'information' and with the necessity for distinguishing it from experience. Yet this seems unavoidable. God is not a state of mind, an attitude, a psychic experience. He is, according to the conviction of all the great religions of the Book, a reality utterly independent of anything we may think or do, indeed He is the very foundation of the possibility of our thinking or feeling anything because He is the Source of all being. To form a right attitude about God I need to know something genuine about Him. This knowledge of a reality existing independently of me is what I mean by *information*. Now the tradition does hand down information about God. Information about God obviously cannot be very much like information about geological strata. What kinds of information does the tradition hand down?

a) Through Holy Scripture, the tradition informs us of God's revelations of Himself. This includes descriptions of a number of theophanies, pictured in varied and wonderful language. (A systematic perusal of these theophanies turns up an impressive variety of descriptions of the divine presencing, through which runs a consistent strain of information about the nature of these divine initiatives). It includes definite divine instruction, impinging on our behaviour. What God wants of us becomes quite discernible, "Let those with ears to listen hear!"

b) Again through Holy Scripture, we are informed of a multitude of details about the most contentful (if I may so put it) of all the theophanies, the Incarnation of the Son of God in Jesus. The New Testament contains what we need to know about Jesus. Little biography, perhaps, and as St. John tells us at the end of his account, only a fraction of what he said and did, but that fraction contains an immense amount of material to digest, to inform us, to guide us, to challenge us. Again, in this way the Divine Will makes quite clear what it wants from us in the way of performance. A concrete model of behaviour is held up to us. At the same time the power and the glory of the Lord shines out from many a page. We learn how perfect human existence, under perfect divine leadership, manifests itself in a significant variety of situations. We learn of the founding of the Church, the sacraments, and of eschatalogical prophesy.

c) From the Fathers and the Doctors, we are handed theological elaborations of all the matters revealed in the Scriptures. To the extent these theological efforts yield genuine insight, they too provide a kind of information, about God, Being, man, and society. Moral illumination, psychological insight, ontological frameworks are all a kind of content demanding to be judged and if found to stand up in the light of the totality of our knowledge and experience of the world, to be absorbed into a global view of things, in terms of which we ought to direct our action.

d) The lives of the saints and the example of others provides a kind of information about what is possible and achievable. There is indeed something to learn about and from the life of a John Henry Newman or a Theresa of Avila. Their accomplishments provide an ontic stuff which throws light on the limits of human existence, as the ontic both shows forth and obscures the ontological. It is a great mistake to underemphasize the revelatory power of the ontic. The utterances and the acts of the saints elicit from us broadened horizons of interpretation which have to be opened out in order to take account of their factual accomplishments in corporal works of mercy, spiritual adventures, and heroic behaviour. The whole of Christian art and culture is a treasury of such ontic illustrations, information, inspiration. The sedimented, informed results of Christian work transforming nature down through the long sweep of historical epochs.

Without such information, we would not know what there is which we are called to possess. But information, while necessary, is not sufficient. Enter the role of experience! Only through the experience of communal life in the liturgy and in working together and in the experience of prayer do we come to realize what it means *to take possession* of the treasures of the tradition. Through such experience we learn what all the information is for. Only in this way—through living the faith—does one come to understand that what is revealed is the possibility of communion with the Source of life which is present in and through the communal life of the Church as Christ's presence on earth. Experience of the life of the Church reveals the need for appropriation to be a response to the elicitations of the concrete possibilities for love and insight which are handed down by the living tradition. This responseability of course involves an essential critical moment. To be able to respond to *genuine* possibility we have to be able to distinguish it from the false solicitations of fantasies and degrading possibilities. To do this, we have to call upon all of our knowledge of the world and all of our experience of what is fructifying (our total "natural faith"). Each possibility that is held out to

us by the tradition must stand the test of critical scrutiny in the light of our
natural faith, that is according to the way in which it fits into the totality of
our experience embraced by our basic, on-going operative judgment of "how
it stands with the world." "By their fruits you shall know them" is the
criterion offered by Jesus himself. The judgment as to what among the possibilities opened up to us by the tradition are indeed genuinely fruitful is
made by coming to grips critically with the *meaningfulness* of the sacramental
life, prayer, corporal and spiritual works of mercy and Christian ethics generally. Meaningfulness is achieved when a possibility makes sense to us in
terms of our overall assessment of our total experience.

When the knowledge of God is considered in this way, that is with regard
to the integration into our personal lives of the possibilities regarding the
divine that are handed down to us by the tradition through its institutions,
we see that the appropriation of the tradition of revelation in its fulness is
nothing less than a fundamental encounter with God. Participation in the
sacramental life is becoming one with the Mystical Body of Christ. "Knowing God" is here growing together with Him through active participation in
the Community through which He has willed to be present in the world in
a special and very full way. This is not basically a propositional kind of
knowing, even though it may be talked about in explicit expressions. It is
that Biblical kind of knowing, as when it was said, that "Mary knew not
man," not of course in the restricted sexual sense of this particular passage,
but in the root meaning of a total participation. It demands a certain critical
discrimination, for we must be one with the mind of the Church and we need
to discern the genuine core of its practice in the midst of a mass of pious
practices, some of dubious alloy.

Similarly, through *imitatio Christi per sanctis,* the following of the model
of a given saint whose experience is most relevant (as Louis Massignon, for
instance, followed the example of Saint Francis in his mission to Islam), we
attain knowledge of the divine that is revealed through following a way of
action in the practice of which alone the implications of the divinely ordained
virtues are revealed to us. Only the handing down of the model by a tradition
and our own thorough appropriation of it makes this kind of knowledge of
the divine possible.

It is the same with the life of prayer. Spontaneous prayer, of course, opens
us to God and requires no tradition, no appropriation to be effective. But the
higher forms of prayer are most often learned, great traditions of spirituality
(sufi'ism, Franciscan spirituality, the Spiritual Exercises of St. Ignatius) are
passed on—often through texts—and practised by *imitatio.* Through them the
Spirit will often come into the recesses of the heart in a fashion that changes
the orientation of men's lives. This then is another way in which the tradition
opens up a way to a knowledge of God that again is not theoretical, not
primarily propositional, but a knowledge through encounter in the depths of
the soul's interiority. The tradition of spiritual exercises, while itself a grace

in the sense defined earlier, cannot in any way guarantee the divine response to the properly prepared soul. But, the tradition teaches, without such disposition through careful ascesis, a certain kind of encounter is unlikely in the extreme.

Finally, there is knowledge of God to be attained through the handed down texts. Holy Scripture witnesses the tradition and reveals not only the saving events but the divine teaching itself. In this instance the knowledge is propositional ("I am the Way, the Truth and the Life") but also performative, ("Go ye therefore and baptize . . ."). At the same time it is descriptive. The model of Christ is held up as the man for all seasons, the point of ultimate imitation by all Christians. Other non-biblical texts bring the Christian masses of information and many detailed prescriptions for his conduct. The authoritative expressions of the Magisterium down through the ages, the theological elaborations of the fathers and doctors, pious writings, catechisms and manuals, all provide precious guides to a Christian life, vastly enriching the fund of possibilities open to us, a fund of spiritual discoveries, fruit of a massive reflection on ultimate things, without which the Christian life would be remarkably diminished. Appropriation of all these symbols requires not just hard study on our part but again an effort to live according to the prescriptions and to encounter the living realities which they proclaim.

III. *Conclusion*

In this brief outline the multi-faceted role of tradition as the handing down of possibilities and the revelation of needs has been explored in a very general fashion and discovered to be an immensely rich source of knowledge of God. That important parts of this knowledge are quite other than theoretical, drives home the importance of *participation* as condition for an adequate appropriation of the tradition. At the same time, the importance of the critical moment for discerning the genuine in the tradition has been underscored. The transition from that stage of our lives when we are more appropriated by the tradition than appropriating introduces a fundamental change in our way of relating to the truths that are handed down. The realisation of the need to pursue explicitly and knowingly a course of deepening our participation and for sharpening our critical evaluation is the birth of that process of *fides quaerens intellectum* which the Fathers recognized from early on to be central to the Christian tradition. That into the openings favored by the tradition's prescriptions the supernatural graces of faith, hope and charity may or may not flow, we have acknowledged. But without the appropriative effort to open ourselves to the fullness of the possibilities handed down by the tradition, it is doubtful that anything much above a primitive religious experience is likely to occur.

University of Toronto

5 PROOF AND PRESENCE

Frederick Crosson

It may be helpful to note some preliminary reference-points in order to give a sense of the orientation of these reflections, and so to provide the reader with some of the conscious assumptions and perspectives within which they unfold.

I take the notion of the presence of God to˙be a constitutive element of both religion and faith, these two terms being used in the senses that Thomas Aquinas expounds. But I want to avoid any understanding that the concept of presence is, on my own part or that of the reader, appended to an autonomous ego cogitans or transcendental subjectivity. Hence I am trying to anchor that concept and its relevant corollaries into historical strata which underlie the emergence of the cogito and the emphasis on consciousness in the modern period. I have elsewhere tried to explore that anchoring in the *Confessions* of St. Augustine,[1] and here I shall be concerned primarily with some of Thomas Aquinas' discussion of these issues. For similar reasons, I want to keep the exploration of the notion of presence within a social context and a tradition, which will serve as dialectical complements to keep that notion from standing in itself and by itself.

I choose Aquinas for many reasons, but important among them is the common view that he is an intellectual believer, who gives reasons for his faith, so far as possible, by rational arguments. Yet Aquinas' doctrine is one in which faith-knowledge is the paradigm of knowledge, so that it serves as the touchstone for rational assessment. Nor is this position arbitrary or unfounded, for the God whom he affirms is Truth and Goodness.

In the third book of the *Summa Contra Gentiles*, in the course of considering a *per impossibile* argument, he remarks in passing,

---

[1] "Religion and Faith in Augustine's *Confessions*" in *Rationality and Religious Belief*, ed. C. Delaney, (Notre Dame Press, 1979). I am grateful to Gary Gutting, whose critical comments helped me to formulate my thoughts about proof and presence more clearly.

it is not possible for the knowledge of faith to be false and empty, as is evident from what we have said in the opening Book.[2]

Intrigued by such a statement, one turns back to the referenced locus and finds four arguments, of which the first is typical:

It is clear that those things [the principles of rational discourse] which are implanted in reason by nature, are most true, so much so that it is impossible to think them to be false. Nor is it permissible for that which is held by faith, so evidently divinely confirmed, to be believed to be false. Since therefore only the false is contrary to the true, as is apparent from their definitions, it is impossible for these principles naturally known by reason to be contrary to the truth of faith.[3]

Note that it is the principles of reason—the laws of noncontradiction, transitivity, parts and wholes, etc.—which cannot be contrary to the truth of faith. Whatever is not so self-evident, but appears to follow according to them, if contrary to faith must be wrong:

any arguments alleged against the teachings of faith do not follow correctly from these self-evidently known primary principles of nature. Hence they do not have demonstrative force, but are either probabilistic or sophistical, and hence there is a basis for refuting them.[4]

So must say any scientist when confronted with an alleged fact or argument

---

[2] Non est autem possibile fidei cognitionem esse falsam neque vanam, ut ex dictis patet in principio Libri. *Op. cit.* III, 40.

[3] Ea enim quae naturaliter rationi sunt insita, verissima esse constat: in tantum ut nec esse falsa sit possibile cogitare. Nec id quod fide tenetur, cum tam evidenter divinitus confirmatum sit, fas est credere esse falsum. Quia igitur solum falsum vero contrarium est, ut ex eorum definitionibus inspectis manifestis apparet, impossibile est illis principiis quae ratio naturaliter cognoscit, praedictam veritatem fidei contrarium esse. *Ibid,* I, 7.

[4] quaecumque argumenta contra fidei documenta ponantur haec ex principiis primis naturae inditis per se notis non recte procedere. Unde nec demonstrationis vim habent, sed vel sunt rationes probabiles vel sophisticae. Et sic ad ea solvenda locus relinquitur. *Ibid.* There is a species of reciprocity here, in that the same claim can be turned around to discriminate what only appears to be the implications of faith. Two factors can mitigate the reciprocity: a long-examined and traditionally accepted faith-doctrine places the burden of proof on a challenge to it, and a *magisterium* speaking out of the community can set parameters for interpretation. Compare Newman's *Essay on the Development of Christian Doctrine.*

which contravenes the premises and criteria of evidence of rational inquiry into nature.

It is important, I think, to stress here that it is his confidence in reason as well as his confidence in faith that marks Aquinas' position. There is no double truth doctrine, or more pertinently, reason is not a merely human faculty which must falter and yield when it inquires into the Divine Truth. The principles of human reason are based on the intelligibility of being and thus are not alien to the understanding of God. No more than we can God understand—or make—something to be both four and greater than four. This claim carries recursively all the way back to *any* exercise of reason. If God could make something self-evident to us to be not true then no evident judgment can be known to be true. Descartes' admission of this possibility underlies the well-known circle which his argument for God's existence exhibits. Aquinas' contention is not, like that of Descartes, that a benevolent God did in fact endow us with reliable insight, but that He could not not do so.

The affirmation of faith that God is Truth thus meshes perfectly with the exigencies of rational insight. And as the Author of our rational nature He cannot not have "taught" us rightly in endowing us with reason: "it is not possible to say of God that he taught us misleadingly" (*ibid.*). The *malin genie* appears only when faith is doubted or set aside.

Nevertheless, the affirmations of faith are more encompassing, more fundamental and more imperative. They are self-grounding, not requiring confirmation or validation by rational insight or argument. Indeed, Aquinas holds that the merit of faith is diminished if a person believes only when human reasons are provided. Even though one may have reasons confidently based on demonstrations of the existence of God, he should be willing to believe on the authority of God alone.[5] Similarly, although the knowledge of the existence and unity of God is a necessary condition to further matters of faith, it is not necessary that these be established by demonstration, but "those who do not hold them by demonstration must at least posit them by faith."[6]

Those truths about God which are in principle susceptible of being rationally known he calls the "preambles" of faith. But it should be noted that these truths are not necessary conditions for a judgment of the reasonableness ("credibility") of the propositions of faith. St. Augustine's famous remark that no one believes anything unless he already understands it to be believable is relevant here.

---

[5] II-II, 2, 10c: all references are to the *Summa Theologiae* unless otherwise noted.

[6] oportet ea saltem per fidem praesupponi ab his qui eorum demonstrationem non habent: *Ibid* 1, 5, 3m; cf. 2, 10, 2m.

Let us examine several of Aquinas' statements about the relation of these preambles to faith.

Theology makes use of philosophy "to demonstrate those truths that are preambles of faith and that have a necessary place in the knowledge of faith. Such are the truths about God which can be proved by natural reason: that God exists, that God is one; such truths about God or about His creatures, subject to philosophical proof, faith presupposes."

God's being one insofar as it is demonstrated is not said to be an article of faith, but presupposed to the articles: for the knowledge of faith presupposes natural reason, as grace does nature.

The existence and unity of God "are not articles of faith but preambles to the articles."[7]

Now these texts might be understood—and historically have been understood—to mean that for the act of faith to be warranted, reasonable, one must already have attained on rational grounds the knowledge of God's existence, unity, etc. But in fact as we have seen, Aquinas explicitly says that they may be posited by faith itself.

For a long time, beginning in the seventeenth century and down to our own time, commentators on St. Thomas and Catholic apologetics have held such a rationalist position, namely that the credibility of revealed truths required a prior demonstration of God's existence, truthfulness, etc.[8]

The confusion with respect to Aquinas' position arose by taking him to mean that the preambles are necessary conditions to the *act* of believing, whereas Thomas takes them to be logically necessary conditions to the *articles* of faith, that is the specifically revealed truths of Christian doctrine. Hence the preambles, as the intersection of the areas of faith and reason, can either be held by belief or by demonstration, and must be held (as necessary conditions) in one way or the other.

Even this schema however, as we shall see, makes Aquinas seem more of

---

[7] ad demonstrandum ea quae sunt praembula fidei, quae necesse est in fide scire, ut ea quae naturalibus rationibus de deo probantur, ut deum esse, deum esse unum et alia hujusmodi vel de deo vel de creaturis in philosophia probata, quae fides supponit. *In Boet de Trinitate* II, 3c.

   Deum esse unum prout est demonstratum, non dicitur articulus fidei sed praesuppositum ad articulos: cognitio enim fidei praesupponit cognitionem naturalem, sicut et gratia naturam. *de Veritate* 14, 9, 8m. . . . non sunt articuli fidei sed praeambula ad articulos. *Summa Theologiae* I, 2,2,3m.

[8] For an examination of the changes which emerged in the seventeenth century in the conceptualization of this issue, cf. G. deBroglie, "La Vraie Notion Thomiste des 'praeambula fidei'," *Gregorianum* (1953) pp. 345–389.

a rationalist than I believe he is. For the area of intersection can, in fact, only be adequately delineated by the knowledge of faith.

So it is that Aquinas distinguishes as one of the component parts of the act of faith, believing in a God, along with believing God and believing in God.[9]

It is not inconsistent with this for him to hold not only that strict demonstration of the existence of God is possible, but that

> natural reason tells man that he is subject to a higher being on the basis of the defects which he perceives in himself and by reason of which he needs help and direction from someone above him: and whatever this being may be, it is that which is called God by all men.[10]

Such an apprehension is not a logically necessary condition for faith but manifests a converging gradient in human experience, one which testifies again to the fundamental compatibility between faith and reason.

Compatibility does not mean agreement: the inclination of natural reason toward such a recognition may remain so general as to ground quite diverse religious beliefs ("called God by all men"), and Aquinas is quite willing to say that those who do not have faith do not succeed in referring to God whatever they may call Him:

> Those who do not have faith cannot be said to believe in a God as we understand it in relation to the act of faith. For they do not believe that God exists under the conditions that faith determines; hence they do not truly believe in a God, since as the Philosopher says, to know simple things defectively is not to attain them at all.[11]

This is one of the corollaries of his understanding of "religion" as distinguished from "faith". He adopts Cicero's definition of religion as consisting in "offering service and ceremonial rites to a superior nature that men call divine." As distinguished from faith, which is a "theological virtue" having God as its object, religion is a moral virtue (indeed the chief moral virtue) which has God as its end, but not as its object:

---

[9] II-II, 2, 2c: credere Deo.

[10] naturalis ratio dictat homini quod alicui superiori subdatur, propter defectus quos in seipso sentit, in quibus ab aliquo superiori eget adjuvari et dirigi. Et quicquid illud sit, hoc est quod apud omnes dicitur Deus. *Ibid* 85, 1c.

[11] Credere Deum non convenit infidelibus sub ea ratione qua ponitur actus fidei. Non enim credunt Deum esse sub his conditionibus quas fides determinat. Et ideo nec vere Deum credunt, quia ut Philosophus dicit, in simplicibus defectus cognitionis est solum in non attingendo totaliter. *Ibid* 2, 2, 3m. For a discussion of this failure of reference, cf. Peter Geach, "On Worshipping the Right God" in *God and the Soul* (New York: Schocken, 1969) pp. 100–116.

the acts whereby God is worshipped do not attain to God Himself, as
when we believe God we attain God by the believing.[12]

Several things are worth noting about his conception of religion. First, it
is interesting that he takes over the definition of a pagan philosopher, although
not surprising precisely because for him religion is a natural virtue, one
whose origin and intent are wholly within the human sphere.

Second, religion is a moral virtue: it is concerned with behavior and indeed
with social behavior. It is concerned with service and cult, with prayer and
sacrifice, with oaths and oblations. Like Durkheim, Aquinas locates religion
in actions which relate to the good of the social community, although that
good and the right actions with respect to the divine which it entails will
differ as the good is differently perceived. Unless it is instituted by God,
religion will be diversified in the same way that political regimes are diversified, which does not mean that there are no natural norms underlying it.
Hence, God is the "end" but not the "object" of religion.

Third, "religious experience" is not an integral component or goal of
religion (in the sense in which William James speaks of the varieties of
religious experience). Aquinas does refer, in a text cited above, to the sense
of dependence on God's help which he contends is common to all men, but
the object of religion is the behavior which is perceived to be appropriate
toward God. The essence of religion does not consist of that sense of dependence, but rather of a way of life, whether always accompanied by feelings or not.

To sum up: faith (and the same can be said of religion) is not logically
dependent on a prior demonstration of the existence of God. In fact, natural
reason was not in Aquinas' view able to determine adequately the nature of
God's unity:

> by faith we hold many things about God which the inquiries of the
> philsophers by natural reason were not able to discover, for example
> about his providence and omnipotence and that he alone is to be wor-
> shipped.[13]

The "common and confused" knowledge of God (communis et confusa
cognitio Dei) which he thinks inclines most men to the acknowledgement of

---

[12] cui cultus exhibetus non quasi actus quibus Deus colitur ipsum Deum attingant,
sicut cum credimus Deo, crendendo Deum attingimus. *Ibid* 81, 5c and 1c.

[13] multa per fidem tenemus de Deo quae naturali ratione investigare philosophi non
potuerunt, puta circa providentiam eius et omnipotentiam, et quod ipse solus sit
colendus. *Ibid*. 1, 8, 1m.

a superior being does not make clear who or what sort of being He is, or whether He is one (Quis autem, vel qualis, vel si unus tantum: S.C.G. III, 38).

It may indeed be possible for unaided human reason to demonstrate the existence of God, and something of His unity;

> But if there have been any men who have discovered the truth about divine things by way of demonstration without any admixture of falsity, they have certainly been very few . . . and this knowledge includes much uncertainty, which is shown by the diversity of conclusions about divine things among those who have tried to discover them by demonstration.[14]

When reason is illumined by faith, the probability of finding an adequate demonstration is significantly increased, since we already know what it is we want to prove. Logically speaking, this is not a unique case, as Galileo's Salviati shows: Aristotle, he says, first obtained his conclusions in natural philosophy by observation and then

> he sought means to make them demonstrable. That is what is done for the most part in the demonstrative sciences; this comes about because when the conclusion is true, one may by making use of analytical methods hit upon some proposition which is already demonstrated, or arrive at some axiomatic principle; but if the conclusion is false, one can go on forever without ever finding any known truth—if indeed one does not encounter some impossibility or manifest absurdity. And you may be sure that Pythagoras, long before he discovered the proof for which he sacrificed a hecatomb, was sure that the square on the side opposite the right angle in a right triangle was equal to the squares on the other two sides. The certainty of a conclusion assists not a little in the discovery of its proof.[15]

Galileo would appear to provide support for Michael Polanyi's contention, as against Karl Popper, that the inquirer into nature seeks to prove what he holds to be true, rather than to falsify it. In our context, it would seem to be

---

[14] Si autem aliqui fuerunt qui sic de divinis veritatem invenerunt demonstrationis via quod eorum aestimationi nulla falsitas adiungeretur, patet eos fuisse paucissimos . . . cognition autem praedicta multum incertitudinis habet: quod demonstrat diversitas scientiarum de divinis eorum qui haec per viam demonstrationis invenire conati sunt. *S.C.G.* III, 39.

[15] *Dialogue Concerning the Two Chief World Systems.* (Berkeley: University of California Press, 1962) p. 51.

appropriate to say that Aquinas' conception of the logical place of proofs for
the existence of God is fundamentally Anselmian. That is, although the premises of the proof are not held by faith, the conclusion is: the proofs are sought
retrospectively. And this is the case not just factually or historically, but on
the logical grounds referred to: only by knowing what it is we want to prove,
on other grounds, do we stand a chance of finding a proper demonstration.

So it is that what has been called the "principle of charity" in recent
discussions of convergence of theories in the history of science functions also
for Aquinas. Although nothing corresponds exactly to the inadequate conceptions of the divine which earlier philosophers and religions elaborated, we
can see what they were trying to attain, to refer to, and make use of adapted
forms of earlier proofs.

Just because of the retrospective character of the proofs, and their resting
in the sense indicated on the firmer ground of faith, the elaboration of them
is not a central concern for Thomas. And this is why, I believe, he lumps all
five "ways" into one article of one question of his *Summa*.

Do we have any demonstrations in the case of the existence of God?
Negative rejoinders to this question are often based on the observation that
alleged demonstrations are not universally accepted. By itself, that non-acceptance is not logically sufficient ground for abandoning an apparent proof,
and might simply send the demonstrator back to his work more cautious and
more determined to scrutinize each step of the argument. But when it is
observed that virtually no one accepts such a proof who does not already
believe in the existence of God, the pertinence of non-acceptance is given
more weight. For it tends to suggest that the belief has surreptitiously found
its way into the demonstration, so that not simply is the conclusion known
by faith in the way that Salviati approves, but that some of the premises or
steps also rely on belief, and hence the proof as a whole does not, as it
purports, rest simply on what is knowable by human reason.

I think that this common view is not as cogent as it appears. My reason
for so thinking is derived from a reading of several controversies in the
history of science in which demonstrations were presented and rejected, but
later came to be accepted as demonstrations. What is perceived as an argument may come to be seen as a demonstration when it is placed in a different
context. That is to say that the notion of a proof is relative to a context, and
that context is not merely logical (an axiomatic system, for example) but
may be constituted by a specifically different attitude toward the world, and
toward the way in which we understand and even perceive the sense of things.

A brief discussion of two of these controversies will illustrate my reading.

The starry sky above has been from earliest ages perceived as totaliter
aliter, as a region of power and unchangeableness. We can still recapture
some of that sense of glory, when we find ourselves at night far from the
city lights and gaze up at that imperceptibly, majestically moving pageant of
the sky. It has always been perceived as related to, if not the home of,

divinity. Galileo wanted to establish the earth-like nature of those heavenly bodies, and to prove the Copernican theory. But he found that in order to do so, he had to de-mythologize the heavens. It is, he said, "vanity to imagine that one can introduce a new philosophy by refuting this or that author. It is necessary first to teach the reform of the human mind, and to render it capable of distinguishing truth from falsehood," which no mere observations could do.

That reform must go very deep indeed, for the conviction of the inalterability and perfection of the heavenly bodies is linked with man's deepest fears and emotions:

> Those who so greatly exalt incorruptibility, inalterability, etc., are reduced to talking this way, I believe, by their great desire to go on living, and by the terror they have of death.[16]

The Copernican revolution is often described as a revolution in our way of conceiving the universe and of locating ourselves within it. But I think it would be difficult to overestimate the power, both perceptual and effective, of the phenomenon referred to here. It can be put contrastingly by saying that we today no longer *see,* with our own eyes, anything palpably immutable, a visible sign of the eternal and unchanging God. It was the very way in which man inhabited the universe, the claim of the "higher things", the very evidence of the senses which blocked the way to seeing another significance of the stars.

Cannot the seeing of sunspots show that the sun is a changeable body? "An illusion of the telescope", "a fallacy of the lenses" reply his critics.[17] The difference which Aristotle postulates between the natural motions of heavenly and terrestial bodies (which Galileo says underlies all the other differences), viz. circular and linear motion, can be shown to be possibly relative to the position of the observer, i.e., standing on a rotating and orbiting earth. But even if we grant that this is mathematically possible to demonstrate, can we succeed in *seeing* a dropped cannonball move in a circular path, or the horizon sink beneath the sun at "sunrise"? And the Bible, Aristotle, tradition are all against such a view.[18]

The required reform of the human mind must be pursued by something like persuasion, assisted by arguments which will eventually turn into dem-

---

[16] Sagredo, in *op. cit.* p. 59; cf. p. 57.

[17] *Ibid.* pp. 52, 336.

[18] *Ibid.* pp. 18, 37. The analogy of Gestalt perception, the switching of visual perspectives which Norwood Hanson invoked in *Patterns of Discovery* is thus not pertinent. Cf. the discussion in Thomas Kuhn, *The Structure of Scientific Revolutions* (Chicago, 1965) p. 85.

onstrations, i.e., be accepted as such. It is not by accident that Galileo's great work on this takes the form of a dialogue. Wittgenstein remarks,

I can imagine a man who had grown up in quite special circumstances and had been taught that the earth came into being 50 years ago and therefore believed this. We might instruct him: the earth has long . . . etc.—We should be trying to give him our picture of the world. This would happen through a kind of persuasion.[19]

My second instance may conveniently be linked to Galileo, who noted that the positive integers may be placed in one-to-one correspondence with the even integers, although one would intuitively suppose that the latter set must be smaller than the former. He puzzled over this and seems to have decided that it was impossible to compare infinite quantities. "Infinity and indivisibility are in their very nature incomprehensible to us" he wrote. There is something indeterminate about the notion of the number of infinite numbers, and if we try to give it definiteness we get self-contraditions. Those parts of mathematics which dealt with the notion of infinity, such as the infinitesimals of the calculus, lacked a satisfactory theoretical foundation for several centuries, and suffered the guerilla attacks of philosophers and cantankerous mathematicians. Not until Cauchy's work on analysis in 1821 which formulated the concept of a limit did the calculus acquire such a foundation. But even then, one simply replaced the notion of infinitesimals with that of approaching a limit as closely as desired, thus circumventing the talk of an infinitely divisible interval. Gauss, the foremost of the 19th century mathematicians, protested against the use of "infinite magnitude", which he said was never permissible in mathematics.

But in the 1870's, Cantor began to publish a series of articles in which he proved the existence of transfinite numbers, showed how different transfinite numbers could be distinguished from each other with sufficient determinateness to formulate theorems about their relationships with each other and with their parts. His work was, however, rejected by the mathematical and academic community and bitterly attacked by such eminent mathematicians as Kronecker and Poincaré. A large and indeed fundamental part of the basis for rejecting his work was the weight of the centuries-long traditional understanding of infinity as implying the possibility of going on indefinitely. Cantor's critics felt that these puzzles i.e. contradictions, would undermine the certainty of mathematics. The contradictions of infinite magnitudes (or the paradoxes, as they came to be called) aroused the same sort of scornful

---

[19] *On Certainty* (New York: Harper and Row, 1969)

rejoinders which the Copernican theory aroused in Galileo's day.[20]

Cantor was keenly aware of the philosophical context which set his understanding apart from that of his peers, and of what he saw as its theological implications. He corresponded with several Cardinals in the Vatican about theological pronouncements on actual infinities and even wrote to Pope Leo XIII on the subject.[21]

Were his proofs proofs? They are certainly so accepted now; they were certainly rejected then. As a mathematician colleague once commented to me in discussing this question, "Well, we understand infinity differently now." For a proof to be accepted as a proof, one is tempted to say, its conclusion must be possible and plausible, intellectually admissible, and the criteria for those qualities are related to one's *Weltbild*. But while the *Weltbild* is not merely a conceptual framework—its roots may be very deep, as we have seen—neither is it a *Lebensform* which encloses its own justification and hence is impervious to rational criticism. Cantor himself commented of his discovery, "I was led on step by step, almost against my will"; he had, in fact, started out to show that the notion of an infinite magnitude was untenable. "Je le vois mais je ne le crois pas" he wrote to his friend, Dedekind, in recounting the steps of the demonstration.[22]

But if this casts some light on a possible reason why proofs for the existence of God are not generally accepted, it has not yet been made clear why such a proof is neither a necessary nor a sufficient condition for faith. That it is not necessary for Aquinas is clear. I want to say that the proof is not sufficient because what faith affirms is the *presence* of a living God, and no proof can establish that. He cannot not be thought of as present to the believer, and it is this intellectual affirmation which grounds our direct address to Him in prayer and our union in love:

the thing believed is not made perfectly present to the intellect by the knowledge of faith, since faith is of things absent, not of things present

---

[20] N. Bourbaki, *Elements d'histoire des Mathematiques,* (Paris: Hermann, 1960) pp. 42 ff. and Galileo, *op. cit.* p. 336.

[21] Cf. Jos. Dauben, "Georg Cantor and Pope Leo XIII", *Journal of the History of Ideas* 38 (Jan.-Mar. 1977) pp. 85–108.

[22] *Loc. cit.* There may seem to be a kind of disanalogy here, since some believers accept the conclusion but reject a proof of any part of it. But it would appear that either they reject such and such a proof, *de facto,* or they reject the possibility in principle of a proof on the grounds that God is not a reality to which the notion of proof applies at all. Gabriel Marcel and Wittgenstein are examples of this position. This is a view radically different from Aquinas, which involves rejecting the "principle of charity" referred to above. We cannot pursue it further in this essay.

. . . Yet God is brought into the presence of love through faith.[23]

So long as we are in the body, we are said to be absent from the Lord, in comparison with that presence whereby He is present to some by the vision of sight . . . Nevertheless even in this life He is present to those who love Him, by the indwelling of His grace.[24]

But doesn't the affirmation of something's presence logically depend on the affirmation of the thing's independent existence? Only if the presence is contingent with respect to the reality, i.e., if the reality is knowable apart from its presence to someone. Compare proving that the external world exists. Can we say, it's present but does it really exist? For a long time this seemed a real problem, and the present-world was taken to be separate from the real world, internal to consciousness or to the theater of the mind. Today we find it hard to give more than a notional assent to that problematic: the very language in which the present-world was described betrays its rootedness in the perceptions of things in the world, and not apparent things. The reality of the world is existentially and cognitively inseparable from its presence: the world is what is given to me in perception.

Similarly, Aquinas argues in the First Part of the *Summa* that God by His very nature is present to all things (He is everywhere by essence, presence and power). But like Augustine's discussion in the first book of the *Confessions*, presence here is construed as unilateral omnipresence. It is, so to speak, a metaphysical presence (as causally sustaining) which carries no implication of being recognized by what is sustained (I, 8c). Only when he comes to discuss faith and religion does he delineate the reciprocal of that presence, namely the way in which God is experientially present to man's awareness in a *unio affectus*. God is present to man by nature, we can say, but man is present to God in the exercise of the natural virtue of religion as well as by faith. The acknowledgement of His presence is implicit in prayer (an act of religion), which has as a necessary condition that "the person who prays should approach (accedere) God to whom he prays."[25] I think "approach" here must be construed in the sense of "turning to", rather than of proximity: far and near are both dimensions of presence. Jesus on the cross

---

[23] Per cognitionem autem fidei non fit res credita intellectui praesens perfecte: quia fides de absentibus est, non de presentibus . . . Fit tamen per fidem Deus praesens affectui S.C.G. III, 40.

[24] quamdiu sumus in corpore dicimur peregrinari a Domino in comparatione ad illam praesentiam qua quibusdam est praesens per speciei visionem; . . . Est autem et praesens etiam se amantibus in hac vita per gratia inhabitationem. II-II 28, 1, 1m.

[25] II-II, 83, 17c; cf. 83, 1, 2m.

felt abandoned by God, but He expressed that in a prayer, i.e. by direct address.

The natural sense of the presence of God Aquinas traces not to one of the "Five Ways", all of which begin from observations about the way the world is, but to the apprehension of man's dependence on a power not his own. That apprehension opens a space of encounter, an intentional space characterized by the numinous quality of its intentional object. It opens or discloses, that is, a dimension of meaning which events and actions can come to participate in. Occurrences, objects, behavior can acquire the intentional quality of the praeternatural by virtue of their reference to the divine. We can speak of encountering the divine in such events.

But the sense of the presence of the divine itself is, in this sphere, unstable. The "high gods" may be absent: prayers may not be heard. Or power may not be undivided: heard prayers may not be efficacious because, as Vergil muses, other powers may harbor animosity.

The God announced by Christianity is One who is present by his nature, whose power is undivided, whose goodness is unqualified. But the knowledge of that God is mediated: it comes through hearing.

One who believes gives assent to things that are proposed to him by another person, and which he himself does not see. Hence, faith has a knowledge that is more like hearing than seeing.[26]

Faith is not a mystical or direct apprehension, it is an act of rational assent to what is heard.

So it is that Aquinas allots the experiential component of faith to the affective domain of the will. *Believing* in the irrevocable presence of the God whose nature specifies and fulfills the empty intention (to borrow Husserl's language) of natural apprehension, the heart of the hearer leaps up in joy, for what is naturally loved as the highest good is with us. Joy is the awareness of the presence of the beloved.[27]

While that awareness is personal, it is not merely subjective in a psychological sense. For it derives not from private intimations, but from a public source: the propositions which are handed on to us by an historical tradition. And the affective union of love is kindled and quickened not merely by the hearing, but in the communal rituals and celebrations and symbols of Emmanuel.

University of Notre Dame

---

[26] Qui credit, assensum praebet his quae sibi ab alio proponuntur, quae ipse non videt: unde fides magis habet cognitionem auditui similem quam visioni. S.C.G. III, 40.

[27] On union in love, cf. I-II 26, 2; 28, 1 and 2.

6 THE LOGICAL ROLES OF THE ARGUMENTS FOR THE EXISTENCE OF GOD

Bowman Clarke

Immanuel Kant has been almost alone among philosophers and theologians in proposing that the classical arguments for the existence of God are not different arguments attempting to support one common conclusion. Too frequently these arguments, although divided into *a priori* and *a posteriori* arguments, have been presented like parallel, but distinct, columns supporting one common architrave of a Greek temple. The critics of the arguments then point out the weaknesses in each argument leaving us to follow one of two courses: To conclude, either that the architrave, too heavy to be supported by such weak columns, collapses; or that each column, although weak in itself, adds strength to the others so that the architrave, too heavy to be supported by any one alone, manages to be supported by all in concert.

As is well known, Kant goes beyond merely denying that the classical arguments are distinct, parallel attempts to support one common conclusion. He proposes a distinct logical relationship between the argument from design, the cosmological argument, and the ontological argument—namely, that they necessitate each other like three building blocks, each resting upon the next, so that the argument from design necessitates the soundness of the cosmological argument, which in turn, necessitates the soundness of the ontological argument.[1] His conclusion that the ontological is unsound necessitates, he thinks, the collapse of the other two arguments. In this essay I agree with Kant that these three arguments, or kinds of arguments, are not three different, parallel ways of supporting one common conclusion. However, I propose a quite different logical relationship between the three arguments and, consequently, propose different logical roles for them.

Beginning with what Kant called "the oldest, the clearest, and the most

---

[1] See Immanuel Kant, *Critique of Pure Reason,* trans. Norman Kemp Smith (London: Macmillan and Co., 1963), p. 524.

accordant with the common reason of mankind,"[2] the argument from design, it is generally recognized that all its formulations rest upon an analogy—ignoring for the moment John Stuart Mill's denial of this fact. The argument rests upon the "seeing" of a similarity between human artifacts, which are the result of intelligent designing of means toward ends, and the universe. Take, for example, William Paley's classical formulation of the argument in his *Natural Theology*. Paley begins,

> In crossing a heath, suppose I pitched my foot against a stone, and were asked how the stone came to be there, I might possibly answer, that for anything I knew to the contrary, it might have lain there forever. . . . But suppose I found a watch upon the heath, and it should be inquired how the watch happened to be in that place, I should hardly think of the answer which I have before given—that, for anything I knew, the watch might have always been there. . . .[3]

Then Paley raises this question, "Yet, why should not this answer serve for the watch, as well as the stone?" Of course, the answer is obvious: The watch is the sort of thing that requires a designer. As he puts it, "When we come to inspect the watch, we perceive (what we could not discover in the stone) that its several parts are framed and put together for a purpose, e.g., that they are so formed and adjusted as to produce motion, and that motion so regulated as to point out the hour of the day . . . ."[4] So, Paley concludes, "This mechanism being observed, the inference, we think is inevitable, that the watch must have had a maker."[5]

Paley then points to an analogy between the watch and the universe based upon common properties, which he calls indications of contrivance,

> Every indication of contrivance, every manifestation of design, which existed in the watch, exists in the works of nature; with the difference, on the side of nature, of being greater and more, and that in a degree which exceeds all computation.[6]

Paley believes we are led to conclude that the universe too, had a designer. What is the kind of reasoning that so leads us? I suggest that such analogies

---

[2] *Ibid.*, p. 520.
[3] William Paley, *Natural Theology* (New York: American Tract Society, n.d.), p. 9.
[4] *Ibid.*, p. 9.
[5] *Ibid.*, p. 10.
[6] *Ibid.*, p. 20.

in the various formulations of the argument from design function logically in the same way in which certain kinds of models and analogies commonly function in scientific reasoning.

The term 'model' is used in many different ways by practicing scientists and there are differing views of their function among philosophers of science. The type of model and its use which I have in mind is what Ernest Nagel calls the "heuristic" use of "substantive"—in contrast to formal or mathematical—models, or analogies.[7] The heuristic use of a model, or analogy, may involve the use of the model (1) as an aid in teaching, or (2) as an impetus to further investigation. More specifically, it is the latter which concerns us here. Granted that the use of models and analogies can sometimes be as misleading as leading, Nagel is quite right,

the history of theoretical science supplies plentiful examples of the influence of analogies upon the formation of theoretical ideas; and a number of outstanding scientists have been quite explicit about the important role models play in the construction of new theories.[8]

Our concern here, in the logical analysis of the argument from design, is with the function of models, or analogies, in "the formation of theoretical ideas" and in "the construction of new theories," or in what C. S. Peirce has called abductive inferences. The argument from design, after all, purports to be an inference. What I would like to suggest is that the argument is an abductive inference and that the conclusion of the argument is an hypothesis, in Peirce's sense of these terms.

It would be instructive here to avail ourselves of one of Peirce's forms of abductive reasoning, a form which he has called a perceptual abduction. His form, with slight modifications, is as follows, where P, P', P'', etc., are the common properties,

1) A well-recognized kind of object M has for its ordinary properties, P, P', P'', etc.

2) The suggesting object S has the same properties, P, P', P'', etc.

---

[7] See Ernest Nagel, *The Structure of Science* (New York: Harcourt, Brace and World, 1961), pp. 110–111 and pp. 113–114. For an excellent short summary of the use of the term, 'model,' in science see Frederick Ferré, "Mapping the Logic of Models in Science and Theology," *The Christian Scholar*, XLVI (Spring 1963), No. 1, pp. 9–23. For a lengthy discussion of the role of models in both science and theology and a comparison, see Ian G. Barbour, *Myths, Models and Paradigms: The Nature of Scientific and Religious Language* (London: SCM Press, 1974).

[8] Nagel, p. 108.

3) Hence, it is plausible that S is a kind of M. (8.64)[9]

It is a simple task to put Paley's argument in the form of a perceptual abduction; it naturally falls into the following form:

1) A well-recognized kind of object, one requiring a designer (e.g., the watch), has for its ordinary properties, such things as its several parts are . . . so formed and adjusted as to produce motion, and that motion so regulated as to point out the hour of the day, etc.
2) The suggesting object, the universe, has the same properties, etc.
3) Hence, it is plausible that the universe is the kind of object requiring a designer.

To treat the argument from design as an abductive inference throws fresh light on some of Philo's criticisms in Hume's *Dialogues Concerning Natural Religion* and sharpens the difference between his position and that of John Stuart Mill. It was pointed out above that Mill rejects the thesis that the argument from design is based on an analogy. He writes, ". . . it is more than analogy. It surpasses analogy exactly as induction surpasses it. It is an inductive argument."[10] He justifies his thesis in this way:

The circumstances in which it is alleged that the world resembles the works of man are not circumstances taken at random, but are particular instances of a circumstance which experience shows to have a real connection with an intelligent origin—the fact of conspiring to an end. The argument therefore is not one of mere analogy.[11]

In short, unlike Paley, who sees "indications of contrivance," or common properties which by analogy suggest contrivance, Mill appears to be maintaining that the universe shares with human artifacts the distinct property of being "instances of conspiring to an end." For the purpose of analyzing these various forms of the argument from design, I am making no distinction between such phrases as 'exemplifying design,' 'exemplifying contrivance,' 'exemplifying the adaptation of means to ends,' or 'conspiring to an end.' I take, for our purposes, all these to be equivalent phrases. I do, however,

---

[9] All references are to C. S. Peirce, *Collected Papers,* Vols. I–VI, eds. Charles Hartshorne and Paul Weiss, Vols. VII–VIII, ed. Arthur Burks (Cambridge: Harvard University Press, 1966). Peirce uses the term, 'predicates,' in his formulation; I have substituted the term, 'properties,' primarily for literary reasons.

[10] John Stuart Mill, *Theism,* ed. Richard Taylor (New York: Liberal Arts Press, 1957), p. 29.

[11] *Ibid.,* p. 29.

want to make a strong distinction between such phrases as '*exemplifying* design,' or '*being an instance* of conspiring to an end,' on the one hand, and '*indications* of design,' or '*being an indication* of conspiring to an end,' on the other hand.

An ambiguity along these lines seems to run through almost all of the historical formulations of the argument from design. Kant, for example, speaks of the "clear *signs of an order* in accordance with a determinate purpose," but in the next sentence he says "*this purposive order . . .* belongs to them contingently."[12] There appears to be a move here from "signs of" (indications of) to "belonging to" (instances of). Should not Kant have spoken of "this *apparent* purposive order" which "belongs to them contingently"? Also, Cleanthes in Hume's *Dialogues Concerning Natural Religion* speaks of "*the* curious *adapting* of means to ends throughout nature" which he says "*resembles exactly . . .* the productions of human contrivance."[13] Would it not be better to speak of "the *apparent* adapting of means to ends" or "what we take to be the adapting of means to ends" in nature which resemble (i.e., have common properties with) the productions of human contrivance?

It is quite clear, however, that Mill, in contrast to Paley as we have interpreted him, is arguing in this way:

1) s, s', s'' . . . form a subset (those we have examined) of the set of things which are instances of conspiring toward an end.
2) s, s', s'' . . . are found to have the property of having a conspirer (or designer).
3) Therefore, probably all the members of the set of things which are instances of conspiring toward an end have conspirers (or designers).
4) The universe is a member of the set of things which are instances of conspiring toward an end.
5) Therefore, probably the universe has a conspirer (or designer).

This argument could surely be classified as an inductive argument. There are, however, some serious difficulties with it, and these turn on the phrase, 'the property of being an instance of conspiring toward an end.' Step three, for instance, is taken to be an inductive generalization; it is, according to Mill, "a circumstance which experience shows." Does not something's "being an instance of conspiring to an end" necessitate a conspirer, or designer? Could something be an instance of conspiring to an end without a

---

[12] Kant, p. 521 (Italics mine).
[13] David Hume, *Dialogues Concerning Natural Religion,* ed. Henry D. Aiken (New York: Hafner Publishing Co., 1969), p. 17 (Italics mine).

conspirer? It seems very odd. Mill must, however, maintain this in order for his argument to work as an inductive argument. If this were not the case, he would be hard pressed to justify his fourth premise. He could only justify it, it seems, by observing the universe being the result of something's conspiring to an end. He then would have to face Philo's question to Cleanthes,

Have worlds ever been formed under your eye, and have you had leisure to observe the whole progress of the phenomenon, from the first appearance of order to its final consumation? If you have, then cite your experience and deliver your theory.[14]

But what would the property of being an instance of conspiring to an end without a conspirer be? What could this be but what Paley would call "indications" of conspiring, rather than "instances" of conspiring? But then we are back with an analogy.

Philo, on the other hand, holds firmly to the thesis that the argument from design is based on an analogy. In order to justify this thesis, he points to the disimilarities in the analogy by pointing, with perhaps feigned piety, to the radical difference between human designers and the conjectured designer of the universe. He tells Cleanthes that he is "scandalized . . . with this resemblance which is asserted between the deity and human creatures, and must conceive it to imply such a degradation of the Supreme Being as no sound theist could endure."[15] Thus for Philo, the conclusion to the argument from design could only be an hypothesis, or conjecture. And Hume seems to have enjoyed having Philo point out that other hypotheses could likewise follow from the same basic analogy:

A great number of men join in building a house or ship, in rearing a city, in framing a commonwealth; why not several deities combine in contriving and framing a world? . . . if foolish, such vicious creatures as man can yet often unite in framing and executing one plan, how much more those dieties or demons, whom we may suppose several degrees more perfect.[16]

Paley, himself, recognized that this polytheistic hypothesis likewise plausibly follows. When speaking of the watch found on the heath, he writes "there must have existed . . . an artificer or artificers who formed it . . .."[17] But Philo is not willing to stop here; there are other hypotheses. Consider these,

---

[14] *Ibid.*, p. 21.
[15] *Ibid.*, p. 20.
[16] *Ibid.*, pp. 39–40.
[17] Paley, p. 10.

This world . . . was only the first rude essay of some infant deity who afterwards abandoned it, ashamed of his lame performance; it is the work only of some dependent, inferior deity, and is the object of derision to his superiors; it is the production of old age and dotage in some superannuated deity, and ever since his death has run on at adventures, from the first impulse and active force which it received from him.[18]

The God-is-dead theologians have gotten some mileage out of this last hypothesis. Philo's final conclusion in the *Dialogues,* since, according to him the other arguments fail, is that

the whole of natural theology . . . resolves itself into one simple, though somewhat ambiguous, at least undefined, proposition, *That the cause or causes of order in the universe probably bear some remote analogy to human intelligence.*[19]

Natural theology, then, is left with this plausible, but "somewhat ambiguous, at least undefined," hypothesis, or conjecture.

I disagree with Philo that this "somewhat ambiguous, at least undefined" hypothesis is the whole of natural theology and suggest that, on the contrary, it is only the beginning of natural theology. As Peirce was aware, hypotheses of this type are usually very vague and the next step in theoretical construction is to clarify, or explicate, them for theoretical purposes. And I would like to suggest that it is precisely at this point that the ontological argument becomes relevant to the conclusion of the argument from design. For the purposes of the following discussion, I shall limit myself to the theistic hypothesis, "There exists a unique designer of the universe," and shall use the term, 'God,' to refer to this unique individual.

By the ontological argument, I mean any argument concerning the existence of God which turns upon the analysis of the modal terms, 'necessity,' 'possibility,' 'contingency,' and 'impossibility' in their relation to a definite description for the singular term, 'God.' It is this fact which gives one the impression that all that is at stake in the ontological argument are mere words or mere concepts. Listen, for example, to Descartes,

When the mind afterwards reviews the different ideas that are in it, it discovers what is by far the chief among them—that of a Being omniscient, all powerful, and absolutely perfect; and it observes that in this idea there is contained not only possible and contingent existence, as in

---

[18] Hume, p. 41.
[19] Ibid., p. 94.

the ideas of all other things which it clearly perceives, but existence absolutely necessary and eternal. And just as because, for example, the equality of its three angles to two right angles is necessarily comprised in the idea of a triangle, the mind is firmly persuaded that the three angles of a triangle are equal to two right angles; so, from its perceiving necessary and eternal existence to be comprised in the idea which it has of an all-perfect Being, it ought manifestly to conclude that this all-perfect Being exists.[20]

The various forms which the historical arguments take depend upon two things: 1) how the term 'God' is explicated, e.g., as 'that than which nothing greater can be conceived,' 'the Necessary Being,' 'the Perfect Being,' etc.; and 2) how the modal terms are conceived—that is, do they function as predicates of concepts, of acts of conceiving, of individuals, of existence, or of propositions, or as sentential or propositional operators, or what have you. Frequently there is an ambiguity in this second element. The argument itself is based on the fact that an analysis of the modal terms reveals that 'necessity,' 'contingency,' and 'impossibility' are mutually exclusive terms. And the argument involves the denial that the term 'contingency' applies in the case of God because of the way in which the term 'God' is explicated for theoretical purposes. This leaves only the other two alternatives, either 'necessity' or 'impossibility.' The other move is to show that 'impossibility' is not applicable, since possibility is applicable, leaving only 'necessity.'
    Take, for example, the simplest ontological argument, that of Leibniz in the *Monadology*. Leibniz writes,

Hence God alone (or the Necessary Being) has this prerogative, that he must exist if he is possible. And since nothing can hinder the possibility of that which possesses no limitations, no negation, and consequently, no contradiction, this alone is sufficient to establish the existence of God *a priori*.[21]

If we think of the modal terms as operators on sentences, then Leibniz's argument can be translated as follows:

1) If it is possible that God exists, then it is necessary that God exists.
2) It is possible that God exists.

---

[20] Rene Descartes, *The Meditations and Selections from the Principles*, trans. John Veitch (La Salle, IL: Open Court, 1964), p. 137.
    [21] G. W. Leibniz, *Selections*, ed. Philip P. Wiener (New York: Scribner's, 1951), pp. 541–542.

3) Hence, it follows that it is necessary that God exists.

This is obviously a clear-cut case of modus ponens. The first premise of the above argument is by definition logically equivalent to the sentence 'It is not contingent that God exists.' This premise is justified by Leibniz on the basis that the term, 'God,' is explicated as 'the Necessary Being.' In short, the modal term 'contingent' is not applicable in the case of the Necessary Being: "God alone (or the Necessary Being) has this prerogative . . . ." St. Anslem, for example, justifies his form of this first premise in this way:

> . . . if that being can be even conceived to be, it must exist in reality. For that than which a greater is inconceivable cannot be conceived except as without beginning. But whatever can be conceived to exist, and does not exist, can be conceived to exist through a beginning. Hence, what can be conceived to exist, but does not exist, is not the being than which a greater cannot be conceived. Therefore, *if such a being can be conceived to exist, necessarily it does exist.*[22]

Here the first premise is justified on the basis that any individual to which the term, 'contingent' is applicable cannot be "that than which nothing greater can be conceived."

Premise (2) in the above argument denies that the modal term, 'impossible,' is applicable to God and this premise is logically equivalent to the sentence, 'It is not the case that it is impossible that God exists.' Leibniz's justification for this premise is in terms of his own explication of the term, 'God'; it refers to the being which contains all positive perfections and thus possesses "no limitation, no negation, and consequently, no contradiction." If there is "no contradiction," then nothing can hinder the possibility of its existence, or 'It is possible that God exists' is true. St. Anselm's justification is somewhat different. In his reply to Gaunilo, for example, he argues in this way:

> But I say: if a being than which a greater is inconceivable is not understood or conceived, and is not in the understanding or in concept, certainly either God is not a being than which a greater is inconceivable, or else he is not understood or conceived, and is not in the understanding or in concept. But I call on your faith and conscience to attest that this is most false. Hence, that than which a greater cannot be conceived is

---

[22] St. Anselm, *Proslogium; Monologium; etc.*, trans. Sidney Norton Deane (La Salle, IL: Open Court, 1959), p. 154 (Italics mine).

truly understood and conceived, and is in the understanding and in concept . . . .[23]

Thus, such a being can be conceived to exist. From this and the final sentence in the above quote from St. Anselm, it follows that necessarily it does exist.

I am not here interested in the differences between the various formulations of the ontological argument; e.g., the difference between St. Anselm's 'if such a being can be conceived to exist,' and Leibniz's 'if he is possible'; or between those and my formulation, 'if it is possible that God exists.' All of these are interesting historical and logical problems. But I do not think their resolution is relevant to my general argument about the logical role of the various arguments. Likewise, I am not interested in the soundness or the validity of these various formulations. I am only interested in what I earlier suggested that they all have in common and what this means for our original theistic hypothesis; that is, the conclusion of the design argument, 'There exists a unique designer of the universe.'

These historical arguments, it seems to me upon analysis, are attempts to explicate the theistic hypothesis. This explication of the theistic hypothesis is accomplished by introducing a definite description (the so and so) for the term, 'God,' formulated within a theoretical framework; that is, a cluster of consistent and related terms. This definite description is then analyzed further with reference to the modal concepts, or terms. The outcome of this analysis, it is maintained, is: 'it is necessary that God exist,' or 'necessarily it does exist,' or 'the existence of God is established *a priori*,' or some such. In short, our original theistic hypothesis, when clarified, or explicated, within a certain theoretical framework, cannot be a contingent, or empirical, hypothesis.

This should, however, have been expected even when our theistic hypothesis was cast in its vaguer form, 'There exists a unique designer of the universe.' Suppose that most, or all, of the observable characteristics of the universe could be, and were, quite different. How could this be relevant to our hypothesis that God, whom we are calling the unique designer of the universe, exists? At most, it could only mean that he designed the universe differently. The situation here has been characterized by Nicolas Rescher in this way:

The issues involved are not "internal" but "systematic" to the study of nature, that is, they do not deal with *specific facts* regarding what takes place *within the course of events in nature,* but rather with certain *general principles* operative *with respect to the course of events itself.*[24]

---

[23] *Ibid.,* p. 154.
[24] Nicholas Rescher, *Scientific Explanation* (New York: Free Press, 1970), p. 141.

In short, the answer to Philo's question, "by what phenomena in nature are we to decide the controversy?"[25] is: by none. It is this fact, along with the logical empiricist's criterion of meaningfulness, that brought forth the charge of meaninglessness for the theistic hypothesis. The history of this problem is well known and need not be repeated here. The logical empiricist's criterion in its earlier forms, however, turned out to be too narrow for empirical science. And this has resulted in, as Carnap put it, "not only disagreements with respect to the exact location of the boundary line between the meaningful and the meaningless, but some philosophers are doubtful about the very possibility of drawing any boundary line."[26]

There is a very suggestive way of facing this problem of the hypothesis of the existence of God in Peirce's "Additament" to his "A Neglected Argument for the Reality of God." Peirce compares the hypothesis for the existence of God with an ordinary scientific, or empirical, hypothesis. He points out that,

. . . although it is a chief function of an explanatory hypothesis . . . to cite a clear image in the mind by means of which experiential consequences of ascertainable conditions may be predicted, yet in this instance the hypothesis can only be apprehended so very obscurely that in exceptional cases alone can any definite and direct deductions from its ordinary abstract interpretation be made. (6.489)

What the "exceptional cases" are which Peirce had in mind, I do not know. We have no clue. What interests us here, however, is the way in which Peirce gets around this problem which he would call the absence of "any ordinary definite and directly deducible experiential consequences."

Peirce seems to suggest the possibility of explicating the hypothesis of the existence of God within a very general metaphysical, or cosmological, theory and then showing that the hypothesis itself is deducible within this theory. He writes, for example,

Among the pertinent considerations which have been crowded out of this article, I may just mention that it could have been shown that the hypothesis of God's Reality is logically not so isolated a conclusion as it may seem. On the contrary, it is connected so with a theory of the nature of thinking that if this be proved so is that. (6.491)

---

[25] Hume, p. 40.

[26] Rudolph Carnap, "The Methodological Character of Theoretical Concepts," *Minnesota Studies in the Philosophy of Science*, I, eds. Herbert Feigel and Michael Scriven (Minneapolis: University of Minnesota Press, 1956), pp. 38–39.

Is this not, however, the function of the traditional cosmological arguments? To explicate the hypothesis of the existence of God by producing a definite description for the term, 'God,' in a general metaphysical, or cosmological, theory and to prove within that theory the statement asserting the existence of the individual so characterized? The hypothesis, so explicated, stands or falls, then, as Peirce suggested, with the theory itself. Let us examine, for example, St. Thomas' first four ways.

In this analysis of the first four ways, we are not interested in questions of soundness or validity, but with the logical machinery made use of in the arguments. St. Thomas' first way may be summarized as follows:[27]

A. Some things are in motion.
B. Whatever is in motion is moved by something.
C. Nothing moves itself.
D. Therefore, whatever is in motion is moved by another.
E. In any series of movers and things moved, subsequent movers are moved only in so far as they are moved by the first mover of the series.
F. No series of movers and things moved can go on infinitely; that is, have no first movers, or final members of the series.
G. Therefore, it is necessary to arrive at a first mover, moved by no other.
H. And this everyone understands to be God.

In examining the logical machinery used in this first argument, we will find that St. Thomas has made use of the following:

(1) A general relation and the field of that relation; in this case, the relation, 'x moves y' and its field.
(2) A definite description of an individual constructed on the basis of that relation; in this case, 'the first mover, moved by no other.'
(3) The assertion that the field of the relation, 'x moves y' is not empty (A, above).
(4) A series of sentences giving the properties of the relation; in this case, the relation, 'x moves y,' is irreflexive (B,C,D, above), transitive (E, above), and any subset ordered by the relation has a first member (F, above).
(5) The assertion that the existence of the first unmoved mover necessarily follows (G, above).
(6) A sentence maintaining that the singular term, 'God,' names the individual characterized by the definite description (H. above).

---

[27] See St. Thomas Aquinas, *Summa Theologica*, I, Q. 2, A. 3, ed. Anton C. Pegis (New York: Modern Library, 1948).

If we examine St. Thomas' next three ways, we find him making use of virtually the same logical machinery. In the second way, the relation is 'x is the efficient cause of y' and the definite description involved is 'the first efficient cause.' In the third, the relation is 'x is contingent upon y' and the definite description is 'that which is not contingent upon anything else' or 'the absolutely necessary being.' In the fourth way, the relation is 'x is greater in being than y' and the definite description is 'the greatest in being.' In the case of the fifth way, I take it to be a form of the argument from design. Thus, what the first four ways have in common might be summarized as follows and might be referred to as the cosmological argument:

I. There is a relation, R, and a set of entities, S, ordered by R.
II. We can specify, in terms of R, a unique individual by formulating a definite description, 'the so and so.'
III. The axioms, A_1, . . . , A_n, governing the relation, R, necessitate the existence of that unique individual, the so and so.
IV. That unique individual, the so and so, is what we refer to with the term, 'God.'

There are several points that must be made with reference to these four elements of the cosmological argument. First, the relation, R, must be a very general relation and its axioms, 'A_1, . . . , A_n', must be such that they characterize, to use Rescher's phrase, "general principles operative with respect to the course of events itself," and not be concerned with "specific facts regarding what takes place within the course of events in nature." Despite the fact that these first four ways are generally characterized as *a posteriori* proofs, these arguments do not rest upon particular contingent facts. St. Thomas' first way, for example, depends upon motion in general and its characteristics. What particular things move what particular things is irrelevant to the argument, for we are concerned with the concept of motion. That St. Thomas is aware of this fact is evidenced by his remarks concerning the irreflexivity of the relation, 'x moves y,' in the *Summa Contra Gentiles*. The Angelic Doctor, for example, writes,

> It is to be noted, however, that Plato, who held that every mover is moved, understood the name motion in a wider sense than did Aristotle. For Aristotle understood motion strictly, according as it is the act of what exists in potency inasmuch as it is such. So understood, motion belongs only to divisible bodies . . . . According to Plato, however, that which moves itself is not a body. Plato understood by motion any given operation, so that to understand and to judge are a kind of motion.[28]

---

[28] St. Thomas Aquinas, *On the Truth of the Catholic Faith,* Book I, trans. Anton C. Pegis (Garden City, NJ: Doubleday and Co., 1958), p. 88.

In short, then, what is needed for a cosmological argument is a metaphysical or cosmological framework in which we can construct a definite description for the term, 'God,' and show that our theistic hypothesis, as explicated in terms of the definite description, is necessitated by the metaphysical or cosmological framework.

We cannot, however, rely on outdated and repudiated metaphysical, or cosmological, frameworks. As Whitehead points out in *Science and the Modern World,* "Today we repudiate the Aristotelian physics and the Aristotelian cosmology, so that the exact form of the argument manifestly fails."[29] What is needed is a new twentieth century form of the cosmological argument. Unfortunately, I have none to offer. I would like to maintain, however, that when we view the traditional arguments for the existence of God in terms of what they can deliver, and not expect too much from them, they become logically very interesting. And seen in this light, they fall into a very natural logical relationship and suggest an outline for the constructive task of natural theology in the twentieth century.

University of Georgia

---

[29] A. N. Whitehead, *Science and the Modern World* (New York: New American Library, 1960), pp. 156–157.

7 RIGHT AND WRONG COSMOLOGICAL ARGUMENTS

Frank B. Dilley

The task of placing the cosmological style of argument for God in proper perspective is very difficult in modern times for two reasons. In the first place it is hard to find post-Kantian treatments of cosmological arguments which really contain a proper understanding of them. Readily available discussions almost always contain serious misunderstandings of what those arguments do, having twisted those arguments to fit a post-Newtonian framework. In their altered form they are disposed of easily. I have discussed this point elsewhere and will not repeat the documentation here.[1]

A second reason for the difficulty moderns have in understanding the classical cosmological arguments is that most of us find it very difficult to think of nature as purposive, accustomed as we have become to mechanistic thinking in the sciences. This means that the very style of metaphysical analysis which ought to be correct if it is true that there is a God is very difficult for moderns to practice. We assume categories of explanation which presuppose the sufficiency of *physicalistic* analyses of motion, whereas if there is a God we should really expect that physicalistic categories would not be adequate. Once purpose explanations have been replaced by mechanistic ones, it is difficult to think "religiously" any more.

So modernity not only presents us with distorted views of what the classical

---

[1] Elsewhere I have attempted to show where contemporary critiques of cosmological arguments have broken down, and how the supposed success of those critiques depends upon assuming that there is no God. Anyone interested may consult my "An Analysis of Some of J.J.C. Smart's Objections to the 'Proofs'," *Religious Studies,* 4,2 (1968), pp. 245-51 and "Misunderstanding the Cosmological Argument," *New Scholasticism,* 50, 1 (1976), pp. 96-107. William Lane Craig has published an interesting, but incorrect, discussion of the latter article in the same journal 53, 3 (1979), pp. 388-92. Craig does concede that amidst my astounding obscurity and serious misunderstandings I succeed in showing that the usual critics of Thomas misunderstood what he was doing, although not as badly as I do.

cosmological arguments were, but it has almost deprived us of the ability to think along the lines the arguments require.

In this paper I wish to discuss a modern example of the cosmological argument. I will argue that Richard Taylor's version of that argument is not cogent, and is seriously inferior to the classical versions.[2] By transposing the argument from an attempt to explain purposive motion (its Platonic, Aristotelian and Thomistic form) into an argument to explain bare existence, Taylor robs it of whatever persuasive power it once had and might still have. What applies to Taylor's argument applies, I think, to all versions of the cosmological argument which proceed from bare existence alone. I will also try to sketch briefly my claim that classical forms are much better.

I. Taylor's Cosmological Argument

Taylor argues for God on the basis of the principle of sufficient reason, a principle which states "that, in the case of any positive truth, there is some sufficient reason for it, something which, in this sense, makes it true—in short, that there is some sort of explanation, known or unknown, for everything" (p. 86). He goes on to contrast contingent truths with necessary truths, defining necessary truths as ones which "are true by their very natures." He illustrates a necessary truth by saying "if the stone on my window sill is a body, as it is, then it has a form, since this fact depends upon nothing but itself for its confirmation." Thus, apparently, sufficient reason is provided for the stone's having a form by the fact that it is a body. If it is a body it necessarily has a form.

Care must be taken that the point about the stone is not used to prove too much. Taylor's point is merely that it is necessarily true that if there is a stone, and it has a body, then it has a form. Its having a body is sufficient reason for its having a form. One is not entitled to draw from the truth of that claim, however, any inferences about whether there is in fact a real (bodied) stone on Taylor's window sill. To find out whether the stone which seems to be there really is, Taylor would have had to look, and looking is

---

[2] The Taylor argument is contained in Richard Taylor, *Metaphysics* (Englewood Cliffs, N.J.: Prentice Hall, 1963), pp. 84-102. Subsequent citations will be given in the text. The crucial part of the Taylor chapter is included in Donald R. Burrill, ed., *The Cosmological Arguments* (Garden City, N.Y.: Anchor Books, 1967), and in Keith E. Yandell, ed., *God, Man, and Religion* (N.Y.: McGraw-Hill, 1973). Both volumes also contain Paul Edwards' discussion of the cosmological argument which makes the same point I do about the type of cosmological argument Taylor uses. My second article noted above is a full scale treatment of the inadequacies of Edwards' discussion as an interpretation of the classical cosmological argument, but I do think Edwards' critique of Taylor's sort of argument is correct.

an empirical rather than a logical task. Failure to observe this difference between logically necessary truths such as "if X has a body, it has a form" and "there is an X which has a body, hence a form" is what gave the ontological argument its pseudo-plausibility. If the stone has a body it is logically necessary that it has a form, but there is no logical necessity that there be any stones in the world at all.

Taylor observes, correctly, that there is no apparent necessity to the existence of any particular things in the world, or to the existence of things as a whole. "That no world should ever exist at all is perfectly comprehensible and seems to express not the slightest absurdity" (p. 87). Therefore the nature of the world does not provide a necessary reason for its existence, and we must look for something which does, something "which exists by its own nature." If that something cannot be found in the world itself, Taylor argues, then it must be sought outside (p. 90). But why can't it be found in the world?

If the world existed by its own nature, if it were by nature eternal and indestructible, it would supply a reason for its own existence, and the principle of sufficient reason would let us stop there. However, Taylor claims, there is nothing about the world which would suggest that by its very nature it must be such. To make that point he notes that we can think of the world as never having existed in the first place. Also, he says, as if it were another way of reinforcing that same point, we can think of the world as being annihilated (p. 90). If it can be thought of as never having existed and as being annihilated this means that it is not imperishable by nature, Taylor claims.

At this point more careful analysis needs to be made. While it *is* true that one can easily think of the world as never having existed in the first place (there is no necessity that there be any world at all), is it true that one can think just as easily of the world's "coming into being" or its "being annihilated"? To think of the world as "being annihilated" one first has to think of there being a world and then has to think of that world's totally ceasing to be, but that is not easy to think. Nor is it easy to think of the world's "coming into being," as if at one time there were nothing and then, a moment later, there is a world. What did it come to be out of? Where did it go? Those questions spring almost automatically to mind. How can absolute nothing be followed by something and something be followed by absolute nothing? What about such propositions as "matter can neither be created nor destroyed" or "from nothing comes nothing"? It can plausibly be argued that those propositions present necessities of thought also.[3]

---

[3] The notion of necessities of thought is troublesome. I do not know how to draw up a list of them. That nothing can happen without sufficient reason seems to be one

It looks as though a claim which *is* true, namely that we can easily see that there is no necessity that there be any world at all, has been interpreted as though it were equivalent with another claim which *is not* true, that we can easily see that the world is the sort of thing that can come into being and pass away. This latter claim does not seem to be so easily accepted. In fact, it is difficult to give it clear meaning. In our experience, at any rate, the coming into being and passing away of things is not absolute origination or absolute annihilation, but instead is a combining and dissolution of various elements of matter. Those elements pre-exist the combination we call a particular thing and they post-exist the dissolution of that combination. No particular thing exists necessarily, but once there is matter it is difficult to see how there could ever be absolutely nothing again.

So, there is no necessity that matter combine itself into any particular specified form, hence we can easily imagine a world without stones. Moreover, we can easily imagine that there never was any matter at all. There is no contradiction involved in there being nothing at all. What we cannot easily do is imagine a world which *has* something in it ever ceasing to have something in it, or easily imagine absolute nothingness beginning to be something.

In short, my claim is that while there is no logical necessity that there be any world at all, *if in fact there is one,* then it is necessary that there always has been one and that there always will be one. There is a great deal of difference between "never having been" and "having once been but now being no longer." The latter seems difficult to accept just for the reason that while things are perishable their constituents are not and it is difficult to think of this situation as being merely a matter of happenstance.

Taylor's argument proceeds. The world is not necessary because one can conceive of its never having been and one can conceive of its being annihilated, so one must look outside the world for a sufficient explanation of its existence. We must look for something which "exists by its own nature and which is, accordingly, eternal and unperishable" (p. 92).

In case anyone doubts whether that notion is intelligible Taylor observes that it plainly makes sense to think of things which are *impossible* by nature (square circles, formless bodies), hence it is hard to see why the opposite notion would fail to make sense. He supplies as content for the idea of something which is necessary by nature, "a being which is imperishable and

---

of them, and if so, it seems reasonable to argue that something could not emerge out of nothing without a sufficient reason. Now if God exists, there is never nothing, and if God has power to create things *ex nihilo* the principle that something cannot come out of nothing is preserved since it takes a something (God) to create something else out of nothing. What is troublesome is whether creation *ex nihilo* is intelligible at all and therefore impossible for even a God to perform. Fortunately in this paper I am not required to answer the latter question, but I thank Robert F. Brown for raising it.

dependent upon nothing other than itself for its existence'' (p. 93).

It is not clear from the text whether Taylor means by such a statement to refer to two qualities or merely one. He repeatedly refers to something which is imperishable and depends upon nothing else for its existence—that could mean something which is both imperishable *and* depending for nothing else for its existence or it could mean something which is imperishable hence depends upon nothing else for its existence. I have interpreted him to mean the latter because he offers no arguments as to why an imperishable being would *need* a cause and I can think of none which would fit the type of cosmological argument Taylor is presenting.[4]

The key to Taylor's argument is, then, that a being which (who) was imperishable by nature could not be imagined as coming into being and passing away, hence its nature provides sufficient reason for its existence.

What happens if we ask the other question Taylor asked of the world? Could we easily think of there never having been any imperishable being at all? To cut the argument short, is it intelligible to say that God or any other conceivable imperishable being might *never* have existed at all? It seems to me the answer must be yes. One can easily imagine a reality empty of perishable beings and one can equally well imagine reality empty of imperishable beings as well. Neither the non-existence of the world nor the non-existence of God is inconceivable.

On the other hand, there is *grave* difficulty in imagining a world containing imperishable matter (or a world containing God) to become one empty of matter (or empty of God). One can imagine neither God nor matter coming into being or passing away, but one can imagine a world in which neither ever was.

There are logically conceivable worlds which are empty, and logically conceivable worlds which have imperishable things in them, that is why logic cannot tell us which sort of world we have. But logic can tell us that if we have a world with imperishable things in it, then those imperishable things could provide an explanation for their continuing existence and their past existence.

What Taylor has claimed is that because individual things have no necessity, there must be something else which *does* have necessity and which is responsible for the existence of individual things. I have argued that Taylor

---

[4] St. Thomas Aquinas' argument is superior to Taylor's in this respect because Aquinas *does* have such an argument, an argument as to why first causation is required even for some sorts of imperishable being. Thomas' argument has to do with specific features of the world *as we know it* and does not work for just any world at all. Why this makes the Thomistic argument right and the Taylor argument wrong will become more apparent as the paper develops.

has made a mistake, that he has converted the observation that "individual things have no necessity" which is true, into the observation that "there is nothing at all necessary about things" which is not true. Once things exist they have a necessity about them—they just change form and cannot pass into absolute nothing again.

Perhaps Taylor might want to turn to the difficulty of establishing that the world has any necessity at all about it by any *examination* of that world. Could you by examining matter *show* that it is the sort of thing that cannot be destroyed? By no manner of looking over time could you show imperishability, for reasons we all know are inherent in empirical method. But it is equally obvious that we could not show by examination of God *either* that He is imperishable and for the same reason. (The complication as to whether God *can* be examined will be waived.)

Could we perhaps know that some sort of being has logical necessity just by *thinking* about it? But how could that be? We could imagine that there was never a God at all just as we could imagine that there never was a world at all. Whatever kind of imperishable being we imagine, God *or* world, we can imagine that there never was such a being. Here we must be careful again. Having ruled out experience as a source of our knowledge that a particular sort of thing (matter or God) has the quality of imperishability among its collection of qualities, we must appeal to thought as the basis of our judgment that something (God or world or both) is necessary. But there are two ways to appeal to thought on this matter, one wrong and one right. The wrong way is embodied in the ontological argument.

The lesson to be learned from the ontological argument's failure that is relevant to the point under discussion is that no being is logically necessary. The ontological argument was an attempt to prove that a necessary or imperishable being with the *qualities of God* must exist. Certain of their critics said that the argument, if valid, would work for almost anything that could be said to be perfect, but Anselm and Descartes both offered good reasons why the argument, if valid, would apply only to God. They may have won on the issue of whether any other being besides an all-perfect being includes imperishability in its essence, but they lost on the issue that mattered. Critics noted that the ontological argument was unable to supply a bridge from the concept of a being which includes imperishability as one of its attributes to the actual existence of such a being. God's existence is not logically necessary and cannot be deduced from the concept of God.

It is true that a being than which nothing greater can be conceived would have to be imperishable, the concept of an all-perfect being alone among our concepts, contains eternity. But if the existence of that concept does not entitle us to claim that God actually exists, we can only look to the world to find out whether anything exists that even comes close to embodying divine perfection. Perhaps the actual thing that most closely fits that definition is that man from the planet Krypton. Such a being falls far short of being God, and is actually not imperishable by nature, but might be the wisest, most benevolent and strongest being that actually exists. Of course if it turned out that Superman were the best, wisest and strongest being that there is, the sufficient reason for his existence would turn out to be the imperishability of matter.

Once you look at the realm of fact you have to see what sorts of beings there are, and look to see what qualities are exemplified by them or can be inferred to be exemplified by them. We find bodies and see by logic that they must have forms. Similarly we see things apparently being born and dying and realize that we *must* think of them as having predecessor and successor states in which that matter is conserved. Imperishability in anything is not something we could directly establish of course, because we cannot experience it for the appropriate time span, but imperishability can be inferred from the fact that every state of matter must be conceived to have a predecessor and a successor. The situation is the same with real gods, not supermen. If we "found" a God and observed that it was a spiritual being, we could infer that what is equivalent to its spiritual matter or substance also must be imperishable because any observed state of that spiritual matter must have a predecessor state and a successor state. Neither divine substance nor material substance can be conceived to come into being and pass away. Both spiritual substance and material substance provide imperishability. Neither guarantees that individuals composed of that substance will be imperishable. We might try to muster arguments to show that gods could not come apart the way stones do, but that would not be of any help since the perishability of stones is compatible with the imperishability of their atoms.

Application of the principle of sufficient reason to matter and spirit has led us to distinguish two kinds of imperishable being (and there conceivably could be other kinds as well). Taylor nowhere offers an argument that there cannot be more than one type, and I know of no argument that imperishability could not be a quality which peacefully coexisted with a wide range of other qualities as well. It could coexist with divine qualities and also with material qualities. It can coexist with continually changing qualities and with changelessness. It can coexist with omniscience and with not having the power to know at all. There is no sound reason for limiting imperishability to gods.

In short, Taylor's problem is that *nothing* provides a reason why we must conceive that it exists. In the case of any sort of thing whatever there is no *logical* reason why it might never have existed. We can think of the universe as absolutely empty of anything, gods or worlds. Whether the things we think of it as empty of are things which are capable of being born and dying, or things like the imperishable matter out of which things are born and into which they pass on death, or things composed of spiritual substance like gods who also are made of imperishable materials, makes no real difference to logic. Taylor's appeal to "sufficient reason," therefore, does justify the claim that something must be imperishable, but does not justify the conclusion that the something which is imperishable must be God.

II. *The Cosmological Argument of Thomas Aquinas*

To summarize the argument so far, Taylor argues that the existence of a logically contingent world requires explanation. This explanation must be in terms of a necessary or imperishable being. His argument was that nature is not *logically* necessary, so we need to look for something outside the world that is. The problem with his argument is that no sort of existence is logically necessary. What slew the ontological argument slays Taylor's.

If instead of looking for a logically necessary being we turn to one which is factually imperishable, a being which logically just happens to exist but whose existence *factually* explains its never having come into existence and its never ceasing to exist, Taylor provides us no reason for going beyond the world itself. Matter *can* provide all the necessity needed by the principle of sufficient reason to account for its own existence.

If what I have argued so far is correct, how could there be a *good* cosmological argument for God? Unless we can contend that the world needs a cause which transcends the world, and that that transcendent cause must have the qualities God has, how could there be a good cosmological argument for God? One of my footnotes has maintained that the cosmological arguments of St. Thomas are much better. What is the difference between Taylor's argument and Thomas' that would justify the difference in conclusions?

Taylor's problem is that he was claiming that the existence of just *any sort of world at all* proves God, and that is not correct. Let us compare Taylor's proof and the classical cosmological proof as offered by Aquinas (and before him, Aristotle and Plato). Thomas did not think that a perfect imperishable being was needed to explain the bare existence of things. He thought it quite rational that things might *always* have existed. What he did argue is that the particular sort of world we have requires explanation in terms of a being which is not merely imperishable but perfect as well. Let us go back to Taylor's paper once more.

Taylor specifically states that he is not contending that the principle of sufficient reason implies "that there must be some purpose or goal for everything, or for the totality of all things; for explanations need not, and in fact seldom are, teleological or purposeful. All the principle requires is that there be some sort of reason for everything" (p. 87). It is no particular feature of things from which he argues, merely their bare existence.

What do classical forms of the cosmological argument claim that Taylor's does not? Careful attention to Thomas, particularly his "third way" shows the difference. Thomas is willing to concede that there possibly are many sorts of necessary beings, and the over-all purpose of the third way is not to show merely that there must be a necessary being, but rather that a *particular sort* of necessary being is required if it should turn out that there are several kinds. I will not try to prove my case by examination of texts, because quite frankly the examination of texts does not really settle my point explicitly. My case has to rest on deductions from positions Thomas explicitly held.

In the first place he held that creation in time was a revealed truth, not a rational truth. This means that he knew of no way to *prove* that the world had a beginning in time. Moreover the arguments which he was using, which were borrowed from Aristotle, were arguments which presupposed the eternity of motion, and he was obliged to defend himself against that specific charge. He did not deny it (as I presume he would have if he could have) but he makes a virtue of it. It is easy to prove a first cause if time began, but much more difficult if it did not, he said. So, he said, it is expedient to use proofs for God which would work even if time (and the world) had no beginning.

The text itself requires interpretation. The "third way" explicitly requires for its completion the second way, and the "second way" argues there must be a first *efficient* cause. Commentators sometimes make the mistake of thinking that a first efficient cause must *precede* others *in time,* hence that Thomas' argument offers a proof that the world began in time. This is wrong for several reasons, including the fact that it is unlikely that Thomas would have been so muddled as to not notice that he had in fact developed a proof that time began when he in fact had. Moreover, the proof from first efficient causes is taken bodily from the *Summa Contra Gentiles* where Thomas had noted in the text itself that this argument depended on Aristotle's *metaphysics!* This admission by Thomas makes it quite clear that even his proof from "efficient causes" is an Aristotelian proof, hence is a proof compatible with eternity of motion.

How *did* such a proof work? Well, Aristotle's worked by invoking the necessity of certain sorts of causes as needed to explain motion. It is no accident that ways one and two of Aquinas refer to explanations of *motion,* that way five calls for an explanation of things moving in such a way as to achieve design, and way four calls for the existence of a perfect being in order to explain degrees of perfection in things. Thomas never provides a proof for God from the bare existence of things, but always proceeds from their qualities or activities or motions to a perfect being.

Motion is reduction from potentiality to actuality, it can only be understood in terms of causation by something which is fully actual so far as the quality sought by the motion is concerned. Aristotelian and Platonic analysis *both* use final causation as ultimate explanation. Things are moved by their vision (or, in Plato's case, memories) of perfection to seek for it themselves. The analysis of purposive motion requires the existence of perfection, or so it is claimed. Nothing St. Thomas says denies that he is invoking the same set of principles of explanation.

Suppose we offer a proof from the principle of sufficient reason to explain *motion of this sort.* Suppose we argue from features of *this* world, not from features of just any world at all, to a perfect being which causes by "luring" the world not beginning it. We now have an argument that metaphysical analysis of the world there actually is requires an imperishable being *of a certain sort* in order to provide sufficient reason for its purposive motion. Imperishable beings which lacked the qualities of perfection could not serve as explanations or reasons for the perfection-seeking behavior of things. If you have only imperishable things which are themselves involved in perfection-seeking you would not yet have provided a sufficient reason for the perfection-seeking activities of those things because you still have their motions to explain. Imperishable but seeking things are not self-explanatory because you are led outside them in order to explain their motion. The argument is complete and consistent. The fact that things (even imperishable things) move in particular ways requires explanation in terms of some necessary being which is not in motion because perfection-seeking requires the existence of the perfection which is sought. Such a line of metaphysical analysis *does* get us beyond an imperishable world of changing combinations of things *if to explain their activities* you need an unmoving cause. Any cause which is not unmoving still has its own motion to explain, hence we cannot stop short of one which is perfect and unmoving.

No attempt will be made in this paper to *defend* the analysis of motion as striving for perfection against mechanistic accounts of motion. It does seem rather obvious, though, that if religious accounts of the universe are true then it is highly likely that *some* sort of analysis of motion as seeking will be correct. It also seems rather obvious that non-religious accounts of the universe would make it highly unlikely that such accounts would be correct. If one had other reasons to show whether the universe was created by a God or not, it would be very helpful in deciding which kind of metaphysical analysis of motion would be correct. Logic by itself will not decide which view of the world is correct, for reasons already discussed. No positive facts can be deduced *a priori*. In that particular sense of necessary, there are no necessary beings. Cosmological proofs of God do not start *a priori,* however, but with existing things, and the right cosmological arguments do not just start with *any* existing things (as Taylor says) but they start with things which allegedly *behave* in particular ways. If these good cosmological arguments have their facts wrong they will not support their conclusions, but if they have their facts right some version of God should work.

To turn the fact that the cosmological arguments do not work just of any world at all into a criticism of those arguments, or to imply that they are not really good arguments because they depend for the truth of their conclusions on the correctness of their starting points, is surely misguided. The only proofs about actual things that we *can* have are proofs of this sort. You cannot prove God from just *any world at all.* Some worlds that seem logically possible would neither require God nor even support arguments for God's existence. It is just because *this* world is the sort that could *only* have occurred if there is a God that the good arguments work.

This approach to the matter is not really arbitrary, or so I would claim at least. Suppose one were asked to prove the existence of other minds but were not permitted to use the purposive activities of bodies to develop such a proof. Such a prohibition would be a clearly arbitrary one. To prove the existence of other things you need to begin with some things. Pure *a priori* arguments are not really possible, as the failure of the ontological argument shows. A proof of other minds may fail to be fool-proof because of the possibility that a *different* interpretation of the behavior of bodies is correct, but no other sort of proof is possible. It is not regarded as a defect in arguments for other minds that such arguments must begin with a correct interpretation of the behavior of bodies. It should not be regarded as a defect in proofs for the divine other mind that they must start also with a correct apprehension of the activities of things which are not God.

The enterprise of metaphysical thinking is usefully seen as one way of trying to test out our initial apprehensions of starting points, and provides us a way of exploring whether some of the things that we initially experienced were correctly analyzed or not. We test partly in terms of whether our apprehensions of some things jar against our apprehensions of other things. When we find conflicts we have to decide which apprehension has to give way. Primitive and criticized ethical experience and ordinary scientific analysis conflict, because ought implies can and scientific analysis implies cannot, and these conflict, to give only one example. On the basis of this conflict I have to decide which to reconstruct, my science or my ethics. If I reconstruct on the basis of ethics and qualify my scientific construction of the world, I may be right or I may be wrong, but there is no way to tell for sure in this life except by looking again, and analyzing again, and resolving conflicts the best I can—but I never get beyond tested experiences as the beginning point for what conclusions I finally work out as proved.

If God created the world, then that world will be correctly experienced only when it is experienced as matter exhibiting that peculiar sort of God-seeking behavior that the good cosmological arguments attempted to analyze. Not just any sort of world at all will do, only *our* sort (or others which share functionally similar features) will do.

Taylor himself addresses aspects of this problem in proposing teleological arguments as well, but teleological arguments are basically different from the cosmological styles of arguments under discussion. Teleological arguments, as Taylor points out, are arguments that the character of the world points to some "purposeful" being who fashioned it. He calls these "guiding hand" arguments and his conclusion about them is that they "are for the most part unconclusive" (p. 96).

This argument is different from the classical cosmological arguments that I have been addressing, however. The "good" cosmological arguments are not basically "guiding hand" arguments because they do not attempt to prove overall design. Good cosmological arguments move from a type of activity in things to an unmoving mover of those things, and not from designed things to an architect or designer who externally imposes a design upon those things. I do not find fault with Taylor's judgment on the teleological argument, only with his treatment of the cosmological.

One other argument that Taylor gives some credence to is that our trust in our own faculties of sense and cognition presupposes something about the nature of the world. He observes that it is difficult to *justify* that trust without at the same time accepting those presuppositions. This argument is a good argument, Taylor concludes, but the results are inconclusive. I would agree that that argument is inconclusive but I would not fault it on that score. In a way, what I have just said about good cosmological arguments assimilates them to arguments of just that sort. Proofs for God can be good proofs while at the same time not be conclusive (fool-proof) proofs, but that was the subject for another paper.[5]

III. *Right and Wrong Cosmological Arguments Summarized*

My argument then has been, no logically necessary being exists, so the claim that the existence of just any world at all requires the existence of a cause outside the world breaks down. Neither gods nor worlds are logically necessary. We can easily imagine that neither of them existed or that either of them provides sufficient reason for their bare existence. Given some particular sorts of world however, and we exist in the midst of the right sort of one, some necessary and perfect being must be supposed by the principle of sufficient reason in order to account for that particular sort of world.

If we consider the world merely *as existing* the principle of sufficient reason does not require us to go outside the world for its reason. Since it can always be supposed that matter is imperishable, once a world means always a world and never a non-world. No argument for *God* is thereby provided, and that is why bad cosmological arguments fail.

If we consider the world as containing things exhibiting purposive motion, the principle of sufficient reason leads us outside it to a world which contains an imperishable and perfect thing. There is nothing in the bare existence of the world that supplies a sufficient reason for its purposive activities, at least that is what good cosmological arguments contend.

---

[5] In "Fool-Proof Proofs of God?" I argue that no proofs for God can be fool-proof and that the proofs for God of the sort represented by the "right" cosmological arguments are just the sorts of proofs that we should expect to have if such a God exists. That paper is published in the *International Journal for Philosophy of Religion*, 8, 1, pp. 18–35.

It is this *latter* claim that was the central feature of classical cosmological arguments but which Taylor's modern version lacked, to its detriment.

Whether analysis of activities in terms of purpose is correct or not we cannot prove by logic alone, but cosmological arguments never attempted to do that and no argument conceivably could. In one sense Taylor is right. From the logical point of view there *might* have been nothing at all. From the factual point of view there is something, but whether this something requires God depends upon whether the view when behavior is apprehended purposively it is apprehended correctly is true or not.

IV. *An Afterword*

To leave the matter as though the analysis of motion in terms of final causes worked as Aquinas (and Plato and Aristotle) thought it worked, would conceal a problem that needs to be brought out. To believe that cosmological arguments do point to God because the particular activities that we find in our world require God as their sufficient reason is not necesarily to believe that these philosophers were right in all basic respects about perfection. It is one thing to argue that nothing in the world explains purposive motion in the world, and another to claim that the cause of that motion which lies outside the world must be unmoving. None of the perfections that we know involve immutability in the human case, and it is not clear that the claim that they must do so in the perfect case has ever been compelling. Perfect love must be all-reaching, and perfect knowledge must include knowledge as to what time it is now. Classical doctrines of God opted for immutability and qualified all other aspects of perfection in terms of it, but that need not have been so. There is no logical incoherence in the notion that all things are moved by a perfection which itself moves in some respects. That is a topic for another paper contrasting cosmological arguments based on moving first movers with ones based on unmoved movers.

University of Delaware

8 SCIENCE, RELIGION AND EXPERIENCE
Frederick Ferré

It is a significant feature of our times that neither scientists nor theologians exude the kind of assurance today that once gave rise to the familiar stereotypes of cocksure empiricist and dogmatic prelate. One lasting benefit of this changed climate might be the recognition, across disciplinary fences, that the grass on the other side is not that much greener, after all. This could be a most useful outcome, since recognizing one's own vulnerability as shared also by one's neighbor might well lead to less defensive posturing and to more compassion among similarly finite human inquirers.

Inquiry must and should go forward, however, despite the more modest current mood in both science and theology. This means that qualified persons will be and are inquiring about some object or reference of interest. It means, further, that such inquirers will be seeking to obtain as much knowledge about their subject-matter as possible. And in this process they will point to certain grounds as warranting such assurance as is available for making their claims to knowledge.

My purpose in what follows is to explore, in connection with the enterprises of scientific and of theological inquiry, the concepts of "knowledge" and "warranted assurance" in hopes of seeing as similar what is similar (and of distinguishing what is distinct) in the application of these crucial concepts to the pertinent endeavors. When this is done, I shall attempt to draw some implications and offer some conclusions about the current cognitive situation.

I. "Knowledge"

We should consider, first, what any claim to knowledge must involve. In this theologians and scientists, insofar as they claim knowledge at all, will be operating within the same general guide-lines.

There are three elements to any knowledge-claim, each a necessary condition for the state of knowledge to exist. First, there must be something that is believed. Knowledge is more than mere belief, of course, but it presupposes some belief. If I do not even believe that the cat is by the fireside, then I cannot be said to know that the cat is by the fireside. If I have serious doubts that Dr. Moriarty is the villian, then I certainly do not *know* that he is to blame.

Besides belief, however, knowledge requires that the content of belief be true or correct. If what I believed turns out to be mistaken it is possible to say: "Well, I believed it, just the same; now I know better." But it is a solecism to say: "Well, I knew it, all the same; now I know differently." In the latter case we would say, instead: "Well, I *thought* I knew, but I see that I was wrong." Knowing, in other words, carries with it an implication of success. To know (unlike believing, which is purely descriptive of a state of mind) is a normative matter. Even though I might be ever so sure that the capital of the State of Illinois is Chicago, I could not know it—nor can anyone know it apart from a change by the Illinois legislature—since it is not a correct belief.

Thus (1) believing and (2) believing what is true or correct are necessary conditions for any valid knowledge-claim. But these are not enough, in themselves, since there are many true beliefs which are yet not known. If I believe that my new colleague is untrustworthy for no particular reason and—as it happens—he turns out to be untrustworthy in fact, it is not legitimate to claim that I *knew* it beforehand. I *believed* it and it was *true;* so much I can say. But knowledge demands more than a lucky coincidence. Without grounds for my belief, I am shooting in the dark: I may hit something, but that can hardly be credited to my marksmanship.

My grounds, furthermore, need to be adequate (another normative consideration). If, for example, I drew the conclusion about my new colleague's untrustworthiness from the swarthiness of his skin or from the close-set character of his eyes, I should still not be entitled to claim knowledge on these flimsy warrants, even if they were sufficient to stimulate my rather irrational belief and even if (as it happened) my ill-founded mistrust unfortunately turns out to be correct. Only reasons that are relevant and evidential can be counted as warranting a knowledge-claim.

I shall soon (Part II) return to discuss more fully what is involved in this last requirement, but first it is important to ask whether knowledge-claims play an important part in theology and science. It may seem odd even to ask this question in connection with science. The very word for science derives from the Latin noun *scientia,* meaning "knowledge." Science represents, we hope, the best knowledge we have about the natural order.

And yet, on reflection, we may well wonder whether any given claim to scientific knowledge will stand up under the test of time if the three necessary conditions for knowledge in general are taken with full seriousness. In the past we have become used to seeing scientific principle after principle fall as scientific inquiry, in its advance, discards its own previous achievements. What was once *thought* to be known about heat or light or electricity or even space and time is now recognized as incorrect in fundamental ways. We have no doubt that there exists a great, fluid history of scientific *belief*; but is there any comparable history possible of scientific *knowledge*? If a necessary condition of scientific knowledge is that it must be correct, as well as believed for relevant evidential reasons, then how do we know that today any more than yesterday there is anything within scientific doctrine that will stand as genuine scientific knowledge?

Science, by its very nature, is corrigible. That corrigibility is one of its greatest strengths. But in that very strength we find the problem for scientific knowledge-claims, if taken strictly.

From a theological point of view, of course, claims for knowledge may seem essential in inverse proportion to the degree of corrigibility offered by theological statements. It is much harder to find places where theologians, as compared to scientists, make themselves vulnerable to disconfirmation, as the protracted "theology and falsification" discussion has illustrated.[1] This has both advantages and defects for the theologian. A primary advantage, of course, is that the second necessary condition of knowledge, that the substance of knowledge be true or correct, is less likely to be shown lacking. A primary disadvantage, conversely, is that the third necessary condition, that knowledge be grounded in relevant and evidentiary warrants, is correspondingly harder to fulfill.

It might be tempting, under these cirumstances, for the theologian to withdraw altogether from claims to knowledge. He speaks, after all, for a community of faith. May it not be enough for him, rather than claiming knowledge, to make faith-claims?

I think it would not be enough. The theologian, like the scientist, is engaged in the enterprise of making claims about reality. These claims are alleged to be true. To anyone who makes such allegations about reality it is appropriate to ask: "How do you know that?" or "Why do you say such a thing?" If these utterances are not to be utterly arbitrary, and if the ideal of reality-reference is operative, there must be some point at which the responsible inquirer will answer: "Here I stand; this much I know." He may be wrong, of course, in thus claiming knowledge. It may turn out that he only *thinks* that he knows. Only time and further inquiry will tell. But without a knowledge-claim to undergird it, the act of assertion loses its moorings. Though a theologian, in asserting that God is love, may not be making a simple knowledge-claim in that complex act, he at least must stand responsible for knowledge that Scripture can be interpreted to support such a state-

---

[1] The literature is too extensive to cite in a footnote, but the start of the discussion is to be found in A. Flew and A. MacIntyre, *New Essays in Philosophical Theology* (London: SCM Press, 1955), and further bibliography may be found in F. Ferré, *Language, Logic and God* (N.Y.: Harper & Row, 1961).

ment. At some point he must know why he is speaking as he is or admit that he is merely blathering.

Scientists and theologians, then, are each involved in their own way with knowledge-claims. Knowledge, however, involves both true belief and adequate warrant. If this is so, how can there ever be real knowledge in either science or theology? Perhaps we have knowledge, but, on the other hand, how can we know that we know? What is to guarantee that the truth we think we hold on strong evidentiary grounds will never need amendment or correction?

I submit that there is no such guarantee, and that none is needed. Looking for a guarantee is a misconceived search. In its place we should recognize that the nature of knowledge is an ideal limit. *Knowledge is what we would have, that is, if our best warranted beliefs never needed to be corrected.* Never needing correction, after all, is what is meant by the complete truth of an idea. In every context, from every point of view, under all circumstances, a true idea is one that is perfectly reliable; and a perfectly reliable idea—in the strong sense of "perfect"—is one that is true.

When a scientist claims knowledge about nature, then, he is trusting in the strength of his warrants enough to place his belief into the context of ideal, perfectly warranted assertions. He is betting that in the long run his belief will not need to be revised except to be enriched by further connections and applications. He is offering his personal conviction that the matter before him is not merely a personal (and momentary) belief but that—as knowledge—it will take its place in the permanent store of reliable conceptual representations of reality, forever corrigible but forever not needing correction.

Likewise the theologian in claiming knowledge is asserting that the assertions he makes will withstand every testing that is possible, including the testing of infinitely prolonged experience. His assurance is not that his conceptions will copy reality in every detail, but that nothing that happens or could happen will fail to illustrate and extend the central vision he has been granted.

"Knowledge," then, is the ideal limit of warranted assurance in the conceptual reliability of one's beliefs. Scientists and theologians, however, may look to their beliefs for different sorts of "reliability." In this their standards of warranted assurance may well differ. Our next step, consequently, must be to address directly the quest for warranted assurance in science and theology.

II. *"Warranted Assurance"*

The first step in clarifying the concept of warranted assurance of any kind is to ask the prior question: assurance about *what?* The sort of assurance one is looking for will depend upon the sort of interests or purposes that one has.

And the sorts of warrants that one will require will, likewise, vary with the functions of the enterprise one is following. It is a mistake to suppose that all sorts of assurance are alike or that there is only one overriding logic of providing warrants. There is a considerable difference, for example, in the sort of assurance I am seeking when I want assurance that the square root of 2,025 is 45, on the one hand, and that my lover loves me, on the other. Similarly, there will be a great difference in the sorts of warrants that will be acceptable or appropriate in the two different contexts. A meaningful glance or tender touch will not and should not bring assurance to the mathematical question; but a demonstration from first principles will not go far toward warranting assurance in romance.

Since warranted assurance is always relative to the purpose at hand, it is important to look at our question in terms of the basic purposes or functions of science and of theology. We cannot tarry here to go deeply into details, but the general outlines at least should be clear. What is it that is being *done* in science and in theology? What do they want assurance about, respectively; and what sorts of warrants are appropriate to provide such assurance?

Let us begin with purposes and warrants in the sciences. There are, of course, immensely many purposes at the concrete level of specific scientific research projects. We must abstract from the welter of these particular purposes and classify them in broad terms. If we do so, I think we shall find three primary and irreducible sorts of purposes that scientists share and that define, in fact, the scientific enterprise.

The first general purpose shared by scientists is to provide an accurate and reliable description of natural regularities. Ideally these descriptions will take the form of mathematically expressible law-statements, subject to prediction and replicable confirmation. In practice these ideals may not be attainable; experimental control is hard to come by in astronomy, for example, and prediction is notoriously difficult in sociology as well as in classical biology. But the aim at accurate and reliable description of the observable is a unifying and essential element wherever science is practiced. I shall call it the *descriptive* purpose of science. Under this purpose fall all the efforts at enhancing the accuracy of observation, including the development of instrumentation to push back observational horizons. Under this purpose, too, we find the development of precise languages, often mathematical, in which to express accurately what is observed to be the case. Also, as I have suggested, the predictive efforts of scientists may be seen, at least in part, as serving the descriptive purpose of science; if a law is indeed as it is described, then it should be able to be confirmed experimentally under a variety of clearly controlled conditions. Accurate description is possible without prediction, but predictive power adds mightily to our confidence in the accuracy of our descriptions.

The first function of science is essential, but it is by no means the only essential purpose that we find. Observation, classification and prediction alone leave us merely with the facts. Scientists want also to understand the facts. Why should these particular regularities be as they are? How do these laws relate to others? What best makes sense of the descriptions we have reached? The second defining purpose of science, in other words, is its *explanatory* function. Here creative conceptual activity is brought into play. Relationships are sought; "subsurface" connections are considered and debated. The ideal is an explanatory scheme that will unify the descriptive data in a satisfying whole.

It must not be supposed that these two purposes can or ought to be pursued in isolation. The directions of explanatory speculation will of course be stimulated by the descriptive findings of controlled observation. But also the language that classifies phenomena (descriptive function) will be shaped by the explanatory categories that are currently being employed to unify them (explanatory function). And, most strikingly, perhaps, the ancillary function of prediction will attach itself both to the confirmation of suspected natural regularities (descriptive function) and—often more dramatically—to the suspected implications of unobservable theoretical constructs (explanatory function).

None the less, the purposes of scientists in *describing* and in *explaining* what is described are distinguishable in principle, even though not neatly separable in practice. And each of these purposes carries with it an appropriate but distinct sort of warrant as to whether the purpose has been well enough satisfied to justify assurance.

The crucial sort of warrant evidentially relevant to the descriptive purpose of scientists is intersubjective sensory verification. Where prediction is possible, of course, this is highly valued as a type of controlled experience capable of being repeated on demand at a variety of times and for a variety of observers. But where it is not possible to predict, at least it is important for one scientist to be able to say to another: "Do you see what I see?" The saying and the sharing demand a language and a community, of course; and so it may be said that the grounds for warranted assurance in scientific description are offered by community consensus based on a common language and analogous personal experiences.

A different sort of warrant is evidentially relevant to assurance concerning the explanatory purpose of scientists. Explanations are not simply descriptions to be supported (or not) by observation, although they must be harmonious with the observations. Instead, a good explanation is warranted by its conceptual coherence in drawing together our thoughts concerning not only the phenomena in question but also the larger range of beliefs and concepts that constitute the scientific—and sometimes metaphysical or religious—background for the scientific community. If an explanation fits in well with the forms of thought that are current in other areas it is naturally adopted with more assurance than an alternative that must remain out of relation and relatively *ad hoc*. Criteria of adequacy to the descriptive data, then, and coherence both internally and externally—that is, within its own conceptual network and between that network and the larger conceptual field within which it must take its place—constitute the grounds for warranted assurance in scientific explanation.

Penetrating both these essential purposes shared by scientists is the aim to be applicable or useful to human beings. The scientific enterprise is being done, after all, by human beings for human beings. Descriptions must be relative to human powers of observation augmented by humanly invented and applied instrumentation. Explanations must be meaningful and satisfying to human minds. In consequence, the simpler, more applicable procedure, concept, or explanation will properly be preferred, all other things being equal, to the more complex. Aesthetic preferences for symmetry and elegance will prevail over alternatives that are perceived as malformed or merely ugly. Grounds for warranted assurance in science must not, then, be assumed to be inhuman; it is appropriate that the full humanity of scientists, including affective and practical interests as well as sensory and logical, be satisfied as far as possible when scientists claim to know reality.

How does this account of scientific purposes and their appropriate warrants compare with the purposes and warrants of theology? Both are human enterprises; both need to satisfy the full range of human interests represented within their respective concerns; but the specific functions we find are distinct as well as, in some respects, quite similar.

First, the theologian's function is not to describe and explain the regularities of the natural order, but is, instead, to articulate and relate the value-laden vision of a religious community. Theologians, I submit, are spokesmen for those who see themselves and their world in the light of a central *mythos*. The *mythos* itself is not primarily made up of doctrines and dogmas; those are derivative from past theological work. Instead, the focus of the worshipping community is a mosaic of images provided, for the Christian churches, through the vivid stories of the biblical saga. These stories include not only the whole fabric of human experience but also the larger framework of the natural and the divine, offering a structure of meaning for the whole.

But this meaning is not wholly explicit, nor is it self-evidently relevant to the beliefs and concerns of any given age. The theologian's job is to bring into explicit articulation what is implicit in the *mythos* taken as focus for worship, and so to articulate the images of faith that they relate coherently to the whole of human experience. His or her aim, that is, is to say for the church what was "on the tip of its tongue" and to say it in such a way that theological categories and concepts not only fit the primary, inarticulate sense of the *mythos* but also illuminate the human condition and the cosmic order as these are experienced in a given era.

This is a tall order, but theologians historically have succeeded brilliantly in their daunting task. St. Augustine, finding useable concepts in Platonic thought, not only spoke for the Church of his time in ways it found deeply

acceptable but also spoke to the experience of Classical Rome. And he succeeded in both aspects with such penetration that we read him today with
enduring profit. St. Thomas, later, articulated the Christian *mythos* with Aristotelian conceptual tools in ways that the Catholic Church, though shocked
at first at his radical departure from Platonism, eventually came to embrace
for many years as though his was the only possible proper articulation. And
his *Summa* at the same time provided a synthesis of faith with sophisticated
thought—scientific, psychological, metaphysical—that was the capstone of
medieval culture.

Theologians today are in various ways at work on the same project. This
means that there must be a dual set of warrants for theological assurance
corresponding to the two major aspects of the theologian's task: first, the
task of being articulator for the faithful community of their central *mythos*
and, second, of being spokesman to the world concerning the basic interpretation of human experience.

Corresponding to the first of these two functions there is, I believe, a
standard of *appropriateness* which, when well satisfied, warrants one sort of
assurance in theological claims. This is assurance concerning the authenticity
of the theologian's words from the point of view of the community of faith
he represents. The very function of theologian as articulator makes this an
internal matter, to be decided in the long run by those for whom the *mythos*
of worship shaped personal and communal consciousness.

In principle there can be no clearly formulated rule for the application of
this criterion of appropriateness. In principle, that is, appropriateness must
be a *felt* congruity between what is pre-articulately present to religious intention and what is post-articulately published by the theological inquirer. If
there were a clear rule to apply, this would require that both sides of the
comparison be clearly laid out in advance of its application; but this is exactly
what, in nature of the case, cannot be achieved. I once tried to express this
as follows:

> Each of us engages in the activity of judging the appropriateness of his
> own choice of words: ''Such-and-such a way of putting my thought was
> not quite right; this other way would be better.'' But we cannot possibly
> judge the appropriateness of the manner of our articulation of thought
> by any precisely articulated standard, as though our thoughts were al-
> ready articulated somewhere for purposes of comparison before we
> started articulating them. No, it is the very process of *first* articulation
> that we are judging; and therefore the judgment must be by means of
> some prearticulate—essentially unformulable and imprecise—sense of
> confidence (''That time I said just what I meant'') or of discomfort
> (''No, that wasn't quite the right way to put it'') that guides us.[2]

---

[2] Frederick Ferré, *Basic Modern Philosophy of Religion*, (N.Y.: Charles Scribner's
Sons, Inc., 1967), pp. 382-383.

In this manner, then, the believing community, or substantial segments of it, give the verdict of appropriateness on various theological proposals for fresh articulation. At the current time existentialist, Marxist, "process," and other categories are being used by theologians to recast in fully explicit theoretical ways the "old, old story" of the Christian *kerygma*. Time will tell how the verdict from the community of worship will be given. But it is an essential part of the theologian's task that he seek that verdict and that it not go against his work. The concrete measure of his success in meeting this criterion will be the extent to which his concepts are actually used or reflected in sermons, prayers, and other ongoing activities of the church. When this acceptance is high, then the first, internal ground for warranted assurance is present. The language of theological theory has proven its appropriateness to become the vehicle for living faith.

On the other hand, however, the theologian's function is to speak meaningfully and illuminatingly to the general categories of human experience. A church theology that is not also a theology for the world is a parochial exercise of little interest. In this respect, theology's purpose overlaps with all general explanatory conceptual activities, particularly those of philosophy on its ethical and metaphysical sides. This is why, I think, theologians have so often made use of philosophical frameworks to carry out their interpretive role.

If so, it will not be surprising that the same warrants that offer assurance in general theoretical contexts will be found to function also on the "external" side of theological activity. Since the purposes are the same, the warrants should also be held in common. These are, stated most comprehensively, the warrants provided by theoretical coherence and theoretical adequacy.

Theoretical *coherence*, first, has already been identified as significant in the explanatory function of the sciences. It is the capacity of a conceptual scheme to permit thought to flow unhindered by gaps or obstacles within the scheme (to provide internal wholeness) and to relate thought in other domains to the concepts of the scheme itself (to provide grounds for additional unification of thought). In the theoretical stratosphere where theology and metaphysics mingle their functions, however, there is in principle no need for additional unification. All must be included, since the subject matter itself is of unlimited comprehensiveness. Therefore the coherence criterion offers its relevant evidential warrant primarily in terms of the wholeness it is capable of providing for human thought at the very limits of its capacities. Warranted assurance for this aspect of theological work comes from the demonstrable ability of a conceptual framework to bring a sense of unity and comprehension ("holding together") to the minds of those who think within it.

Coherence, however, is empty if it is based upon a set of concepts that fail to reflect the fulness of human experience taken as a whole. A conceptual scheme must not only be coherent within itself but also must be *adequate* to all the data needing illumination. Here the theologian needs to be able to deal with the heights and depths of human expression, with the nobility and the squalor of existence, and—not least—with the findings of the most careful descriptions and explanations of the observable world available to us, the sciences. If his, the theologian's, claims are to be made with warranted assurance, that is, they must be fully conversant with and relevant to our most reliable source of data about the empirical order. This requirement is built into the function of the theologian in attempting to speak to the world with general illumination. He or she cannot abandon this role without fleeing to the ghetto and thus forfeiting religious responsibility.

Therefore, we find, the need to harmonize the science-theology relationship returns with redoubled force once more, as a necessary condition of warranted assurance within theology itself. We have in this section seen that the purposes and warrants of science and theology are clearly distinguishable, but for all their distinctness they cannot finally be sealed off from one another. What implications may we at last be able to draw? What guidance may these implications provide?

III. *Conclusions*

Perhaps the most general conclusion to be drawn from this line of thought is that although a number of specific sciences may legitimately do their proper work without taking explicit notice of theology, the reverse is not the case. Theology cannot be faithful to its fullest internal aims without taking account of the existence and the findings of the sciences. Given the theological purpose to speak a meaningful word to the world, which brings with it the requirement that theological claims be adequate to all the data of the world, the methods and findings of the sciences become literally part of the subject-matter of theology. This is unlike the situation of, say, physics, in which explicit notice of Trinitarian controversies is not necessary for either descriptive or explanatory purposes. True, Trinitarian and other theological predilections may be at work in the background of the physicists' thinking—as in preferences for or against the three-in-one model of the quark, or the like—but these considerations belong to reflections about the work of the physicists (to philosophy of science) rather than to the work itself.

Theology, on the other hand, cannot do its own job without relating the religious vision it articulates to the best warranted beliefs of the age. And its mode of relating cannot merely be negative, excluding or denying what the sciences claim to be the case. The descriptive rigor of the scientific enterprise requires that at a very minimum the findings of empirical research be taken by theology as setting forth how the world presents itself to human observation. When theologians have been so unwise as to set themselves up as head-on rivals in the matter of describing the domain of empirical regularities, they have again and again suffered ignominious confusion.

The explanatory role of science, on the other hand, prompts a somewhat different story. Theologians had better be attentive to this function of the sciences; it represents, after all, an expert approach to the profound human quest for understanding. It is based on penetrating thought about the observed and described phenomena, and it is warranted by networks of connections not only among the specialized concepts employed but also between domains of observation. Challenging its results had better not be done lightly. But since it is in regard to their explanatory functions that the sciences and theology principally intersect one another, the relationship established by theology to scientific explanation should be expected to be complex.

On the one hand, the concepts employed by theologians in any age need to be able to incorporate or illuminate the specific explanatory claims of the sciences when the value implications of such claims are compatible with the fundamental religious vision itself. This is one of the most pressing needs of religious believers in any age: to be able to think responsibly in terms of the abiding images of personal and community commitment. The theologian's task is to make such coherence come about by articulating a scheme of concepts capable not only of being judged appropriate to these images of commitment but also of being found comprehensive enough and illuminating enough for thinking the world through the images of faith. If aspects of the world are also being understood through the models of various sciences, the theologian is required to employ concepts that can link these models and theories into a larger framework wherein a sense of understanding is provided.

On the other hand, however, theologians must not only find ways of incorporating current scientific explanations in their wider conceptual schemes but must also have a way of distancing themselves from the theories and models of science at any given time. It is naive to suppose that the scientific vision of any given time must be taken whole into the theology of that day. First, the scientific vision itself *is not* "whole," but is particular and fragmentary. This, I think, is no accident but is due to the specialized nature of the special sciences themselves, and to the effective methods developed by particular research communities intent on the understanding of very specific domains. However this may be, it is no doubt the case today, and has been the case throughout the history of modern science, that although the vision of a "unified science" has been an ideal to many, it has not been and is not even close to realization. Therefore the theologian is not only not obliged, but is properly unable, to swallow the mélange of theories, concepts, models and methods uncritically in one gulp.

Second, the scientific enterprise itself, as we have repeatedly noted, is highly corrigible both in principle and in practice. The history of scientific explanation is a flux, involving sudden reversals and radical revolutions as well as evolutionary development. No theologian with this in mind ought to feel intimidated or forced into accepting the current deliverances of the sciences as final. Clearly, as we have noted, the theological enterprise requires that what is being claimed in the sciences must be related to religious thought, but it cannot be foundational. Where there are compelling reasons to criticise, the theologian should feel his obligation to point out the incompatibility of current scientific claims to fundamental spiritual perceptions. He should not suppose himself to be a match for the scientist on scientific grounds, but in the wider flux of cognitive constructs, the theologian may well stand firm as critic of the abstractions of some proposed scientific theory in terms of principles derived either from the value intuitions of the religious community for which he speaks or from the articulated conceptual framework from within which he attempts to understand the world.

Standing sometimes as a principled critic of the actual assertions of particular scientific research traditions, the theologian may indirectly also influence a rethinking of the descriptive adequacy of scientific work within that tradition. As we have noted, the work of description does not in fact go forward without major influence from the conceptual structures and pre-observational expectations of scientists. It may be that some features of the observable world are not being adequately noted, if conceptual structures themselves seem from some thoughtful theological point of view to be faulty. If important human intuitions are being ignored or run over roughshod, then the theologian's critique may, in the larger cognitive context, be just the warning that is needed for more adequate conceptual construction and more accurate empirical description. A word grounded in faith, that is, may well have a therapeutic value to the disciples of reason.

This mention of faith brings me to my final set of observations concerning the implications of this paper for science and theology. There are, I believe, epistemological applications of the great Pauline triad of virtues: faith, hope, and love.

The place of *faith* in this context has already been hinted. Theology is anchored, by its purpose and by its criterion of appropriateness, to certain fundamental value intuitions and thereby to data drawn from large domains of human experience supplementary to those typically recognized by the several sciences. It is vital that the theologian insist, in the marketplace of ideas, that these experiences are in fact data. They are vague and hard to measure and therefore easy not only to overlook (by crisp intellects to whom the quantifiability of data is the *sine qua non* of their respectability) but also, given a trenchant set of categories derived exclusively from the readily measurable, to deny. Faith, however, as the stubborn determination that evidence not "seen" is yet there, remains a counterweight in retaining cognitive and valuational balance.

Particular scientific research traditions, too, are anchored in what can only be called faith. I am not now speaking of the larger confidence in the orderliness of the observable world, or in the powers of conceptual creativity to bring understanding to human inquirers. These, shared by scientists, philosophers, and theologians alike, we have been taking for granted. Rather, the specific workers within a particular research community have and must have a more particularized faith, both in the adequacy of the general framework of their research paradigm and of their fellow-workers in the field. The latter faith is principally moral and cannot concern us here, but the former is essential to the epistemological possibility of the normal scientific enterprise itself. Without it, as Thomas Kuhn points out, each worker would need to reestablish his field *de novo,* and confident advanced specialization of research could not go forward.[3] Such faith is necessary and legitimate. What is vital, however, is that faith of this sort be recognized as such. This is particularly important when the faith undergirding the practices of some research tradition has larger implications for fundamental human values as, for example, Skinnerian psychology has built into its procedures, instrumentation, and theories. The faith that human phenomena are in principle capable of being adequately described and understood without reference to intentions, purposes, aims, and goals (the realm of the supposedly fictitious "inner man"[4]) is essential to the entire enterprise. So be it. The Skinnerian research tradition should go forward as far as it can with its project, but not without acknowledging the difference between its actual research results to date and its basic, far from established faith. Clarifying the presence of faith in the sciences will reveal much that is useful both to the theologian and to the scientist. Instead of strife between "science and theology," as such, we shall find that often there are faiths in conflict. Untangling them from the other functions of science and dealing with them on their own terms will be helpful both to the needs of science and to the clarification of faith itself.

The place of *hope* in the scientific and theological enterprises is closely allied to that of faith, but is not identical. In the sciences, the labor of research within a community committed in faith to a given paradigm is carried on in hope. The solution promised at the end of the research trail is elusive and often delayed. Anomalies are found that test the firmness of one's commitment to the shared expectations of one's community. But hope, the readiness to act on faith and to see the possibility of desired outcomes even in adversity, sustains the work.

In theology, the role of hope is even keener, to the extent that the theological motive towards a realist intent—the conviction that one's concepts point beyond themselves to some reality to which they are more or less adequate—is even stronger. Since there is no way to compare our conceptual representations directly with some "naked reality," there is no literal way

---

[3] Thomas S. Kuhn, *The Structure of Scientific Revolutions* (Chicago: The University of Chicago Press, second edition, 1970), Chapters II-IV.

[4] B. F. Skinner, *Beyond Freedom and Dignity* (New York: Alfred A. Knopf, 1971).

in which *belief* that our concepts correspond with their referents can be confirmed. Belief, therefore, seems inappropriate to this context. But in so far as the images and theories of theology describe a concerned Thou, a being both in-Himself real and for-Himself aware, it would seem quite fitting for religious thinkers to *hope* that the reality that constitutes the ideal limit of our most reliable conceptions may be at least as great as faith maintains.

Finally we find the place of *love*. Given our understanding of knowledge as the ideal limit of warranted assurance, and recognizing the varieties of warrants operative in our many-mansioned cognitive household, we must expect irreducible differences between knowledge-claims at various levels. At one level, simply between scientist and scientist, there will be conflict based on different professional commitments, different temperaments, different readiness to abandon the familiar status quo for promising but uncertain possibilities, different weighing of the importance of conflicting criteria, different aesthetic sensibilities, and the like. Theologians, too, will differ both in what they take to be essential in the articulation of their authoritative focus of faith and in what conceptual vehicles they prefer for the long, demanding journey of theological thought. And across these levels, as well, between theologians as seekers after coherent explanatory schemes and scientists providing recalcitrant data, between scientists as committed to ultimate visions of what is true and satisfying and theologians speaking for a community's spiritual heritage, and in many other ways, argument will break out.

If any party had unquestionable authority to dictate knowledge, then this tumult of claims might be regrettable. But in the human cognitive situation the reverse is the case. Our need is not merely to "tolerate" the vision and the voice of the cognitive rival, as J. Bronowski finds essential to the nature of science itself,[5] but more positively to nurture the other whose dissent helps us break free from the narrowness of familiar frameworks, the deficiencies of which we might otherwise forever fail to see. Pluralism is not merely a fate to be endured but an opportunity to be cherished. Internal to science and to theology, as well as lying between science and theology, there are built-in stimuli for continuing variety in claims for "knowledge of reality." This fact will be for the good, surely, as long as our response to pluralism is not to retreat nor to dig in but to treasure the intrinsic value of the other's vision for his or her sake, not merely for the contribution it can make to mine. And at the same time, the treasured other is not to be left out of relationship. The fellowship of seekers needs each part, both as valuable in itself and as a contributing element in the larger harmonies of cognitive expansion. The invitation to community without violation of integrity is what we mean by love.

---

[5] J. Bronowski, *Science and Human Values* (N.Y.: Harper & Row, 1956), pp. 58ff.

And so there abide these three: firm commitment to beliefs even when the evidence is not clear; readiness to rise to the creative possibilities suggested by such commitment and to translate them into undiscouraged practice; and tender nurture of human believers both in their singular independence and in their intimate mutuality for yet wider good. These are the epistemological virtues of faith, hope, and love. And still the greatest of them is love.

Dickinson College

9 UNLESS YOU BELIEVE YOU WILL NOT UNDERSTAND

James Ross

Wondering what Saint Augustine might have conveyed with the scriptural maxim "Unless you believe you will not understand,"[1] I explore some infrequently discussed aspects of faith and reason, particularly *ego-situated religious knowledge*. That is a kind of religious knowing that results from religious conceptual sets and one's unpolarized religious self-awareness. Believing certain things which may be thus known is essential to being "of the faith" and the things believed, though not identical with what is revealed, *cannot* be *understood* unless one believes what has been revealed. Furthermore, this kind of religious knowledge shares in the "indeterminacy of translation" (to use a phrase of Quine's from a quite different area of philosophy) that afflicts theology. That is because such self-construals are, like theology, formulated with mixed religious and secular conceptions whose correlation

---

"Unless you believe you will not understand."
[1] This text is taken from *Isaiah,* Vii, 9, and appears in *En.* in *Ps. 111:*

"Some things must be understood before one can believe in God; nevertheless the faith whereby one believes in him helps one to understand more . . . Since faith comes from hearing and hearing through the preaching of Christ, how could one possibly believe a preacher of the faith unless one at least understood his language, to say no more? But conversely, there are things which must first be believed in order to be understood; this is shown by the prophet's statement "Unless you believe, you shall not understand". The mind thus progresses in understanding what it believes." R. A. Markus, also cites *Sermo* 18,3; *Sermo* 43, 3 and 4 and 7 and 9, where the same idea is expressed. ("Augustine", in Armstrong ed. *Cambridge History of Late Greek and Early Medieval Philosophy* [Cambridge: Cambridge University Press, 1970]).

Markus (*op. cit.* p. 350) reminds us that Augustine divided *"credibilia"* (things suitable for belief) into: (1) those that can only be believed, never understood; (2) those where belief and understanding go together—to believe is *ipso facto* to understand them and (3) those things that must first be believed in order to be subsequently understood. Still tracking Markus, *loc. cit.,* historical truths belong to the first class; mathematical and logical truths to the second; and "the third, truths about God which believers will one day understand if they live according to the commandments."

with Scripture admits neither of a scientific nor a religious *final* and *positive* test. Thus ego-situated religious knowledge has interesting attributes deserving philosophical reflection.

Augustine's principle, given that what is believed on divine faith is *known*, seems to be true in at least two senses which Augustine intended and also, and especially significantly, in a third sense (concerning ego-situated religious knowledge) which I think it likely that he intended as well. After distinguishing relevant senses of "understand", I will trace out those three interpretations.

Markus then reminds us that for Augustine you can believe something without understanding it, that is "without having insight into the rational necessity of its truth," because such insight may be impossible, as with contingent historical truths, where there is no rational necessity for their being true. Markus can't reconcile all of what Augustine says because he does not explicitly allow for the many different senses in which Augustine's principle is to be interpreted: the many senses of "understanding the words used" and "having insight into the rational necessity of truth".

Furthermore, we know that Augustine was well aware that expressions adapt in meaning to their contexts of discourse, and that one can speak in *sensus plenior* (see *De Doctrina Christiana*) so that something which is said and is true in a certain context is intended in every sense which it acquires in any compatible context and in which it is true. Even if so grandiose an attitude were not Augustine's, the very fact that his maxim appears in such diverse contexts as are indicated in the references, suggests that it has many different meanings and a *single* statement of the relation of belief to understanding will miss the grand sweep of his design. The works Markus cites at p. 350, are *De Div*. qu. LXXXIII 48(PL 40, 31); cf *Ep*. 147, 6-7 (PL 33, 599-600). And *De Mag* 11, 37 (PL 32, 1216) cf. *Solil*, 1, 3, 8 (PL 32, 873).

The scriptural text is also used in *De Magistro* Xi (pp. 389-390 in Random House Selections from *Writings of Saint Augustine,* ed. Whitney Oates [N.Y., 1948], vol 1.) Referring to the story of Daniel, Augustine said:

"For I already grasp what three boys are, what a furnace is, and fire, and a king, what unhurt by fire is, and everything else signified by these words. But Ananis and Azarias and Misael are as unknown to me as *sarabellae;* these names do not help at all to know these men, nor can they help me. I confess moreover, that I believe rather than know that the things written in those stories were done at that time as they have been written; and those whom we believe knew the difference between believing and knowing. For the Prophet says "If you will not believe, you will not understand." Surely he would not have said that had he not thought that believing and understanding are different. Therefore, what I understand I also believe, but I do not understand everything I believe; for all which I understand I know but I do not know all that I believe. But still I am not unmindful of the utility of believing many things which are not known. I include in this utility the story about the three youths. . . . But referring now to all things which we understand, we consult, not the speaker who utters the words, but the guardian truth within the mind itself because we have, perhaps, been reminded by words to do so."

R. A. Markus cites other places where the idea "Believe that you may understand" also occurs: *De Trin* vii, 6, 12; ix, 1, 1; xv 2, 2 (PL 42, 946; 961; 1057-8). In *JO. EV. Tr* 40, 9; 29, 6 (PL 35, 1691, 1630-1); *C. Faust* xii, 46 (PL 42, 279). And these are not all, but enough for now.

1. UNDERSTANDING. William P. Alston, commenting upon an earlier version of this paper,[2] pointed out the enormous differences between reading Augustine's principle "semantically" and "epistemically", the one kind of understanding being characterized by a "grasp of what is meant" and the latter by a "grasp *that* what is meant is so," with overtones of "grasping *why* what is meant is so." And indeed Alston is right; such distinctions are needed to disambiguate any interpretation of what Augustine intended. But the matter is further complicated by the fact that the "semantic" and "epistemic" senses of "understand" do not form merely equivocal extremes as do "pack" (group of wolves) and "pack" (container for transporting things on one's back); rather the "semantic" and "epistemic" senses paradigmatically represent *clusters* of *meanings* of "understand", clusters along a *polarized continuum*. That is, senses of "understand" can be contrasted along a continuum between extremes of *incomprehension,* extremes of *not understanding:* in one direction, the opposition is to "not knowing *what*" and in the other, to "not knowing that." Thus:

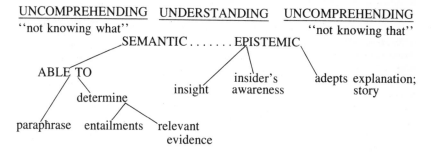

Some semantic understanding is necessary for *any* epistemic awareness of something as *said* or *read* (stated) but semantic understanding is not necessary for all epistemic understanding. Yet, because any semantic understanding requires that one understand *that* certain words mean certain things, all semantic understanding is preceded by some epistemic understanding. Moreover, not all "understanding-that" is verbally mediated. Those observations accord with the position of Augustine in *De Magistro* that our understanding of words must be preceded by illumination as to their meanings.

When Augustine compared Christianity, as a whole, to the pagan philosophies of Epicurus and Plato and applied his maxim, it is evident that he was talking about those kinds of epistemic understanding that can result from

[2] This paper was originally delivered at a Symposium on Philosophy of Religion, "Experience, Reason and God", sponsored by the Franklin J. Machette Foundation and the Department of Philosophy, University of South Carolina, March 3-4, 1978. The present version is considerably modified in light of the remarks of Prof. William P. Alston, University of Illinois. I am most grateful for Alston's help.

the enterprise of philosophy,[3] at least insight into truth, usually enriched with an account of being true. Christianity was said to be a superior *philosophy* because there are truths to which the Christian has cognitive (experiential) access and evidential (epistemic) access and for which he has an account, but which are inaccessible cognitively, evidentially and, therefore, explanatorily, to the pagans.

Augustine does not understand his principle to deny minimal semantic, verbal, understanding of revelation to the unbeliever but to deny what I call "sense" understanding (experiential realization) to unbelievers. There is a polarity between "sense" (experiential) understanding and "epistemic understanding" that contains meaning clusters distinct from those on the polarized continuum between "sense" and "epistemic" understanding. That

---

[3] Rational inquiry is to be undertaken "not in order to reject the faith but to understand by the light of reason what you already firmly hold by faith." (*En Ps.* 120; PL 33, 452).

R. A. Markus (op. cit.) says that for Augustine " 'Christianity' and 'true philosophy' are practically synonymous terms and indeed, Augustine once defined Christianity simply as 'the one true philosophy'." (*C. Julian,* IV, 14, 72; PL 44, 774). See *Contra Academicos,* III, 20, 43 (PL 32, 957): what is taken on faith is to be rationally elaborated: "Via ad Christum Divus Plato" is the way the editors of the Latin-Spanish text (Vol. III of Works of St. Augustine, *Bibloteca de Autores Cristianos,* Editorial Catolica, S.A., Apartado 466, Madrid, MCMLI) titled sections 43-44 of *Contra Academicos.* Here Augustine, having refuted the skeptics, remarks that there are two sources of knowledge of matters religious, the teachings of Christ and the philosophy of Plato.

"But no one doubts that we are incited to learn by the double weight of authority and of reason. Therefore, I am sure that I shall never depart from the authority of Christ. . . . But what ought to be attained by the most subtle reasoning—for at present I am so disposed as impatiently to desire to apprehend truth not only by believing but also by knowing—I trust I shall find meanwhile in the words of the Platonists, what is not in contradiction with our sacred writings."

Augustine thought of philosophy as "everything that was of ultimate concern to man, everything related to the question: how is a man to attain his ultimate fulfillment, that is 'blessedness' (beatitudo)?" See R. A. Markus "Augustine" p. 333. See also *De Civ. Dei,* xxxix 1, 2 where, describing Varro's classification of philosophers according to their ideas about the supreme good, Augustine seems to approve calling any *rationally elaborated account of happiness* (human fulfillment) a philosophy. Markus, op. cit., 345, traces out Augustine's complex conception of philosophy as disciplined rational inquiry and as a way to happiness of which the unlearned believer has often more wisdom than the learned unbeliever).

In *"On the Profit of Believing"* Augustine says, 25, p. 418:

"What then we understand we owe to reason; what we believe, to authority; what we have on opinion, to error. But everyone who understands also believes and everyone who has an opinion believes too; but not everyone who believes understands; no one who has an opinion understands." In 27 "But now *I call wise those in whom there is, so much as may be in a man, the knowledge of man himself and of God, most surely received and a life and manners suitable to that knowledge.*"

can be illustrated by contrasts between semantic or verbal understanding of something said and experiential understanding of something whether or not stated. A tone deaf person can verbally understand "The violin is properly tuned," can understand it to be like in meaning to "The strings are under correct contrasts of tension" and opposed to "The violin is sharp" and distinct from "The performer is *playing* sharp". Yet in a crucial way he cannot understand what is said unless he can correlate such judgments with *sounds* by means, for instance, of an oscilloscope. There are no configurations of appearance that tell him or form the basis for telling him the violin is properly tuned.

Again, when I read "The visceral branches of the first five throacic nerves have their cells of orgin in the lateral column of gray of the spinal cord" my *verbal,* semantic, comprehension is limited, minimal and uncertain. I cannot, beyond syntactic transformations, confidently paraphrase it or recite its entailments or envision definitely what evidence would be relevant to its being found false or true; and certainly I do not know, in a way I can state in other words, its truth conditions. More seriously, I have no accessible experiential basis for comprehending what is claimed. And that lack is something like the defect of the tone deaf. For there are no configurations of appearance that tell for or against what is claimed.[4]

---

[4] I consider configurations of appearance to be the evidence or grounds upon which we make perceptual judgments about things external to ourselves. Thus, the visual sensations have to be organized, along with the auditory (perhaps by the brain which involves both what Aquinas considered the *sensus communis* where such unified impression can be realized and the *vis cogitativa,* a partially innate and partially acquired and experientially modifiable program for organizing the impressions of the *sensus communis*) to seem to be an F (e.g. a person). The results of that organization are configurations of appearance. *It is impossible to see anything that does not seem to be there (or is not included in what does seem to be there).* But *seeming itself* is a product of organization, configuration.

I think J. H. Newman, *Grammar of Assent,* recognized that logically prior to the reasoning processes (deductive and inductive) that characterize men, there is a prior capacity, *that of configuring data,* of projecting patterns in sensations, and patterns *upon patterns* (to ground concepts) and thus, *configuration, at every level of thought is prior to and is the basis for judgment.*

There is an interesting use of an allied idea in *Theology and Meaning,* by Raeburne Heimbeck (Stanford: Stanford University press, 1969) to explain how there can be empirical confirmation of some assertions about God.

Sensory deprivation causes complete absence of those configurations that ground judgements based on such sensations. Similarly, the person who is tone deaf cannot have the data for pitch judgements; and the person who is pathological cannot make certain moral judgements because no appropriate *seemings* occur to him and similarly, the person without certain beliefs cannot make certain judgements because the data of experience are simply not organized so as to provide configurations relevant to supporting such judgements.

There is a difference between the verbal grasp of "I am going to die" and an experiential realization by a person with the symptoms. Sometimes we say "you don't know what you are saying" when we think the speaker does not *realize* what has been asserted. The lack is more like dispositional and irremediable tone deafness, because stimuli cannot be processed to an outcome in experience, rather than like the mystified reader of the medical book who merely lacks appropriate stimulation.

Now I don't mean that the tone deaf cannot *find out* whether the violin is tuned. Someone might tell him. And I don't mean that he cannot *find out for himself* that what was said is so. For he might have an oscilloscope by which to substitute visual displays (substitute configurations of appearance) for the sounds. Thus the tone deaf may know the instrument is in tune just as the person who can judge "heard" pitches knows it; but the tone deaf man cannot know on the basis of what he *hears* as can the other. So some configurations of appearance that are available to others and are information-bearing and evidence-creating, are unavailable to the tone deaf.

Apart from a definite context Augustine's formula is multi-ambiguous because of the many meanings of "believe" and "understand"; and it has different meanings when viewed from different perspectives. But with the aid of the clusters of meanings of "understand" that we can discern, I will consider the maxim from various viewpoints, disentangling its meanings and extrapolating the rationales underling them.

2. THE FIRST INTERPRETATION. The first interpretation of "Unless you believe you will not understand" comes to this: unless you willingly accept the truths that have been revealed, you will not, because you *cannot*, understand (with insight into what is so and an account of its being so in terms of truths available to all men—as the philosophers seek to understand) what is both necessary and *sufficient* for man's happiness. In a word, unless you believe what has been revealed, certain truths essential for an adequate philosophical account of the human condition and of the means to human fulfillment are *evidentially* and *experientially* inaccessible to you.

When Augustine said "Christianity is the one true philosophy," *una vera philosophia* (Contra Julian, IV 14, 72; PL 44, 774), he meant that rational inquiry, illumined by the products of revelation accepted on faith, is the only *wisdom,* the only adequate account of things human and divine. And that is because without the illumination of faith, certain realities are inaccessible for living (experience) and for rational reflection (explanatory understanding); the world cannot be patterned properly so that things fall into their proper *evidential* configurations unless you believe what has been revealed; one is like the child who cannot see the faces of the presidents in the dots of a jungle picture. One consequence of Augustine's position is that there must be a *Christian* philosophy, not in method but in content.

Augustine conceived Christianity, here regarded as revealed truth elaborated with the "spoils of the Egyptians,"[5] elaborated beyond revelation through the conceptions of the pagan philosophers (e.g. Plato's account of the soul), as the victorious competitor over all pagan philosophies because it successfuly accounted for the ultimate structure of reality while describing and justifying the path to human fulfillment.

Thus, the pagan accounts of the origin of the world, the inner structures of human history, the destiny of individual human life and the origin of evil, were manifestly incomplete and unsatisfactory, while the Christian account was satisfying and provided a new configuration within which to employ the best of the pagan ideas.

So the first interpretation imagines "understanding" as pagan philosophers understood it: "the articulate rational account of the truth about the ultimate nature of reality and the means to human fulfillment." And to Augustine it was obvious that such understanding was not possible for a philosopher without the Christian faith because that faith contained access to central pieces of the philosopher's puzzle, pieces necessary for the pattern, the explanatory configuration, to stand out against the background of pagan insights. That is not the same as the second interpretation, which relies upon a different notion of understanding, the understanding of the wise man.

3. THE SECOND INTERPRETATION. The believer, reflecting upon what he believes, comes to know *other* things than those that are revealed, things whose being known is necessary to understanding one's own life, to having insight into and a coherent insider's story about one's fulfillment. For instance, a believer, seeking to understand the revealed truth that all, save one, are sinners, may come to know that his excuses for his own acts mask his resistance to full religious commitment. Similarly, a believer construes the death of a friend as the passage of a person to an everlasting life, rather than as the epicurean judges it, the end of all being for him. Those particular conclusions about individual situations have not been revealed; but without accepting the revelation, the believer could not know those things to be true, for he would lack the experiential and conceptual classifications that make

---

[5] In *De Doctrina Christiana* II, 40, Augustine defends philosophical inquiry to produce a hybrid knowledge of God: just as the Israelites despoiled the Egyptians of their treasures before leaving that place forever, and took them with them into the promised land, so the Christian is to take what he can from the philosophers who have spoken truly, in consonance with the Christian faith, in order to devote it to the preaching of the gospel.

Knowledge resulting from the amalgamation of pagan intellectual disciplines and divine revelation will not merely form two discrete piles of truths with little in common or one great pile merely lumped together, but an *inextricable hybrid of truths* arrived at by configurations projected from beliefs of both kinds (some demonstrative and some not). The spoils of Egypt are an integral part of the treasures of the promised land and like wealth, joined with wealth, further wealth is generated.

things appear that way and lead him to judge things to be as they appear to
him.

Thus particular cognitive states are *causally dependent* upon your having
certain *general* beliefs whose truth neither entails nor is entailed by those
particular cognitive states, except with the addition of independent (contingent) truths. So unless you have those general beliefs ("Christ died to save
all men") you won't *construe your individual case religiously* (according to
the Christian religion). Therefore, you will not make particular religious
judgments (e.g. "I am redeemed"; "Jones has died but hasn't ceased to
be") without those general beliefs, and yet, those *particular* religious judgments belong to the religious construals of the world that make you "*of* the
faith." On this interpretation, "understand" means anything from "realize"
or "find to be so" through "have insight into". And Augustine means that
without willingly assenting to the revealed truth, you will not realize certain
crucial, particular truths to be so, a realization essential to your being of the
faith and, therefore, to your happiness.

In a word the wisdom that makes an individual a wise man, the possessor
of that knowledge of things human and divine that leads him to fulfillment,
is as much blocked from the person who does not believe as the wisdom that
distinguishes a true philosophy is inaccessible to the thinker without faith.
But in this case the things to be understood are logically distinct from the
things to be believed (the revelation).

4. THE THIRD INTERPRETATION: UNPOLARIZED BELIEF. The
third intepretation of the principle concerns a mixture of that understanding
which I called "realizing" something, as contrasted with merely assenting
to it (possibly something like Newman's distinction between real and notional
assent), and that range of understanding that involves insight into something's
being so. Now the idea is that there are some things you cannot understand
(either realize to be so or have insight into the truth of) unless you first
believe them, (assent willingly from trust or love) to those very things. Moreover, in some cases an experiential understanding (realization) of what is
believed is not practicably possible for one who does not first believe the
same thing but *without* experiential understanding. (I am not going to analyze
"same thing" here; whether the statements (propositions) are the same or
merely such that the denial of one entails the falsity of the other is not
important.)

Sometimes a person will never be in a position to know he can play the
piano unless he first believes the witness of a teacher that he will eventually
be able to play; by acting upon that belief his experience will eventually
present configurations that will *evidentially justify* such a judgment about
himself; what was initially a mere belief becomes a realized fact (knowledge),
when one sees from the inside, as it were, that one will be able to play. So
also, with having a high opinion of oneself; high self-esteem must first exist
to be then confirmed in experience.

Believing (willing assent motivated by trust) is often causally necessary for one's later having the configured experience that causes one's *realizing* (and acquiring insight into) what is so. If you refuse to assent to anyone's testimony that the apparently disparate figures in the Miller-Lyre illusion are really congruent, you may not realize that these perceptual structures, physiologically based, constitute "sets" of the visual system, even though their existence is manifested by the nature and constancy of the illusions; nor will one realize that such illusions are byproducts of an otherwise efficient visual construal of the world.

One must believe, to be "of the faith," "Christ by his death redeemed *me*" and "When I die, *I* shall not cease to be." Whether that is a merely verbal belief, a formula uttered thoughtlessly, or a realized belief, like "I have cancer" uttered by a man with diagnosed symptoms, it is still not revealed.[6] Although it is revealed that all those who have died in the faith still live and will rise again to live forever, and it is not revealed that *Jones,* who dies in the faith, will rise again, that is because not everything that follows logically, by the addition of *contingent* truths to what has been revealed is itself revealed. Yet *realizing* some of those truths is essential to *understanding* one's salvation, and that is evidentially possible only if preceded by assent to what is revealed.

To convey the immediacy of the particular beliefs, I italicize the "I", when the very point is the *absence* of reflective polarization into believer and

---

[6] Assuming as did Augustine that in addition to any event-revelation through which God is manifested to his creatures, there is also some propositional revelation, we then have to observe that not everything that is *entailed* by what is revealed is revealed. For instance, if it is revealed that -P, then it is entailed that (Pv-P). But the latter is a necessary truth which would have been true whether or not P is true or revealed and so P's being revealed is not evidentially necessary for our knowing the latter to be true. Of course, some things are revealed which we could also know without their having been revealed. But surely those things that are not included in what is *meant* by what is revealed (assuming that it is statements or propositions that are revealed rather than facts which are without meanings) are not revealed.

Further, not even everything that is meant (in one sense of "means") by what is revealed is revealed. That is, something that is so and is necessary for the truth of another thing is often said to be meant by it. Thus if "all men are promised salvation" is revealed and it is true that I am a man, then it has to be true that I am offered salvation. Yet it does not seem likely to me that it has been revealed that *I* have been offered salvation; for whatever was revealed could have been true had I not existed at all and it would have meant exactly what it does now. And it will not do to say that what was revealed was the conditional "if there is a man named Ross, then he will have been offered salvation," for it is entirely implausible that such *conditionals* form part of revelation and, even if they did, nothing would be revealed about me without the additional claim that there *is* such a man. And surely that contingent truth is not revealed.

thing believed. Such realized belief is an *unreflective construal,* like one's judgmental awareness when one is falling down, making love, pulling a child from the path of a car, staunching the flow of blood from a cut. Unreflective realization of one's concurrent action is paradigmatically ego-situated. It is often accompanied by insight into its being so, often with an explanatory story and vivid awareness of causal or other connections that make it so: "The knife slipped," "They pushed me," "Brakes don't work."

Christianity offers insight into profound truths about oneself, for instance, that one is forgiven, that one is not destroyed by death. Such belief is characteristically accompanied by realizations expressed in accompanying explanatory unpolarized cognitions, "Jesus died that *I* might be forgiven." The chain of such cognitions will trail off, eventually, into larger explanatory stories (e.g. the New Testament story) which provide a background for the concepts and general presuppositions of the ego-situated religious realizations that comprise my present religious understanding (construal) of myself.

In a word, there are some things you can't *realize,* or otherwise epistemically understand, unless you first believe those very things. Not trivially because, logically, any epistemic understanding entails belief (as it does) but significantly because evidentially belief is causally necessary to create the configuration of appearances (the patternings of one's self-construal) from which such judgments appear justified (it being assumed that we are to some extent biased against making judgments which do not appear to us to be justified, unless, of course, we are motivated by trust or love).

Let me distinguish another sense in which you will not understand unless you believe, even though I don't think Augustine would regard it as very important. There are some things you cannot understand to be so about you unless you believe that they are so. For instance, if you do not believe that you are elected for salvation, or have repented your sins, then very possibly it is not true that you have been elected or have repented your sins. That is, there are states which have as a *causally* necessary condition your willing assent that they are so; your not believing will, then, be *causally* sufficient for their not obtaining. In that case, there is nothing to understand (realize to be so and have insight into) unless you believe.

I had in an earlier version considered that a believer's ego-situated religious self-construal involved beliefs about himself (and, therefore, things to be understood) that are undetachably identified with the person who believes them, so that no one else can believe exactly the same thing (as distinct from "have exactly the same belief"); and thus, what is to be understood about oneself, e.g. that I am redeemed would be epistemically accessible only to one who first believes just exactly what is to be understood.

William P. Alston objected that it does not follow from the fact that such a belief cannot be ego-situated for another person, that another person cannot believe the same thing about me that I in an ego-situated belief, believe about myself; and, hence, he objected that it does not follow that no one can understand such beliefs unless he believes them about himself. He is right. Yet I do not accept the sufficiency of his positive test that A and B can believe the *same* thing if A can successfully deny what B asserts; for you need only deny an equivalent or an entailing or an entailed proposition to contradict someone else. Nevertheless, he has shown, and I thank him, that we ought not to locate what is crucial in Augustine's principle in the claim that what is believed about himself by the believer is inaccessible for *belief* to any one else. Further, we ought not to say that what the believer understands about himself is unavailable for understanding (realization and insight) by anyone else. For just as Jones knows he is going to die, so a friend, spouse or doctor might suddenly *realize* it. Thus both would realize the same thing even if they did not share the same beliefs. So also for the most profound religious truths.

Therefore, I restrict this third interpretation of Augustine's maxim to the claim that the willing acceptance of revelation is causally necessary for our being in the position cognitively, to realize (and understand with insight) certain religious truths about ourselves that are essential to our salvation. It is not the realization or the understanding that is essential to salvation, only the believing that is; but what is to be understood is the truth believed. The truths believed are evidentially inaccessible for realization or insight except by one who believes them because without believing the general truths of revelation (about creation, redemption, salvation and santification) you lack the background classification, the conceptual sets, within which to configurally *construe* your experience so that such realizations will occur.

The things to be believed and the things to be understood, in all three interpretations, involve a common syndrome that afflicts theology as well. The objects of understanding characteristically involve conceptualizations that are secular (sometimes pagan, e.g. "soul") in origin; and yet such conceptualizations enter constitutively into the expressed truths to be understood. Is there any *positive* test, religious or scientific, that will determine that a religious reality has been properly restated with such mixed expressions or properly apprehended with such mixed concepts? Is religious truth afflicted with an indeterminacy of translation that parallels the indeterminacy, the lack of a positive test of correctness, that Quine identified for translation between languages, where "meaning" is interpreted behaviorally?

5. EGO SITUATED RELIGIOUS KNOWLEDGE AND CONCEPTUAL SETS. It seems highly unlikely that one comes to an awareness that one has sinned by deductive instantiation: "All men have sinned, save only one: I am a man and not the exception; therefore, I have sinned." Beliefs of that kind are construals rather than conclusions. And construals require conceptual sets, readiness to configure discriminable data in certain ways rather than others, like readiness to configure human faces within moving light and shade rather than leaves only; judgments are justified by warranting configurations.

Even though you accept revelation only by achieving compatible and suitably extensive religious awareness, the conceptual and, possibly, perceptual classifications, logically part of the awareness, do not arise from your own discovery but are learned from the believing community (or some report or record thereof). The idea is that Moses, to have had his experience of God, had to acquire concepts and beliefs about God from his religious environment; they formed the classification and expectation within which his construal occurred.[7] You acquire conceptual sets through learning and application just as we acquire some of our perceptual sets. (Others are in the structure of the perceptual systems, like those that cause the visual illusion.) Conceptual sets are to ego-situated religious construals what perceptual sets are to perceptual judgments.

Whatever is perceived is placed into and achieves its meaning from a class of percepts with which it is grouped.
(J. Brunner, "On Perceptual Readiness," p. 9, *Beyond the Information Given*)

Perceptual organization is powerfully determined by expectations built on past commerce with the environment.
("Perception of Incongruity," p.83, Ibid.)

Perceptual sets influence the appearance of things and, thereby, our judgments. For instance, to poor children, higher value coins appear larger than they do to wealthy children (Brunner, op. cit., p. 50, "Value and Need in Perception") and the more valuable the coin, the more the perceptual distortion.

The best account of conceptual sets I can offer at the moment is this: a conceptual set is an acquired, durable disposition to configure appearances and *classify* awareness according to a limited set of associated general beliefs and their component ideas. This is obviously inadequate, but the inadequacies

---

[7] I argued this point in Chapter 2, of *Introduction to Philosophy of Religion,* (Macmillan: New York, 1970). As Houston Smith points out, persons with strong religious backgrounds more frequently report "God" experiences under drugs than others do.

That kind of act is usually mistakenly interpreted to suggest that there is always a sufficient natural cause for such reported "religious" experiences and, therefore, that there is no reason to suppose that they are veridical, But, of course, an opposed conclusion is more reasonably to be drawn: that the experiential classifications that become established among humans are related to the success of such classifications in founding (evidentially) judgements which are effective for human living. And so, a person for whom God configurations do or did form a useful part of life is likely to find such configurations in the strange experiences produced by drugs. Hence the occurrence of such "experiences" has nothing *evidential* to do with the veridicality of religious experiences which are not drug-caused. (Furthermore, overdetermined causation is possible; so that God may actually be experienced through judgements which are fully explicable as produced non-veridically by drugs.)

are not peculiar to philosophy of religion. We simply do not know how general beliefs function irresistibly, unreflectively, voluntarily but non-deliberately, to produce construed awareness. Yet that is what happens in the formation of ego-situated religious belief. And it is the inseverable connection of our particular religious awareness to general religious belief that makes our highly personal religious belief subject to the same indeterminacy of "translation" and of *judgment* that afflicts theology.

6. THE INDETERMINACY OF TRANSLATION. For theological knowledge *(scientia divina)* to grow out of revealed truth (say, as expressed in the Scripture), elements revealed have to be assigned correlates within conceptual schemes that originate in secular inquiry. For instance, "God made everything other than himself" might be rendered by an Aristotelian as "God created the world without pre-existing matter or form" and by a modern physicist as "God brought into being the matter—energy continuum and all of its laws but from no prior continuum or laws."

The rational inquiry that characterizes theology cannot be carried out without the posing and answering of questions framed in secularly originated concepts. And so it cannot be carried out without our devising "scientific" (theological) correlates of scriptural and creedal expressions; and *they* cannot be produced correctly unless revelation is properly understood. Whatever "understanding" must be here, the final product must "mean the same thing as" the original religious assertion. But is that possible? Or is "means the same thing as" used equivocally of translations?

Evidently there is an analogous problem for ego-situated religious belief which, inevitably, also involves hybrid "scientific" and scriptural ideas. For instance, religious belief that "God will redeem my soul" involves such a hybridization (some secularly originated "soul" doctrine). "God created matter, energy, time and change" also involves secular concepts.

The problem is the same as for the general assertions of theology: what is the criterion for the correctness of a "translation" (I have no better word for the relation) of a privileged religious expression, like "God made the heavens and the earth" into a religious belief expressed in secular categories and with secular assumptions, like "God created the world without preexisting form and matter"?

Maimonides and Aquinas epitomize the puzzle at the level of theology. Maimonides was so certain of both the literalness and the demonstrative truth of secular science (Aristotle's philosophy) that the untranslatability of a scriptural expression, read literally, into a known scientific truth or a proposition compatible with known scientific truth, was sufficient to warrant a revision in any prior form of religious understanding so as to regard it as figurative or allegorical. Thus the creation story was treated as figurative because of its literal discrepancy with the supposed demonstrated eternity of the world. "Correctness" of the translation was not addressed directly in Maimonides' account. But if a literal reading of the religious expression would yield a scientific truth, it was presumed correct.[8]

Aquinas, on the other hand, thought science could be, and sometimes might be, revised in the light of religious belief. Thus, the fact that as Aristotle was understood by the Arabians, there was no place for personal immortality of the soul in current science, did not suggest the revision of religious belief but the reinterpretation of Aristotle's system because science has to be made to accord with what is so. And further, Aquinas thought that although science may help the believer to understand the revelation and even the scriptural expression of it, the Scripture cannot mean what the living Church thinks it does not mean.

Maimonides did not allow for religious belief to have any weight against the conclusions of science. Aquinas did not allow science to have any weight against what religious belief (performatively expressed in the proclaimed faith of the church) *denied;* science simply had to be revised.

Although I am skipping various refinements in both positions, neither provides a positive criterion for "correct" translation of the privileged expression of faith.

Neither science nor religion holds an *affirmative* trump to say finally that a conceptual hybridization of the faith is a correct translation. Religion is in no position to pronounce affirmatively upon the existence of a scientific truth (despite the Council of Trent's adopting "transubstantiation" theory, and of earlier councils' adopting "consubstantiality" theory). A scientist, say a philosopher, is in no position to state that because his rendering of the religious

---

[8] There was a new outbreak of this disease in 1974 when John Post published "New Foundations for Philosophical Theology: Quine with God", *The Journal of Philosophy,* Vol. LXXI, 19, Nov. 7, 1974, pp. 736-748. Here Post proposed a Quinese translation of traditional religious claims, so that he has only sets, properties, quantifiers, etc., and individuals in space-times in his ontology. And, like Maimonides, Post says that what is left over after the Quinese paraphrase of the original religious utterance is what is metaphorical or symbolic, so that we would be well advised to continue using the original utterances and to cherish the broken myths, just as Maimonides did not propose to tell ordinary believers that "God created the world in one week" was literally false because it was not created at all.

Nor is it that I see a virtue in the reemergence of old errors in new disguises. Rather, I see a virtue in the quick detection of old errors regardless of their disguises. The fact is that you can't paraphrase basic religious claims in Quinese and that even if you could get paraphrases, they would not function behaviorally indistinguishably from the originals. The religious believers would still hold the trumps as to whether the paraphrase is good enough. There was something misguided in Quine's behavioral account of meaning in the first place, something that is independently disclosed by the inability of the theory even to account for logical relations among what we utter (since such relations do not hold among the noises). See following notes.

belief yields a true and even coherent scientific picture, that his is a correct translation.[9]

Each side has *negative* trumps, however. The believing community has the last word, regardless of the convictions of the scientist, that they do *not* mean what the scientist offers as a translation, provided, of course, that they understand it. And that is so even if what the scientist offers is a truth. That means that the religious community can, in an extreme case, pronounce substantively about the inadequacy of an ontology, say an ontology exclusively confined to space-time individuals and abstract sets. Reductive analyses of religious claims in terms of such an ontology will not reproduce what the believers maintain, no matter how excellent a correspondence can be achieved with established scientific truths. In this respect I regard Maimonides as mistaken and Aquinas as right. Furthermore, John Post has recently repeated Maimonides' error in modern terms.[10]

---

[9] Even if we introduce the notion of "truth" and assume that there is independent access to the truth of the proposed translation, we will never count mere equivalence (logical equivalence) between pairs of utterances as synonymy. Now it is an obvious Quinean move (if Post could allow us to talk about *logical* equivalence) that equivalence of *all* the pairs in two global bodies of discourse is a different matter. For everything that can be accomplished by the one, in the way of distinguishable behavior, can be accomplished by the other. I think the believers reply, "Call the relation whatever you will, if the product of your 'scientific' rendering does not 'capture' what we mean and, so, could be true even if *our* sentences had quite different meanings, then, you do not say what we mean. Thus you do not paraphrase our claims."

Post's article, though he did not intend it, shows that science holds no trumps over religion. If you can't find a translation of religious claims into the currently respected ontology of science, so much the worse for the science which is probably false anyway, (as history and philosophy of science show even for the best physical theories) quite independently of its attitude toward religion. But religion holds a negative trump on science: if the only available scientific paraphrases make false what the beliefs proclaim to be true, then science has to be revised.

[10] I am not condemning Post for a mere unknowing repetition of Maimonides position. Post's claims that there is a mapping of traditional religious utterances into the desert ontology of Quine, so that God is defined in terms of the Godhead, which is *identified* with a mathematical set, raises a fundamental question in philosophy of religion: *Who is to decide what religious utterances mean?* Is it the scientist-philosopher who can paraphrase them in some scientific ontology or the religious believer who claims priviliged access to the meaning of what he says?

Maimonides obviously thought that the adequacy of the resulting scientific translation is sufficient to guarantee the accuracy of the paraphrase, and in effect, to tell us what the religious utterances mean. Others, like Aquinas, thought truth was a necessary condition of accuracy of paraphrase but that *preservation recognizable by the believing community* of "what they meant" was the final test of the adequacy of a reformulation of religious doctrine. And yet, Aquinas was willing to *teach* the believer the transubstantiation view of the Eucharist, with the result that eventually

Rational inquiry, whether it be "science", broadly, as understood in Augustine's or medieval times or more narrowly as we understand it now, has only a weak negative trump. On the *assumption* that the translation is correct, if the resulting proposition can be decisively falsified, then the original belief is not literally true and must be regarded as allegorical or figurative. That seems to be the furthest extent to which science can competently judge religious faith or religious self-construal.

No positive account exists of the conditions for correctly rendering privileged religious expressions into secular categories. As a result, even if I am right in suggesting that the range of religious knowledge is much broader than is usually remarked, including quite individual, ego-situated religious awareness, because such awareness is inextricably permeated with classifications and general ideas not part of revelation, there appears to be no way, apart from the configurations of experience that believing them helps generate, to determine the extent to which such beliefs are actually knowledge or even true.

University of Pennsylvania

---

the believer's understanding of his claims like "The Eucharist is the body of Christ" would become *theoretically infested,* because subjectively understood with ideas deriving from particular "scientific" theories.

In effect Post puts an old problem in a new way (though he seems not to recognize what he is in fact doing): "Is scientific 'sense' the criterion of religious *meaning*?" For Post claims that what is left out of the paraphrase belongs only to the metaphorical and symbolic meaning, not the literal truth, and to the extent that there is no sensible scientific paraphrase of a religious utterance, there is not only no truth to it, there is no cognitive meaning to it either.

Now I have not resolved all those issues but rather have pointed out that parallel issues arise in one's religious understanding of oneself because crucial ego-situated religious self-construals involve hybrid conceptions, deriving partially from religion and partially from philosophical and scientific views of the world, many of them substantially discredited a long time ago.

10 IRREDUCIBLE METAPHORS IN THEOLOGY

William P. Alston

I

My primary concern in this paper is with the possibility of irreducible metaphor in talk about God, and with the kind of significance such talk would have if possible. But before tackling those problems head on I should indicate why it seems to many that theology needs irreducible metaphors.

The impossibility of literal talk about God has become almost an article of faith for theology in this century. Of course it is not denied that one can *make* a statement in which some term, used literally, is applied to God; that is not regarded as being beyond human powers. The impossibility alleged is, rather, an impossibility of saying anything *true* about God while using terms literally. Various reasons have been given for this sweeping proscription. Perhaps the most popular in our day is the *transcendence* of God, His "wholly otherness". This appears in various forms; Tillich, e.g., holds that (a) God is not *a* being, but Being Itself, since anything that is *a* being would not be an appropriate object of religious worship, and (b) that only what is *a* being can be literally characterized. Those who identify themselves with the mystical tradition emphasize the principle that God is an ineffable, undifferentiated unity. Coming from another quarter is the infamous verifiability criterion of meaning, which has been used to argue the still more sweeping thesis that no theological predication has any truth value at all.

I myself do not regard any of these arguments as successful, but this is not the place to say why. The present point is that arguments like this have been convincing to many contemporary theologians and philosophers of religion. But a sizable proportion of these are not prepared to give up theological discourse. And so they must find some other way of construing what look like literal theological statements, such as,

God created the heavens and the earth.
God spoke to Jeremiah.

God brought the Israelites out of Egypt.
God sent His only begotten Son into the world.
God forgives the sins of those who are truly repentant.
God's purpose is that we shall all enjoy eternal life.

One popular move is to give them some non-cognitive interpretation, e.g., as expressive of attitudes, feelings, or commitments,[1] or evocative of mystical experience, "insight", or "seeing X as Y".[2] But again a sizable proportion are unwilling to give up the idea that it is possible to make *true statements* about God, to articulate something that really does pertain to the divine nature, to convey in words some apprehension, however inadequate, of what God is like.

To those who find themselves in this position metaphor can seem a promising way out. In many spheres of discourse we manage to make true statements without using terms literally. We can correctly describe what Russia did at the end of World War II by saying that she dropped an iron curtain across Europe, even though no iron curtain was literally dropped. Why can't we analogously provide some insight into the divine nature and operations by saying things like "God spoke to Jeremiah," etc., even if none of these predicates are literally true of God? Just as the dropping of an iron curtain across a stage provides a useful "model" for thinking about what Russia did just after World War II, why can't human speech provide a useful model for thinking about God's relation to Jeremiah, and sending one's son to do a certain job provide a useful model for thinking of God's relation to the work of Jesus Christ? But of course if *no* term can be literally applied to God, our metaphorical talk about God will be *irreducible*. A metaphor is *irreducible* if what is said in the metaphorical utterance cannot be said, *even in part,* in literal terms. Obviously, if no term can be literally applied to God, we cannot do *anything* to spell out in literal terms what is said metaphorically about God. Hence theologians who go the route we have been describing will wind up construing talk about God as made up of irreducible metaphors.[3]

---

[1] See, e.g., George Santayana, *Reason in Religion,* (New York: Charles Scribner's Sons, 1905), and R. B. Braithwaite, *An Empiricist's View of the Nature of Religious Belief* (Cambridge: Cambridge U. Press, 1955).

[2] See, e.g., W. T. Stace, *Time and Eternity* (Princeton, Princeton U. Press, 1952), J. H. Randall, Jr., *The Role of Knowledge in Western Religion,* (Boston: Starr King Press, 1958), Ch. IV, and John Wisdom, "Gods", *Proc. Arist. Soc.,* Vol. 45.

[3] I want to emphasize that in this paper we are not asking the (silly) question as to whether it is possible to have metaphors of any sort in talk about God, nor are we asking what status our metaphorical God-talk actually has. It is obvious that much talk about God is metaphorical. For example:
The Lord is my shepherd.

It may seem that very few theologians have followed what I have described as a "natural tendency"; for the term 'metaphor' does not figure heavily in twentieth century discussions of religious language. Nevertheless I believe that in many cases in which writers speak of "analogy", "symbols", "parables", or "models", the basic linguistic mechanism involved is that of metaphor, though they may be envisaging some particular complication or elaboration of the simplest kinds of metaphors. I am unable in this paper to document this suggestion, but I would suggest that writers as diverse as Karl Barth, Rudolph Bultmann, I. M. Crombie, I. T. Ramsey, and Ian G. Barbour are in effect treating talk about God as irreducibly metaphorical, though they rarely use the term.

II

We can effectively come to grips with our central question only if we have an explicit account of the nature of metaphor. To this I now turn.

Despite the frequent occurence of terms like 'metaphorical *meaning*' and 'metaphorical *sense*' in discussions of the subject, I believe that they reflect a confused, or at least a loose, way of thinking about metaphor. To get straight about the matter we need to keep a firm grip on the Saussurian distinction between *language* and *speech*. A (natural) language is an abstract system, a system of abstract sound types or, in principle, types of other sorts of perceptible items. The systematicity involved is both "internal" and "external". The phonology, morphology and syntax of a language constitute its "internal" system—the ways in which its elements can be combined to form larger units. The "external" system is revealed by the semantics of the language—the ways in which units of the language have the function of "representing" things in and features of the world.[4] A language serves as a

---

His hands prepared the dry land.
The Lord is my rock and my fortress.
In thy light do we see light.
The Lord looks down from heaven.
I believe that it is commonly supposed that metaphors like these are reducible, that it is possible to say in literal terms at least part of what is being said about God metaphorically in these utterances. In saying "The Lord is my shepherd" I am saying that God will protect me and see to it that my needs are satisfied; and so on. But we are not concerned in this paper to determine whether this is so. We are concerned with a certain project—interpreting all talk about God, including the more literal-sounding statements just mentioned, as *irreducible* metaphors. We are dealing with a question that is fundamental to that project, viz., whether there can be irreducible metaphors, and if so what status they would have.

[4] This is a very crude way of characterizing semantics, but it will have to do for now. There is no general agreement on what an adequate characterization would look like.

means of communication; that is its basic *raison d'être*. *Speech* is the *use* of language in communication (using speech in an extended sense to cover written as well as oral communication). It is what we *do* in the course of exploiting a linguistic system for purposes of communication.[5]

Now the fact that a given word or phrase has the meaning(s) or sense(s)[6] it has is a fact about the language; it is part of the semantic constitution of the language. Thus it is a (semantic) fact about the English language that 'knit' has among its meanings:

1. To form, as a fabric, by interlacing a single yarn or thread in loops, by means of long thin bluntly pointed rods.
2. To draw together; to contract into wrinkles; as he knit his brow in thought. [7]

The fact that a word has a certain meaning is (part of) what gives it its usability for communication; it constitutes part of the linguistic resources we draw on in saying what we have to say.

The term 'metaphor', on the other hand, stands for a certain way of *using* words, a mode of *speech* rather than a type of meaning or any other feature of *language*. More specifically, it belongs to the family of *figurative* uses of terms ("*figures of speech*", as they are appropriately called in the tradition) that stand in contrast with *literal* uses of terms. Let's make explicit the distinction between *literal* and *metaphorical* uses, restricting ourselves to the uses of predicates in subject-predicate statements, since that is the application with which we are especially concerned.

We may think of each meaning of a predicate term "correlating" the term with some (possibly very complex) property.[8] Each of the definitions of 'knit'

---

[5] Language and speech may also be interrelated in other and more intimate ways. Thus, in my view, langu..ge *exists* only as a set of potentialities for speech; the fact that speech is patterned in certain ways *constitutes* the reality of a natural language; if there were no speech, there would be no *actual* languages. But that is quite compatible with the existence and fundamental importance of the distinction drawn in the text.

[6] We shall not distinguish between *meaning* and *sense*.

[7] *Webster's New Collegiate Dictionary* (Springfield, Mass.: G. & C. Merriam Co., 1959), p. 465. I am far from claiming that this is the best or most adequate way to specify these meanings. Indeed it is far from clear, at this stage of development of the art, what is the most adequate way to specify meanings. But it does seem clear that 'knit' has the two meanings thus specified, however lamely and haltingly, and that it having these two meanings is (a small) part of what makes the English language what it is at the current stage of its history.

[8] I would want this supposition to be compatible with the fact that most (all?) predicate terms have meanings that are vague, have "open texture", or suffer from indeterminacy in other ways. This means that an adequate formulation would have to be considerably more complicated than the one given here.

given above specifies a (relational) property with which 'knit' is "correlated" in one of its meanings. Different theories of meaning provide different accounts of the nature of this correlation. Thus the "ideational" theory of meaning found, e.g., in Locke's *Essay,* holds that a meaning of a predicate term "correlates" it with a certain property, P, *iff* the term functions as a sign of the *idea* of P in communication. It will be convenient to speak of a predicate term "signifying" or "standing for" the correlated property.

Now when I make a literal use of a predicate term, in one of its meanings, in a subject-predicate sentence, I utter the sentence with the claim that the property signified by the predicate is possesed by the subject (the referent of the subject-term), or, if the predicate is a relational one, it holds between the subjects. Thus if I make a literal use of 'knit' in saying, e.g., "My wife knitted that sweater," I would be claiming that the relational property specified in the first of our two definitions holds between my wife and that sweater. And if my statement is true, if that relation does in fact hold between these terms, then we may say that 'knit' is *literally true* of these terms, or does *literally apply* to them.

But suppose I say, as Shakespeare has Macbeth say, "Sleep knits up the ravelled sleave of care." It is clear that sleep cannot possibly do to care, either of the things listed as meanings of 'knit'. Nor, if we surveyed all the meanings that 'knit' has in the language, would we find any relation that literally holds between sleep and care. Hence, if I am sensible, I will not be uttering that sentence with the claim that 'knit' literally applies to sleep. Instead I will be using the term *metaphorically.* But what is it to use a term metaphorically? In presenting a brief answer to that question I shall be more or less following the admirable account given by Paul Henle in Chapter 7 of *Language, Thought, and Culture.*[9]

When I use a predicate term metaphorically, or in accordance with some other figure of speech (metonomy, synechdoche, irony, hyperbole, or whatever), I am not turning my back on the meaning(s) that term has in the language. Even though I am not claiming that the term is literally true of the subject in any of those senses, I am not ignoring those senses. On the contrary, I am using the term in one of those senses, though not in the same way as in literal speech. Instead of straightforwardly applying the term in that sense to the subject, I am engaged in the following multi-stage operation. First, I envisage, and "invite" the hearer to envisage, something of the sort to which the term does literally apply. In the case under discussion this would

---

[9] Paul Henle, ed. (Ann Arbor: U of Michigan Press, 1958) The literature on metaphor bristles with controversy. Nevertheless, I believe that there is widespread agreement on the general lines of the following account; and the agreement would be much greater if everyone were to get straight on the language-speech distinction.

be a person repairing a ravelled piece of fabric. Let's call something to which the predicate literally applies an *exemplar*. Needless to say, we will ordinarily be dealing with *envisaged,* rather than actual exemplars. In the metaphorical statement cited earlier, "Russia has dropped an iron curtain across Europe," the exemplar is a person dropping a curtain (a rather unusual one, made of iron) in front of a stage. In "Life's a walking shadow," the exemplar is a shadow cast by a walking man (among other possibilities). Now what the metaphorical statement most basically "says" is that the exemplar can usefully be taken as a "model" of the subject. The hearer is invited to consider the exemplar *as* a model of the subject, as a way of discovering, highlighting, or rendering salient, various features of the subject.

As so far characterized, a metaphorical "statement" does not appear to be making any truth-claim about the subject, other than the implicit claim that it is sufficiently like the exemplar to make the latter a useful model of the former. So long as I am simply *presenting* a model to the hearer for him to use as he sees fit, I am not myself attributing any particular feature to the subject. Now this may sometimes be a complete account of what the speaker is doing; he is simply suggesting a model that has caught his fancy, that feels right to him. But more typically the speaker is concerned to exploit the model in a particular way; he will "have in mind" one or more particular points of remsemblance (between model and subject) that he intends to be attributing to the subject.[10] Thus, to take up an earlier example, when Churchill said "Russia has dropped an iron curtain across Europe," he wasn't just throwing the image of an iron curtain up for grabs, leaving it to his auditors to make of it what they will. He meant to be exploiting the model in a certain way— to assert that Russia has made it almost impossible to exchange information, goods, and persons between her sphere of influence and western Europe.

Thus in the typical metaphorical statement the speaker is "building on" the relevant meaning of his predicate term in two ways. First, he is presenting the sort of thing to which the term literally applies as a model of the subject. Second, he has in mind one or more resemblances between model and subject, and he extracts from these resemblances what he means to be attributing to the subject. In the Churchill quote, the resemblance is the inhibition of communication. In the "knitting" line from Macbeth the resemblance is that the agent is doing something to restore the patient to a sounder condition, one more nearly in accord with what it is "supposed" to be. And these points of resemblance are just what are being attributed to the subject(s).

Note that the speaker is doing this "on his own". Of course the semantic

---

[10] Of course, these "havings in mind" and these intentions can be of all degrees of explictness and articulateness, just as with other thoughts and communicative intentions.

content of the sentence places certain constraints on him, because that is what he has to work with. But within that framework it is "up to him" *whether* he uses the predicate term metaphorically, and, if so, what features of the model he selects for attribution to the subject.[11]

The sharp outlines of this idealized picture will have to be softened in various ways if it is to faithfully depict the often blurred reality of metaphorical speech. Let me just mention the most important qualifications. (A) "Speaker" will have to be taken in an extended sense to include "hearers" as well. For a hearer may himself exploit the model in certain specific ways, and thus endow the statement with a propositional content not foreshadowed in the speaker's intentions; and do this without abandoning the communicative role of hearer. We can handle this by thinking of the hearer as making a metaphorical statement himself. (B) It is not true that propositional content always gets generated "from scratch" with each metaphorical utterance. There are standard, well-known metaphors with standard interpretations, or at least standard cores of interpretations to which variations may be added. Thus if I were to say "Life's a walking shadow," meaning to assert that life is spontaneous and free-swinging, not "tied-down"nor rigid, that would be a strange use of the sentence. I would be violating a sort of convention, even if it is not strictly a semantic rule of the language. We can handle this complexity by thinking of subsequent utterances of the sentence as simply repetitions or quotations of the utterance of some original or standard speaker, who is the source of the standard propositional content. (C) Speaker intentions

---

[11] Here is another way of making this last point. Let's distinguish between *sentence-meaning*—the meaning(s) that a sentence has "in the language", as a compositional function of the meanings of its constituent morphemes, and *speaker-meaning*, what the speaker means in uttering the sentence. We may identify the latter with *what the speaker is saying* (in a sense of 'saying' in which that is not equivalent to what sentence he is uttering), what "illocutionary-act" he is performing. In terms of our previous distinction sentence-meaning belongs to language, while speaker-meaning belongs to speech. With this new distinction, we may say that in literal subject-predicate statements there is a complete coincidence, so far as the predicate is concerned, between sentence-meaning and speaker-meaning. Since what the speaker is *saying* is simply that the subject has the property that is determined by the relevant meaning of the predicate, *what he is saying about the subject* is fully determined by the meaning of the sentence. Whereas in a metaphorical statement about the subject what is said goes beyond sentence-meaning. What we get out of sentence-meaning, for declarative subject-predicate sentences, is the proposition that the property signified by the predicate attaches to the subject; and that is *not* what the speaker is saying in a metaphor. His speech act utilizes and builds on sentence-meaning, but it "goes beyond" that by virtue of his intentions. Hence he is saying more than, as well as less than, what the sentence means. To use a currently fashionable term, the "pragmatics" of the speech situation plays a much larger role in determining the content of metaphorical than of literal statements.

can be of all degrees of explicitness. The speaker need not rehearse to himself in so many words that he intends to be asserting that . . . In certain cases he may not even be able to say, in literal terms, what it is that he is asserting, but be asserting that nonetheless. (This might be elicited by skillful questioning.) What it finally comes down to is what the speaker would take as truth conditions of his utterance when they are presented to him. Of course, as with all such issues, questions can be raised as to whether his later responses to suggested truth conditions accurately reproduce his dispositions at the moment of utterance. But like practically all interesting concepts, the concept of *what a speaker asserted* does not come with fool-proof decision procedures attached.

One might wonder how a speaker communicates what he is asserting in a metaphorical utterance if that is determined by his intentions, since these latter are typically unannounced. The answer is, of course, that this is effected by a variety of contextual cues. It may be that the verbal or non-verbal context of the utterance points to one rather than another way of exploiting the exemplar. It may be that the speaker can assume that any human being, or anyone in this culture, would be struck more by some of the existing similarities than by others. But though it is "public" features of this sort that make metaphorical communication possible, I would resist any temptation to suppose they determine what was being asserted. That is the prerogative of the speaker, and he may or may not be successful in communicating the content so determined.

It may be helpful to append a few notes to this account.

(1) Talk about "metaphorical senses" is encouraged by the fact that many established senses of terms have historically resulted from what were originally metaphorical uses of the term in other senses. Thus one originally spoke metaphorically in referring to something as the "mouth" of a river, the "hood" of an automobile, a "fork" in the road, or "knitting" one's brow. However, when we use such phrases we are applying the terms in senses they have in the language. The metaphor has "died", has "ossified", and has given rise to a new sense. It can be called a "metaphorical sense" but only by reference to its origin. Insofar as there *is* such a sense in the language, we are *not speaking* metaphorically, not using the term metaphorically, when we speak of the hood of a car.

(2) The term 'literal' has picked up a number of adventitious associations in the course of the rough treatment it has received in recent times. I think particularly of 'precise', 'univocal', ' specific', ' factual', 'empirical', and 'ordinary'. However common the conflation, it is simply a confusion to suppose that 'literal', in the historically distinctive sense just set out, implies any of the features just mentioned. Meanings that words have in a language can be more or less vague, open-textured, unspecific, and indeterminate in a variety of ways. Hence I can be using words literally and still be speaking vaguely, ambiguously, or unspecifically. Again, I can be using my words

just as literally in asking questions, cursing fate, or expressing rage, as in soberly asserting that the cat is on the mat. The conflation of 'literal' with 'empirical' on the other hand, is something more than a vulgar error; it reflects a basic issue in the philosophy of language as to the conditions under which a word can acquire a meaning in the language. If this requires contact with "experience" in one or another of the ways spelled out in empiricist theories of meaning, then only terms with "empirical" meanings can be used literally, for only such terms *have* established senses. But that doesn't follow just from the meaning of the term 'literal'; it also requires an empiricist theory of meaning, and it is by no means clear that any such theory is acceptable.

(3) The other side of this last coin is that various theorists, such as Cassirer, Langer, and Wheelwright, have fallen into speaking of an original "metaphorical" use of language that is distinguished from what Wheelwright calls the "steno" language of science by its "plurisignification", "lack of precision", etc. But this has nothing to do with the metaphorical, as contrasted with literal, use of words. Put unconfusedly, the thesis is that the further back one goes in the development of a language the less precise, specific, etc., the meanings of words are, and the less possible it is to make sharp distinctions between different meanings of a term. In asking about the possibility of irreducible metaphors in theology we will not be asking whether it is possible to speak of God imprecisely, unspecifically, etc. That, obviously, is all too possible.

III

With this background we may turn to our central problem concerning the possibility and status of irreducible metaphors in theology. A metaphor is irreducible if what it says cannot be said, even in part, in literal terms. How we answer our central question will depend, *inter alia,* on how we pick out *what is said* in a metaphorical utterance. So a word on this is in order.

There are, no doubt, various ways of drawing a distinction between *what is said, how* it is said, and other aspects of what is *done* in a speech act. Our way of drawing these distinctions is dictated by the fact that we are interested specifically in the use of metaphors to attribute properties to subjects, with an attached "truth-claim", the claim that the property in question does indeed belong to the subject in question. Hence the "what-is-said" on which we will concentrate is the proposition(s) *asserted* in an utterance, those propositions the speaker is claiming to be true. When we ask whether what is said in a metaphor can be said in literal terms, we are asking whether the *propositional* content of the metaphorical statement can be literally expressed. This is by no means the whole story about a metaphorical statement. As we have seen, a speaker makes a metaphorical statement by using the literal meaning of his predicate to present a model of the subject. Now, by definition, that *way* of asserting a certain proposition cannot be reproduced in a literal utterance; any assertion done that way is, by definition, a metaphorical assertion. And any feature that attaches to a metaphorical statement by virtue of this distinctive mode of statement will likewise fail to survive transposition to the literal mode. Thus it is often pointed out that metaphorical statement is characterized by a certain "open-endedness". However definite an attribution the speaker means to be making via his model, he is also *presenting* the model as a source of hitherto unnoticed insights into the nature of the subject. And so metaphorical statements always have what might (metaphorically) be called a penumbra of inexplicit suggestions that surround whatever definite propositional content is present. Again, this cannot be captured in a literal re-statement. Even if we explicitly assert in literal terms *that* the model may be indefinitely rich in insights into the subject, that is not the same as *presenting* the model with the implied suggestion of untapped resources. Thus we are not asking whether metaphors can receive exact or exhaustive literal paraphrases, as that question has often been understood in the literature.

Moreover we are not even asking whether the propositional content can be exactly or exhaustively expressed in literal terms. It may be, e.g., that the "open-endedness" alluded to in the last paragraph affects the propositional content of a metaphorical statement. It may be that in a metaphorical statement there is no sharp line between what is being asserted and what is only more or less explicitly suggested, so that propositions asserted metaphorically possess a kind of fuzzy boundary that is not shared by propositions expressed literally. But even if that is so it would not prevent the propositional content from being partially expressed in literal terms. Remember that our concern is with the idea that, since no predicates can be literally true of God, God can be spoken of only in metaphors that are wholly irreducible. Our question is, then, whether there can be a metaphorical statement the propositional content of which cannot be expressed, even in part, in literal terms.

In tackling this question it will be useful to consider separately the two strata of truth claims we have found to be contained in metaphors. First, there is the very *unspecific* claim that the exemplar is sufficiently similar to the subject, in some way(s) or other, to make the former a useful model of the latter. (Call this M-similarity.) Second, there is, normally, some more *specific* attribution that is derived from one or more particular points of resemblance.

The first level can be handled very quickly. There is obviously no difficulty in literally applying the predicate 'M-similar' to any pair of entities whatever. Moreover this predicate will be literally true of the exemplar and subject whenever the metaphorical statement is true, or, indeed, whenever the metaphor is successful or appropriate in any way.[12] Thus the literal expressibility of that much of the propositional content unquestionably holds for any metaphorical statement whatever. This gives us a "floor" of guaranteed literal paraphrasability that cannot be gainsaid.

The additional, *specific* propositional content is a more complicated problem. Yet I believe there to be a simple argument that shows that the specific content must, in principle, be expressible in literal terms. Let's restrict ourselves to the predicative part of the propositional content, since we have just been taking for granted the reference to the subject; and let's consider a statement, "God is my rock." Let us say that when a speaker asserts this, the property he means to be attributing to God is P. What would it take to express P in literal terms? There must be some predicate term such that by a literal employment of that term in the frame 'God is _____ ' I can attribute P to God. That is, we need a term that signifies P, so that just by virtue of the term's meaning what it does one can use it to attribute P to some subject. And what does it take for that to be possible? An adequate answer to that question would involve going into the mechanisms by which terms acquire meaning in natural languages—a very murky subject. But at least this much is clear. So long as it is possible for members of the linguistic community to form a concept of P, it will be possible for P to become the meaning of a predicate term in the language. For so long as I can form the concept of P, it will be possible for me to associate an element of the language with P in such a way as to use that element to attribute P to something. How could that be impossible for me to do, so long as I have "cognitive access" to P? And if the property is cognitively accessible to me, then, unless this is by virtue of superhuman powers, it will be, in principle, cognitively accessible to any other normal human being. But if it is conceptually accessible to the language community, there is no bar in principle to a word's signifying the property *in the language*.

And now we are ready for the final turn of the screw. The sufficient

---

[12] If the basic truth claim were only that exemplar and subject are similar in some way or other, then we could say without qualification that it could never fail to succeed. It is *a priori* true that any pair of objects exhibit similarity in indefinitely many respects. Just for starters, each shared non-identity constitutes a point of similarity. But the basic presupposition has a bit more content than that; it stipulates similarity in such a way as to make the one a useful model for the other. It is not clear just what that takes. Presumably the fact that X and Y are both non-identical with Z would not suffice by itself. But since we are often surprised at what ingenious modelers can make of unpromising material, it is not clear that this presupposition cuts out anything that would be allowed by the more unqualified presupposition. Hence it may be that even this presupposition is satisfied by any pair of objects whatever. But I do not feel confident in pushing this point.

condition just uncovered is automatically satisfied whenever a certain property figures in the propositional content of a metaphorical utterance. For, as
we have seen, it cannot so figure unless the speaker has that property in mind
as what he means to be attributing to the subject. And he cannot have the
property in mind without having a concept of that property. No matter in
how inexplicit or inarticulate a fashion he ''has it in mind,'' he will be in
possession of at least an equally inexplicit or inarticulate concept. Therefore
a statement cannot possess a propositional content unless it is, in principle,
possible that a language should contain words that have the meanings required
for the literal expression of that content.

There is one transition in this argument that needs further discussion, viz.,
the step from ''it is possible for members of the linguistic community to form
a concept of P'' to ''it is possible for P to become the meaning of a predicate
term in the language''. The problem is this. What if, although each member
of the community can acquire the concept of P and some or all do, still there
is, in principle, no way of sharing this concept, no way of telling whether
what I call my concept of P is the same, even in part, as what you call your
concept of P. In that case, though one could coin a term for P for one's
private use, it would not be possible to introduce a term for P into a public,
socially shared language, usable for interpersonal communication. Furthermore it may seem that this is a real possibility for talk about God. I might
develop a certain concept on the basis of my experience of God, and so with
you. But how can we compare our experiences and thereby determine the
degree of overlap of our concepts?

It would be tempting, at this point, to fall back on the Wittgensteinian
''private-language argument'', which is designed to show that what was just
presented as a possibility is not possible. From that standpoint I can linguistically express a certain concept only if it is in principle possible that other
people should realize what concept I am expressing. However, since I don't
regard Wittgenstein's argument as compelling, I cannot take this way out.
What is needed here is an investigation of the features of religious thought,
activity, and experience within religious communities that make it possible
to share common theological concepts. There is no time for that in this paper.
(For some suggestions see my ''How To Talk Literally About God'', un-
published.) For purposes of this paper I will have to ask that you take it for
granted that whatever factors are generally available for disseminating socially shared meanings in religious communities are also available for establishing new meanings of terms out of originally metaphorical uses.

It may be thought that we have made our job too easy. ''You have secured
this conclusion only by making the standards for meaning-acquisition too
loose. What if the property in question is one that is not open to our experience, or has to do with another realm of being that is radically beyond our
ken, or. . . .'' But this is not to the point. Our argument assumes nothing
as to what is or is not within our experience or our ken. The point is that

whatever restrictions there are on meanings of predicate terms, they will follow from corresponding restrictions on concepts. If certain features of the world cannot be literally represented in language because they cannot be experienced by us, that will be because their unexperiencability prevents us from forming a conception of them. So that if *P* really does belong to the propositional content of a metaphorical utterance, it is *conceivable,* and hence can be semantically correlated with a predicate term. And, conversely, if it cannot, it *ipso facto* cannot form part of the propositional content of any utterance.

Let's be clear as to what I do and do not claim to have shown. I have argued that the propositional content of any metaphorical statement issued with a truth-claim is, *in principle,* capable of literal expression, at least in part. It is important to recognize that this does not include the following claims.

(1) "Anyone who makes or understands a metaphorical statement can restate it (at least in part) in literal terms." This is *not* part of my claim. Although the unspecific presupposed claim could easily be literally expressed by any minimally articulate person, the specific content is another matter. A careful examination of our argument on that point will reveal its conclusion to be quite compatible with the possibility that one who makes or grasps the statement may not be in a position to bring off even a lame and inadequate literal version. One may have the property "in mind" in too implicit or intuitive a fashion to know whether any term in the language signifies it, or to explicitly associate it with a new term. Or perhaps the most we can come up with is a paraphrase into other metaphors. The "in principle" possibility for which I have argued may not be a real possibility for anyone at this point, or, perhaps, at any point.

(2) "Literal paraphrasability is a necessary condition of any intelligible metaphorical utterance." My conclusion extends only to metaphorical statements that make *truth-claims.* My thesis does not extend to the case in which the speaker simply puts forward, e.g., kingship as a possible model for God, inviting the hearer to make of it what he can. Here the speaker is making no claim that can be evaluated as true or false, and so my argument does not apply. This may be all that is going on in some metaphorical talk.[13]

---

[13] One may wonder why I would bother to throw out the model if I am prepared to make no claims for it. But this is not to the present point and in *any* event there are various possible answers to the question. I might issue the metaphor just because it seems apt to me. Or I might have been seized by a divine frenzy; I may be the unwitting mouthpiece of the muse of poesy; it may be a post-hypnotic suggestion, or some mad scientist may be manipulating my behavior by remote control.

IV

The argument against irreducibly metaphorical statements has been a completely general one. Let's now apply the results to theology. Of course the direct application is obvious; it is just universal instantiation. If there can be no irreducibly metaphorical statements anywhere there can be none in theology. So this way out is unavailable for one who denies the possibility of literal predication. But let us not be too hasty. The distinction between two levels of propositional content may give our quarry some room for maneuver. In particular, we might imagine an opponent of literal predication attempting to construct the following half-way house.

"Let's grant that in order to have any metaphorical truth-claim at all, one must at least be presupposing that the exemplar is like the subject in some significant way(s); and your point that at least this presupposition can be literally expressed is an undeniable one. Nor is this a trivial point; it does show that the unqualified denial of literal predication cannot be sustained, if we are to talk of God even metaphorically. But that denial never was (should have been) issued in so unqualified a form. What we anti-literalists are really concerned about is not those abstract, "structural" predicates like (*significantly*) *similar in some way or other,* but specific predicates like *wise, loving, makes, forgives, commands,* and so on. Therefore if we can make the denial of specific[14] literal predicability stick, we will have gotten what we were after. For in that case it will be impossible to say, literally, what God is like, what He has planned, done, what He would have us do, and so on. We deniers of literal predication will be only minimally shaken by having to admit that God is, literally, *significantly like a king in some way or other.* Again, we will admit that you have shown that if we issue a metaphor with some specific property "in mind" as the one we mean to be attributing to God, then it is in principle, possible to make that attribution in literal terms. Since we are operating within these constraints, the way out is to construe theological statements as limited to the unspecific claim, as far as "propositional content" is concerned. So when one says "God gave me courage to face that situation," he is to be interpreted as simply putting forward the model of one human being encouraging another, with only the unspecific claim that this is sufficiently similar to God's relation to my being encouraged, to be usefully employed as a model thereof. There is no further claim of some particular point of similarity, P. The speaker is simply suggesting that we think of the matter in terms of that model. And hence the assertion

---

[14] It is incumbent on our opponent to say something by way of indicating *how* specific a predicate must be to fall under the ban. But let that pass.

need be literally paraphrasable only so far as the totally unspecific claim is concerned.

This is pretty much what I take to be I. M. Crombie's position, with the extra fillip that we accept these models on the authority of Christ, even though we are unable to interpret them ourselves.[15]

In discussing this attempt at a mediating position, I am going to (1) bring out unacceptable features, features that would be unacceptable to all or most theologians, and (2) suggest that even its proponents do not, in practice, stick to it. These points are not unrelated.

Metaphorical statements about God that are restricted to the *unspecific* truth-claim will suffer from a number of disabilities that render them unfit for theological duty.

(A) Since virtually any such statement will be true, the theological attributions we like will enjoy this status only at the price of sharing it with indefinitely many statements we do not like. Perhaps we can best appreciate this point by starting from the weaker but more clearcut presupposition of *some similarity or other between exemplar and model*. As noted above, since it is *a priori* true that any two entities are similar in indefinitely many respects, if that were all that were being claimed in a statement about God, all such statements would be true alike; it would be just as true, true in the same way, that God is cruel as that God is merciful, just as true that God is a spider, a mud-pie, or a thief as that God is the creator of heaven and earth and that He has reconciled us to Himself. To be sure, the presupposition with which we are working is not as empty as that; it involves the more specific claim that the exemplar is *M-similar* to God, similar in some way(s) that renders it suitable to be used as a model. But since the force of this further restriction is so difficult to assess, we are in a similar position. Though I cannot claim it is *a priori* true that God is M-similar to anything whatever, it is difficult to be confident, with respect to any proferred exemplar, that it is not M-similar to God. The standard way of testing a putative model is by attempting to elaborate it, to spell out the respects in which it is fitted to function as a model. This enterprise is complicated, on the pan-metaphoricist approach, by the fact that all the elaboration will have to be done in metaphorical terms, each of which is subject to the same challenge. Needless to say, this makes it much more difficult to be sure that a given model *doesn't* work. But waiving that difficulty, I will just note that it seems plausible to suppose that, with sufficient ingenuity, virtually any metaphorical predicate

---

[15] See his contribution to "Theology and Falsification" in *New Essays in Philosophical Theology,* ed. Antony Flew & Alasdair Macintyre (London: SCM Press Ltd., 1955), and his "The Possibility of Theological Statements" in *Faith and Logic,* ed. Basil Mitchell (London: George Allen & Unwin Ltd., 1957).

can be elaborated in a theologically plausible way. Thus God is a spider in the sense that He weaves the web of our lives; God is an apple in that we find at the core of His nature the seeds of truth; and so on. Now what I take to be unacceptable theologically is not that God can metaphorically be said to be a spider or an apple, but that these statements are on a par with statements like "God created the heavens and the earth" and "God commanded us to love one another." Not that the position under consideration is unable to make *any* distinction between these groups of statements; it can recognize that those in the latter group are more effective in evoking desired emotional and practical responses, more in line with the ecclesiastical tradition, involve exemplars that are experienced as sacred, and so on. But what this position is debarred from claiming is that these groups of statements differ in truthvalue. The members of our favored group do not correspond to the way things are any better or in any different way than do the innumerably many statements in the less favored group.

(B) The logical relations in which a theological statement stands with other statements (theological and otherwise) are determined by their propositional contents, i.e., on this position, by the unspecific presupposition. And that content fails to stand in the desired logical relations. First consider contradictoriness. For the same reasons that led us to suppose that virtually any statement about God will turn out to be true, we will also be forced to recognize that a given statement about God will be logically incompatible with virtually no other statements about God. "God is loving and merciful" does not logically exclude "God is arbitarily cruel and bloodthirsty." For the fact that a loving and merciful human being is a suitable model for God certainly does not *logically* exclude the possibility that an arbitarily cruel and bloodthirsty human being is a suitable model for God (in some respect or other). Not even straight contradiction works. The fact that human wisdom is a suitable model for God does not *logically* prevent the lack of wisdom (the holy fool) from being a suitable model. Thus "God is wise" is logically compatible with "God is not wise."

(C) Nor does logical entailment fare better. Consider the following apparently unexceptionable argument.

1. A perfectly loving being will forgive the sins of the truly repentant.
2. God is perfectly loving.
3. Therefore God will forgive the sins of the truly repentant.

Surprisingly enough, on the position under consideration one does not fall into contradiction by affirming the premises and denying the conclusion. For even granting the literal truth of the first premise, it is certainly *logically* possible that both a perfectly loving human being and an unforgiving human being are useful models of God, in some respect(s) or other. Thus we must abandon all hope of inferring theological propositions from other propositions, theological or otherwise, or of rejecting some theological propositions because they contradict others; in short, any hope of logically systematizing theology in any way whatever.

(D) One class of putative consequences of theology that is of particular interest to many religious people comprises predictions of the future course of the world, human life, or of this or that human life. I believe that it is universally acknowledged by thoughtful religious people in our society today that no very specific predictions can be derived from theology, in however full-blooded a way it be understood. We cannot infer from Christian theology that Joan will recover from her illness, that democracy will triumph in Africa, or that the church will greatly increase in numbers over the next fifty years. Nevertheless it is widely supposed by traditional Christians that predictions of a less specific sort can be derived—e.g., that the church will prevail on earth (some day), that Christ will return in glory (some time), that either some or all human beings will enjoy eternal blessedness in the knowledge and love of God. These consequences are supposed to follow from premises like the following:

1. It is God's purpose that. . .
2. God's purposes are unchanging.
3. God is able to carry out any purpose.

But clearly from the fact that God is M-similar to a human being that unvaryingly has a certain purpose he is able to carry out, it does not follow that this purpose *will* be carried out. For the respect(s) in which God is like such a person may not be such as to have anything to do with the actual course of events. That gap in the argument could be filled only by spelling out the points of similarity (and their being of the right sort). But this we are debarred from doing.

(E) Predictions of the future course of events are viewed as unworthy by some of our more advanced religious thinkers. However even thinkers of this degree of advancement are likely to set great store by another class of consequences, practical consequences concerning how we ought to act and feel, or what attitudes we should have. But these fare no better. The proposition that God is M-similar to a human being who commands us to love one another or to refrain from commiting adultery, provides us absolutely no ground for loving one another or refraining from adultery, until that proposition makes more specific in what way God is like a human being who has issued such commands. Pending some clarification on that point, it is completely up in the air whether God is like the human issuer of injunctions in a way that is relevant to the question of what we ought to do.

I take it that these consequences are radically unacceptable to the "religious attitude", or to speak less pretentiously, to the bulk of those in the mainstream of the Judeo-Christian tradition. A theology the propositions of which are logically compatible with anything else sayable of God, which can be true only in the same way virtually anything one might say of God is true, which have no determinate consequences either for theory or for practice, so eviscerated a theology is stripped of virtually all its impact for human life.

Now for a consideration of what happens when those who begin taking a tough pan-symbolist or pan-metaphoricist line come to the actual working out of details. My observation is that in the crunch they either give up the idea that theological statements provide a true insight into the nature of things, or they, in effect, relax the ban on literal predication, or sometimes, I am sorry to say, both. Let me document this judgment by a brief look at two cases.

The first reluctant witness for the prosecution is Paul Tillich. Tillich does not fall squarely within the scope of this paper, for his view does not represent theological statements as making truth claims about God. But Tillich does not really stick to this, and that is why he must be counted among those who inconsistently combine both of the moves just mentioned. On the one hand, the official line (to fill out Tillich's often inchoate remarks in what seems to be the most natural way) is that theological predicates get that status by virtue of the fact that they literally denote "places" in the natural world at which Being-Itself is encountered. Thus what a theological statement does is to direct us to something through which the Ultimate can be experienced. On this interpretation the theological statement tells us nothing of what the Ultimate is like or what it "does". But Tillich is not satisfied with this; he wants his theology to come closer than that to satisfying the traditional requirements of theology. Therefore he sets himself to tell us, in terms of his ontology, what religious symbols really *mean,* what is being said about the Ultimate in theology. And so we get statements like the following:

> Divine will and intellect are symbols for dynamics in all its manifestations and for form as the meaningful structure of being-itself.[16]

> If we call God the 'living God' we assert that He is the eternal process in which separation is posited and overcome by reunion.[17]

> Providence is the divine condition which is present in every group of finite conditions and in the totality of finite conditions. . . . It is the quality of inner directedness in every situation.[18]

This sounds like just the sort of thing we are familiar with from Hegel and others, viz., using the more abstract language of ontology to say in literal

---

[16] *Systematic Theology* (London: Nisbet & Co., Ltd.: 1953), Vol. I, p. 274.
[17] *Ibid.,* p. 268.
[18] *Ibid.,* p. 296.

terms what is said metaphorically in religious language. If this is not what is intended, I do not see what Tillich can mean by the claim that he is telling us how to "interpret" religious symbols—telling us what they mean. Thus in the attempt to give theological utterances a more determinate propositional content, Tillich, in effect, revokes his ban on literal predication.

Second, let's take a look at I. M. Crombie, a thinker who represents more unambiguously the kind of pan-metaphoricism I have been discussing. Crombie is quite clear that the terms we apply to God are not literally true of Him,[19] but that we have it on authority (in central cases, the authority of Christ) that there is an underlying analogy between God and the things to which the terms literally apply,[20] though we are not in a position to say, or to know, what the analogy is.[21] Since we are assured that there is an underlying analogy we can justifiably apply the terms to God metaphorically (Crombie does not use the term 'metaphor', but he is obviously employing the concept), and in doing so we are enunciating fundamental truths about God, though we don't know just what truths these are.[22]

Crombie's apostasy is not so blatant as Tillich's. I have not caught Crombie with his finger in the jam-pot of literal metaphysical interpretation. His lapse comes in the form of insisting on implications from theological statements, both theoretical and practical. On the one hand, he insists that our beliefs about God do have implications for the future course of events, albeit of a very indefinite sort. Thus he holds that "suffering which was utterly, eternally, and irredeemably pointless" would count decisively against the assertion that God is merciful,[23] which means that that assertion implies that there is no suffering that is utterly, eternally and irredeemably pointless. He also refers in this connection to looking "for the resurrection of the dead, and the life of the world to come."[24] Again, he recognizes that theological principles function as a guide to conduct, that they mark out certain kinds of reactions as appropriate, others as inappropriate. Thus the parable of the prodigal son

---

[19] *New Essays,* p. 122; *Faith and Logic,* pp. 43, 70.

[20] *New Essays,* pp. 119, 122-3, 127; *Faith and Logic,* p. 70.

[21] *New Essays,* pp. 122, 127, 128; *Faith and Logic,* pp. 70, 71.

[22] Although I am reading Crombie as a pan-metaphoricist, he is susceptible of an interestingly different reading according to which theological metaphors can be literally paraphrased, though not by mere mortals. That is, we might think of Christ, who, according to Crombie, guarantees that the models he provides for us are suitable models, as being able to spell out the crucial similarities in literal terms. This, then, would be an extension of the familiar situation in which a poet uses a metaphor with some definite intention in mind that he could express literally, but where none of his readers could do so, though some of them are "grasped" by the metaphor.

[23] *New Essays,* p. 124.

[24] *Ibid.,* p. 129.

teaches us that "whenever we come to ourselves and return to God, he will come to meet us."[25]. But clearly, for reasons of the sort I have already rehearsed, theological statements will not have implications, even of that degree of determinacy, unless their propositional content is made more specific than just—some unspecified likeness between God and the exemplar. More specifically, if Crombie takes the proposition "God is merciful" to have consequences like those just noted, he must be ascribing a more definite content to that proposition, he must be supposing himself to have some grasp of the respects in which God is similar to a merciful human being, whether or not he has *said,* or even thought explicitly, what he takes those similarities to be. And so once more we see that the burden of making a pan-metaphoricist theology function like a theology has proved too much for the theologian.

V

The main upshot of this paper is that though irreducible metaphors seem to promise a way of combining the denial of any literal predication in theology with the preservation of significant theological truth claims, this fair promise dissipates on scrutiny like mist before the morning sun. Either the pan-metaphoricist abandons the aspiration to significant truth-claims or he revokes the ban on literal predicability. He cannot have both. Which way he should jump depends, *inter alia,* on the prospects for true literal predication in theology.

If I may be allowed such irresponsibility as to merely toss out a possibly outrageous, and hopefully tantalizing, suggestion, I would submit that what pan-metaphoricists like Crombie really need in order to satisfy their (generally commendable) aspirations is something *more* like the Thomistic account of theological predication. What is suggested to me by St. Thomas (and I cannot go into the question of how close this is to his intentions) is that God really (literally) knows, wills, loves, and performs actions. Though the details must differ enormously from human knowledge, will, love, and action, nevertheless when we make our terms sufficiently abstract they do apply literally both to man and God. But we cannot see *how* this is possible. We can be assured that God does will and love, but we cannot see how. Such a doctrine, in my opinion, does a much more adequate job of walking the tightrope between anthropomorphism and agnosticism that constitutes our mission.

University of Illinois at Urbana-Champaign

---

[25] *Ibid.,* p. 127.

11 NEGATIVE THEOLOGY AND AFFIRMATION OF THE FINITE

Louis Dupré

That no predicates can be univocally attributed to God and the creature, is a principle on which all theologians agree. The issue which divides them is whether the negation of the inherently finite leaves room for an ultimate affirmation. Classical Hinduism and Buddhism have mostly denied that it does. Islam, Judaism and Christianity, on the contrary, have attempted to incorporate the negation within a new and definitive affirmation. Yet even here *apophatic* trends have always existed. In mystical writings the denial that positive attributes can be predicated of God reflects an actual inability to express a direct and intensive experience of the divine presence in positive language. In speculative theology the denial results as a logical conclusion from the presumed inadequacy of relative language to absolute Being. I shall concern myself primarily with the former, though the problems and solutions, if there be any, must in the end be identical in the two theologies. Their fundamental objection to any new affirmation, such as the one commonly implied in the analogy of Being, is that no qualification can ever overcome the inherent finitude of predicates which, by their very nature, are conceived for expressing the nature of a finite universe. When dealing with the Absolute one seldom reaches solutions by compromises.

Yet the objections against negative theology are equally formidable. Since negation alone never attains reality, either we inconsistently ascribe positive attributes to God, or we must settle for a total agnosticism. Such an agnosticism would jeopardize religious practice as much as religious theory: if God is totally unknown, prayer and the entire religious attitude becomes meaningless. Man has nothing to say to a God who remains beyond all determination. If we can assert nothing *about* God, we can say nothing to Him— and that marks the end of religion. It is a conclusion that not only mystics should ponder, but also fideists—including those of the modern, Wittgensteinian variety.

Negative theologians will reply that the attributes are negated, but the ascending movement is not and, in fact, gains its momentum precisely from the unceasing negation. This is true, but the movement itself leads nowhere

149

unless in the end *the negation itself be negated*. In the following pages I shall attempt to show how such a final negation entails in fact a new affirmation of the finite *within* the infinite and consequently a new kind of analogy. Spinoza's philosophy here proves to be particularly instructive. From the principle that determination implies negation, the Dutch philosopher concludes that the absolute substance must be beyond all determinations. But he should have gone further and shown how the absolute nevertheless *includes* all determination. Otherwise he is bound to find himself unable to introduce determination at all. It is only by an inconsistency that his system realizes the transition from the infinite substance to the finite modes. The same happens to negative theology: once its negative movement reaches the One Absolute, it merely stops. Yet the Absolute thus attained is an empty indeterminate, unable to justify the determinate being which supposedly proceeded from it and continues to depend on it. A consistent negative theology reduces the creation (or emanation) to an intrinsically unintelligible event and excludes the possibility of any kind of revelation of the divine nature. It must be admitted that some of the early Neoplatonist mystics appear to have been satisfied with the affirmation of a dark void mysteriously present to them in the spiritual experience. But, by and large, Christian mystics, even in the Neoplatonic tradition, have followed a different path. Their God is essentially a *manifest* one even though none of our names adequately describes him. After having declared God beyond predication, they perform an even more radical negation in a final attempt to overcome human limitation altogether and to pass from the dark of unknowing to the light of self-manifestation. Finding the finite incommensurate to God's Being, the mystic ultimately abandons even his right to judge the finite on his own (also finite) terms and asserts its divine, immanent reality. He thus reaffirms the finite, not by qualifying his original affirmation, but by radicalizing its negation so as to include negation itself and by allowing the divine affirmation to shine forth in its own right. The finite is reaffirmed as God asserts it in the identity of his own creative act, *not as it appears* in the opposition of its creaturehood.

> Divine transcendence ceases to mean negation of the creature, and instead becomes its elevation. Transcendence is no longer found *above* creation, but *in* creation. The creature is *in* God and God is *in* the creature. It is as *creature* and not only as uncreated essence that the creature manifests transcendence: God is the ultimate dimension of the finite reality, the inaccessible in the accessible.[1]

The concept of transcendence must itself be transcended and the final word

---

[1] *The Other Dimension* (New York: Seabury, 1979), pp. 524-25.

about God is not absolute otherness but total identity. As George Morel admirably put it, "Man is not only creature, God is not only Creator."[2] It is this attitude which Ignatius of Loyola expresses in the last contemplation of his *Spiritual Exercises* when inviting the exercitant who previously has renounced all creatures for God to consider "how God dwells in creatures."[3] This negation of negation also determines the complex and seemingly contradictory dialectic of St. John of the Cross which on one level denies all proportion between God and the creature, while on a different level asserting their full equality.[4] Even Eckhart, so strongly identified with the Neoplatonic tradition, does not conclude his ascent with the unknowable and merely negative One of Proclus and Pseudo-Dionysius. He does negate all *similarity* between God's *isness* and the creature's being, since likeness can exist only between the creature and God's *manifestation,* not between the manifest and the unmanifest one. Still his negation of all restricted being (and all being is restricted for Eckhart) ultimately results in a principle that includes all affirmations without excluding any one of them. Yet the presence of the ultimate in the finite does not consist in a *likeness,* such as exists between cause and effect, but in the identity of being beneath the essential dissimilarity.

What in the analogy from the creature to God was "likeness" within dissimilarity becomes a sign of identity within distinctness in the analogy from God to the creature. In the latter analogy the degrees of perfection play no part. Eckhart writes: "God is neither good, better nor best." A recent interpreter in English comments: "It is not that God is *more* perfect; there is no 'more or less' in the All-inclusive."[5] Eckhart himself emphatically declares:

Creatures [by themselves] are pure nothings. I do not say that they are either important or unimportant but that they are pure nothings. What has no isness [of and by itself] is nothing. Creatures have no isness of their own, for their isness is the presence of God.[6]

---

[2] *Le sens de l'existence d'après St. Jean de la Croix* (Paris: Aubier, 1960), Vol. II, p. 176.

[3] *The Spiritual Exercises,* trans. Louis Puhl, S.J. (Westminister: Newman Press, 1954), p. 102.

[4] For the former, cf. *Ascent of Mount Carmel* I, 6, 1; II, 8, 3; II, 12, 4; for the latter, *Spiritual Canticle* XV, 2 and numerous other passages.

[5] C. F. Kelley, *Meister Eckhart on Divine Knowledge* (New Haven: Yale University Press, 1977), p. 169. I borrow the expression "inverted analogy" from Kelley.

[6] *Meister Eckhart. Die deutschen Werke,* ed. Joseph Quint, *et al.* (Stuttgart: Kohlhammer, 1938 ff.), Vol. I, pp. 69-70. *Meister Eckhart. A Modern Translation* by Raymond Bernard Blakney (New York: Harper Brothers, 1941 [1957]), p. 185. I changed the term "Being" into "isness" to avoid confusion, since Eckhart declares that God has no being. *Ibid.,* p. 219.

The infinite is present in the finite not through participative likeness, but through identity of principle. The relation from the creature to God is not *ecstatic:* it is *instatic:* God contains all creatures within *his own* unity. Their difference from Him is a merely negative characteristic, a mere limitation of their reality, not that reality itself. "By negating of God something that I assert that he is not—even this negation must go. God is One, he is the negation of negations."[7]

One might object that the preceding discards the well-established tradition of the creature, especially the soul, as image of God. But at the very origin of this tradition we find that the image itself was conceived, not as a likeness but as a presence of, and, ultimately, as an identity with God. To Origen the mind is the image of God precisely insofar as it is the place where the divine Logos resides and it becomes more image as the presence increases. The sensible world presents only signs and shadows to be assumed *and overcome* by the mind. The Platonic ascent from bodily to spiritual knowledge is radically transformed by the immanent presence of the Divine Logos in the soul. While for Plato the Forms reside in the soul, for Origen and the Greek Fathers who adopted his theory of the image of God, the soul at some point actively coincides with the Eternal Logos.

> There is a certain affinity between the mind and God, of whom the mind is an intellectual image, and by reason of this fact the mind, especially if it is separated and purified from bodily matter, is able to have some perception of the divine nature.[8]

The mind resembles God, because it directly *partakes* in divine Nature. Likeness means dynamic presence of the Logos, not mere similarity of structure as in Cajetan's theory of analogy. The Alexandrian and Capadocian Fathers knew both. But they singled out the image of the soul because only the soul reaches a conscious identity. Origen dismisses the similarity between God and the material universe as an inferior likeness. Later Eckhart was to refer to the knowledge of God through the creatures as "the cognition of the evening," in contrast to the matutinal knowledge of God and of the creatures in God. The soul's intrinsic participation in the divine appears even more explicitly in Gregory of Nyssa who, with Augustine, gave the theory of the image its classical expression. To him that the soul is an image of God means that it directly partakes of a divine archetype.

> The eye enjoys the rays of light by virtue of the light which it has in

---

[7] *Eckhart. Die deutschen Werke* I, p. 364, trans. C. F. Kelley, *op. cit.,* p. 170.
[8] *De Primis Principiis* I, 1.7.

itself by nature that it may apprehend the kindred light. . . . The same necessity requires, as regards the participation in God, that in the nature that is to enjoy God there be something kindred to him who is to be partaken of.[9]

Only because the soul partakes in the divine reality, is it able to know God. The mystical life consists in turning more and more in toward "the image," that is, the presence of God in the soul. Significantly Gregory describes this presence as a dark cloud of unknowing, and thereby directly connects the image of God with the negative theology.

We detect a similar trend toward knowledge beyond images in St. Augustine. While in his early *De Quantitate Animae* Augustine attributes to all creatures a likeness of God though inferior to the one possessed by the soul, in the *Confessions* he emphasizes that the soul must turn into itself and leave behind not only all external creatures but even the faculties themselves. God dwells directly only in the soul and there is no proportion between his inner presence and the intimations of likeness in the creatures. The idea that only the mind is a true image of God gained power in the final period of Augustine's writing. In a treatise on contemplative life, the *Commentary on Psalm 41*, he expresses both the inadequacy of the creatures and the need to ascend beyond the self.

For I see the things which my God has made and my God himself I do not see. . . . Having therefore sought to find my God in visible, bodily things and found Him not, having sought to find his substance in myself and found it not, I perceive my God to be higher than my soul. . . . I have poured forth my soul above myself. No longer is there any being for me to touch save my God.[10]

In his own similitude let us seek God: in his own image recognize the Creator.[11]

The self as principle of transcendence must itself be transcended.[12] The soul

---

[9] De Infant, P.G. 46, 113D.

[10] *Enarrat.* in Psalm. 41, 7, P.L. 36, p. 467-9, trans. by Elmer O'Brien in *Varieties of Mystic Experience* (New York: Holt, Rinehart, Winston, 1964), p. 68.

[11] *In Johannis Evangelium*, XXIII, 10, P.L. 35, p. 1588-89.

[12] Sermo CCCXXX, P.L. 38, p. 1457. In Sermon 330 Augustine writes: Return to thyself; but when, again facing upwards, thou hast returned to thyself, stay not in thyself. First return to thyself from the things that are without and then give thyself back to him that made thee.

is an image of God only to the extent that it is related to God and it is related to God by participating in God.

> The true honor of man is the image and likeness of God, which is not preserved save in relation to Him by whom it is impressed. The less therefore he loves what is his own, the more he adheres to God.[13]

The more we know God, the more we love Him and the more we become united with Him. The practice of spiritual life consists not in seeing God in a pre-existing image but in becoming an image through greater unity. "No creature, howsoever rational and intellectual, is lighted of itself, but is lighted by participation of Eternal Truth."[14]

Though religious mysticism always entails an intensive awareness of God's presence in creation, Christian mystics invariably commence their journey by emphasizing the difference (and hence the absence) between God and the creature. Their negative attitude must not be attributed only to practical wisdom but, first and foremost, to an immediate awareness that the creature as such is totally unlike God. For years Newman attempted to explain how through the phenomena of the visible world we gain "an image of God." But more and more he became convinced that only a previous awareness of God's *inner* presence—in conscience—would enable man to detect a divine presence in the world at all. In contrast to this "definite" presence in conscience "the phenomena are as if pictures, but at the same time they give us no exact measure or character of the unknown things beyond them."[15] Man lacks the power to derive an image of God from the cause and system of the world.

> What strikes the mind so forcibly and so painfully, is His absence (if I may so speak) from His own world. It is a silence that speaks. It is as if others had got possession of His work. Why does not He, our Maker and Ruler, give us some immediate knowledge of Himself?[16]

In the moving sermon "Waiting for Christ" this alienation appears even more strongly.

> When he came in the flesh 'He was in the world, and the world was made by Him, and the world knew Him not.' Nor did He strive nor cry, nor lift up His voice in the streets. So it is now. He still is here; He still

---

[13] *De Trinitate* 12, 11, 16. P.L. 42, pp. 1006-7.
[14] *De Trinitate* 14, 14, 18. P.L. 42, 1049-50.
[15] *A Grammar of Assent* (New York: Doubleday, 1958), p. 109.
[16] *Ibid.*, p. 39.

whispers to us, He still makes signs to us. But His voice is too low, and the world's din is so loud, and His signs are so covert, and the world is so restless, that it is difficult to determine when He addresses us, and what He says. Religious men cannot but feel, in various ways, that His providence is guiding them and blessing them personally on the whole; yet when they attempt to put their finger upon the times and places, the traces of His presence disappear. . .[17]

Once again the inner presence must mediate the visible world with its Creator. Whatever divine clarity radiates from the creature is reflected back from the mind's internal light. In this light "things which come before our eyes, in such wise take the form of types and omens of things moral or future, that the spirit within us cannot but reach forward and presage what it is not told from what it sees."[18] The ambiguous signs of the visible world must await the interpretation of the inner voice. God remains "hidden" in a world that does not allow him "to display his glory openly."[19] Like Pascal, Newman concludes that without the "eyes of faith" the mind is unable to recognize God in his creation. Nor is this inner light derived from the mind's reflective powers. Even the voice of conscience becomes the voice of God only to him who knows how to listen to it as to a message originating beyond the self. We are reminded of Augustine's entreaty to move beyond memory and beyond the self.

The more the awareness of God's presence increases, the more the idea of a similarity between God and the creature recedes. The spiritual soul does not look for "God-resembling" creatures. It embraces all beings with equal fervor. Perceiving the divine presence as much in the lowly as in the high, in the bad as in the good, it abandons its preferences for the good and the beautiful in order to seek out an identical presence underneath opposite appearances. Symbols of creation are not analogues of divine attributes: the singing of the nightingale comes no closer to God than the croaking of the frog. Still the absence of picture-likeness does not reduce religious symbols to the status of arbitrary signs. The relation between the religious sign and the divine Signified surpasses in intimacy the one between a picture and its model. For the reality disclosed by the symbol is not an extrinsic one, but *its own:* the finite *intrinsically* participates in the Infinite. Its *specific* nature reveals only God's *outward* (i.e. non-identical) manifestation, not his intimate Being.

Nor does it follow that all creatures are virtually identical as symbols of

---

[17] *Parochial and Plain Sermons* VI, p. 248.

[18] *Ibid.*, p. 249

[19] "The Omnipotence of God the Reason for Faith and Hope," in *Parochial and Plain Sermons.*

the Transcendent. The insurmountable difference between their essential being and the divine reality in no way prevents them from *disclosing* its presence in various and even unequal modes. Hence the particular predisposition of some to become "religious" symbols proper. But this inequality depends on *man's particular openness* to certain signs rather than to others, not on the greater similarity to the divine of the disclosing symbols. Their hierarchy constitutes an anthropological order. Not because their signifying power is purely subjective; that power is real and objective, but it resides in a particular ability to *disclose* a transcendent presence, not in a presumed similarity with that reality. The contrary position makes it hard to understand why a creature of a lower type—e.g. an animal, or a stone—is selected to symbolize the divine in preference to one of a higher type. Symbols privileged with religious significance—such as light, mountains, etc.—are by no means the highest in the hierarchy of being. Man himself owes his unique status as religious symbol, not so much to his elevated rank in being as to his singular *awareness* of the divine presence both in himself and in other beings. To man alone God is present, because he alone lives in a *present*. As the sole interpreter of that presence, he alone mediates the creation with God through his awareness of a divine immanence. Hence the most prominent symbol of the divine has always been the man or woman most intensively aware of its presence.

The thesis argued in the preceding pages should be well distinguished from the position of negative theology and of dialectical theology. Far from denying religious symbols their significant power, I argue that this significance is one of *presence* rather than of similitude. I fully accept not only the possibility of genuinely religious symbols, but even their necessity. Without symbols no religious experience at all would occur, since the experience originates *in* and *through* the symbols. Nor does the power of symbols derive exclusively from individual or communal decisions to single out certain phenomena for special significance. It is true enough that in the major faiths of the West an authoritative "revelation" establishes both the leading symbols and the determining symbolic structures. But such a constitution could not take place if the religious mind were not *by its very nature* symbolic, and selectively so. Even the symbols of a revealed religion do not owe their entire power to the significance given to them by authority but, in an equal measure, to an inherent religious expressiveness. Symbols do not signify because they are thought to be revealed, but they are selected to reveal because they are endowed with a natural significance. Previous to any revelation there exists a religious receptiveness in the mind's very perception of the phenomenal world. To say this is not to minimize the creative impact of the revelatory event, but merely to assert that its structuring and specifying activity is conditioned by the religious symbolizing function of the mind itself.

This conclusion, of course, leaves us with the question: How do phenomena symbolize divine *presence*? It is a question on which the phenomenology of religion has already spent much competent attention, yet for which it has found no satisfactory answer. Yet this much seems clear. Symbols are religious mainly because they convey a powerful, extraordinary *presence*. Theories of the religious experience, from the early "dynamic" ones to Eliade's "ontic" one, all insist on the universality of this awareness of presence. Identical symbols appear in totally unrelated religions because, beyond their specific significations, they are able to manifest a divine presence. Thus phenomena that abruptly distinguish themselves from ordinary being, the high mountain peak, the loud thunderclap, the sudden clearing and, everywhere, the brilliant light, all convey a sense of immediate presence more than they evoke a specific feeling.

To be sure, most of us today live in a bleaker world no longer illuminated by the natural symbols of a sacred presence. If God is still present to secular man at all, He rarely speaks to him with the voice of natural symbols. But that does not necessarily weaken the proposed theory. On the contrary, it appears particularly appropriate to justify the modern attitude toward transcendent Being. For once the sacred has been removed from direct experience, the distinct quality of each phenomenon loses its decisive significance. To men and women forced to find the ultimate religious meaning in themselves or in a limited community of like-minded, rather than in nature or society as a whole, disorder and ugliness provoke as much religious reflection as clarity and harmony. Few reflective believers today would be as shocked in their faith by a natural catastrophe as Voltaire and his contemporaries were by the Lisbon earthquake. In a world that no longer *directly* manifests the divine, the unexpected causes less religious consternation. If man thinks of God at all, it is as a supreme reality that is both omnipresent and unmanifest. Such an attitude refuses to identify the holy one with any single symbol at the exclusion of all others. To be able to believe, our contemporaries must first come to terms with the secular experience of a world in which nothing *appears* God-like. Natural phenomena must pass through inner reflection in order to become religious symbols. Some undoubtedly lend themselves more readily to such a conversion than others, but only because they shock our everyday view of things and thereby more urgently invite reflection, not, or not commonly, because they are exclusive manifestations of God's own nature. Symbols are always needed. But even after he has received them from his religious tradition or personally discovered them, contemporary Western man continues to maintain a distance between his faith and what he knows to be tokens rather than images. Reluctant to view them as "analogous" to the inner presence, to give them a religious significance he has no choice but to invert the analogy from God to the creature and to abandon the analogy of similitude for the analogy of presence. By a strange paradox the secularization of the world has driven him to a higher degree of spiritualization in which he confronts God himself rather than his image.

Yale University

12 NATURAL IMAGERY AS A DISCRIMINATORY ELEMENT IN RELIGIOUS LANGUAGE

Kenneth L. Schmitz

It is sometimes said that nature no longer speaks to us of God, and that it has become increasingly difficult for us to speak of God in terms of natural images and symbols. It is sometimes thought, too, that—in an older and simpler view of the world—God, nature and man stood in easy harmony with each other. It is often supposed that this familiarity has been "done in" by the reasoned assaults of the natural sciences over the past four centuries; so that God is no longer to be found in those dark corners of the world where religious men in their ignorance had once believed Him to lurk. And it is sometimes argued that the sciences have banished God from nature by showing nature to be in a continual process of self-development rather than in an eternal fix ordained by God. According to this widely held view, the once-manifest God of a public world became the God of the "gaps," then passed within to the courts of conscience, thence to the unknown God, and finally absented Himself entirely. Now these understandings may in fact describe the career of certain ideas about God over the past several centuries, especially in the influential but limited circles of some leading intellectual movements. Still, it seems to me that the chain of ideas does not bear close logical scrutiny. Perhaps not much does that carries men persuasively along from one view to another. Nevertheless, ideas loosely put together do not a lasting firmament make; and so a different relation between the ideas of God, man and nature may still be possible. As part of such a relationship I here offer some considerations about the natural element in religious language.

Some adaptation of what follows can be made, I think, to non-biblical religions, and there is no doubt of their importance for a thorough study of the natural element in religious speech. The difficulty of generalization in matters religious is notorious, however, and so I will base my remarks chiefly upon my understanding of the biblical religions.

To begin with, some general remarks need to be made about religious language and its distinction from what I will call discourse.[1] I understand the structure of religious language in a rather traditional way, as having three primary modes of expression within it. (1) A hierophany gives rise to a sacred tradition or text, which is taken to be sacred speech itself, that is, speech sanctioned by the sacred. The prophet proclaims: "Thus saith the Lord. . . ," or Jesus teaches with authority: "But I say to you. . . ." (2) Oriented by this original mode of speech, a community and its individuals respond by invoking the sacred. Prototypical for this second mode is Samuel's reply: "Here I am, since You called me" (I *Sam* 3). Speech to the sacred develops in prayer, liturgy, hymn and meditation. (3) But religious speech does not only invoke; it also implies something about the sacred. This third mode often remains implicit in religious speech, but it may become articulate under challenge, as it does in Christian teaching. Thus the early Christian prayer: "Christ Lord!" is at once both invocation and assertion, acclamation and proclamation. In sum, then, religious speech is the interplay of three modes: *by, to* and *about*. Speech by or sanctioned by the sacred evokes speech addressed to the sacred, and this in turn provides a subject or theme about which assertions can be made.

Speech about the sacred is a mode of expression within religious language itself, but most language about the sacred (including that used in this essay) is not *religious* language; it is *discourse* about religion. The distinction has arisen within language in the following way. A speech community has as its primary members all fluent speakers of the language who live, think and feel primarily by means of the expressive possibilities of the particular language. This *matrix* language is specified as much by future possibilities and past memories as it is by current expression. It takes predominant shape in a so-called *natural* language, often with a standard form and variant dialects; but these determinate forms of the language all fall within the tolerance of the matrix language. Indeed, nothing which violates its minimal conditions can be said or heard in the language. The slow and often unnoticed change in a language is due to the interplay between the structure of the matrix language and the accumulated responses which the speech community brings to its changing life-situation. In addition to the standard and dialect forms, there are colloquial practices, such as slang, patois, etc. Then, too, specialized strains of language evolve which serve the basic enterprises of the members of the speech community. They are technical idioms associated with definite practical interests. *Religious usage,* however, differs from the foregoing. It arises out of the matrix language as a modulation of that language insofar as

---

[1] For an earlier discussion of this and related distinctions, see "The Restitution of Meaning in Religious Speech," *International Journal of the Philosophy of Religion,* vol. v, no. 3, Fall 1974, pp. 131-151, especially pp. 134-136.

it is directed towards the sacred. It can and often does employ technical expressions, but it is not restricted to special interests and can express deep and broad aspects of human life. It stands, therefore, in a more pervasive and fundamental relation with its matrix language than technical idioms do. Religious usage is able to reflect the experience of the speech community in a fundamental and comprehensive speech which interprets the profane in terms of the sacred, the secular in terms of the sacral, the mundane in terms of the ultimate.

I have already remarked parenthetically that the language of this essay is not religious language; neither is it matrix language, technical idiom or religious usage. I have called it *discourse*. Discourse is expressed by statements that assert something to be true or not true about, for example, the sacred and man's relation to it. It is primarily a mode of assertion. It may be descriptive, explanatory or interpretive. Learned speech, such as science, philosophy, theology and history, is discourse. In such theoretical disciplines speech comes to be integrated into a tighter, more systematic and self-conscious order of expression. Discourse is a modification of matrix language which arises out of a theoretical pre-occupation with the conditions of truth, and so with the possibilities of cognition. Discourse organizes matrix language in the interests of definite cognitive ends by means of a more or less explicit theory of truth, criteria of evidence and canons of argumentation. It introduces a more or less definite set of standards which controls what may be said validly in that discourse. The conditions lead back to a theory of cognition that gives to discourse a different sort of selectivity from the openness of religious usage or the relative indeterminacy of matrix language. To be sure, religious usage is often interested in true speech, may even adopt pragmatic tests for reliability, and may appropriate discourse for its own purposes; but it is not interested in a theory of the general conditions of truth as such. Religious usage may appeal to canonical writings, but it is theological discourse that works out a theory of canonicity; religious usage rests upon revealed words, but it is theological discourse that works out a theory of revelation; religious usage may profess faith in God, but philosophical discourse attempts to prove God's existence; religious usage narrates the story of Joshua, but archaelogical discourse expounds the findings at Jericho. A general theory of cognition attempts to determine the conditions for true or meaningful speech; but such a theory does not preside over religious usage. The needs of worship, petition and action preside. Religious usage does not propose to itself a theory about the way in which terms must function in order to achieve cognitive ends. Where pre-occupation with cognition does preside, it gives witness to a distinctive concern: the methodical pursuit of tested, warranted speech that meets the normative conditions for true cognition. Where such a theory determines the limits and selectivity of speech we have discourse; and where it takes up religious themes it is discourse about religion. If it functions within a purpose and context that is primarily religious, it may be viewed as an extension of religious usage. Nevertheless, it derives its intrinsic character from its cognitional interest and not from religious sanction, whether the discourse be theological, philosophical, scholarly or scientific.

Difficulties can arise in discourse about religion from either the religious or the discursive side of the relationship. From the side of religion, some devout persons fear the discursive element within religion, and are even led sometimes to deny it. They point to the tendency of developed articulate discourse to put itself forward as a substitute for the sacred reality of which it claims to speak, and so to mislead believers into a sort of garrulous idolatry. This is a genuine danger that can be met only by an equally genuine religious sensibility. It is the more likely to happen, moreover, if the speech is too self-assured and positive, too easy and familiar, too much at home with the sacred. Quite the opposite difficulty arises, however, if we take the negative element in religious language seriously. For it seems then that we may not be able to affirm anything about the sacred. The greater the sense of transcendence in any religion or religious tradition, the stronger is the insistence that all terms are inadequate. Absolute transcendence condemns all talk of God to absolute inadequacy, so that we are reduced to silence and must face the impossibility of talking about or even to God. Yet this silence to which the religious person may find himself reduced is not the initial silence out of which everyday speech arises; it is the silence out of which a renewed mode of speech will arise, if any does: a deepened religious usage. And speech does arise out of that silence; for the long history of religion shows us that the merely relative and human, sensing its own limitations, still sounds its voice again. The negativity suggests that silence is indispensable for union with the sacred, but the negation does not simply reject speech whole and entire, does not repudiate it indiscriminately; for then speech could go its own way as though it had never encountered the sacred. Instead, the negation returns speech to itself, chastened; for it does not and cannot go its own way, but must proceed under a discipline. No matter how paradoxical, even nonsensical, the speech at first seems to be (as in Zen Buddhist treatises, for example), there is some determinate if unexpressed measure of appropriateness and inappropriateness. Speech about the sacred can never be adequate, for the relative can never express the absolute adequately. All claims to adequacy must be rejected without reservation. But the relative can still speak more or less ineptly about the absolute, so that—and this is the first observation—*there is a discriminating factor at work in religious usage,* sifting the inept from the unacceptable. The factor differs considerably in different religions, but in rejecting some speech about the sacred as inappropriate and selecting other speech as not inappropriate (no matter how inept it may be), the negativity at work in religious usage displays a pre-understanding of the nature of the sacred. The negative that is present in religious speech is not simply negative; it is not a dead-end denial. Indeed, such indiscriminate negation is itself negated, and the negation of such negation is the very act through which discrimination and selection arise within religious speech. Through the denial we receive speech back again,—chastened, still inadequate, but under a constraint that renders it not inappropriate.

Difficulties also arise from the side of discourse. Many biblical religionists agree that all human speech is infinitely inadequate to express the divine glory: the case simply cannot be over-stated. But it can be misstated, and a misstatement can infect the way in which the problem is defined and resolved. Not all theories of human language and cognition are equally open to recognizing the possibility of speech about the transcendent and absolute. Some theories explicitly deny that possibility from the beginning (e.g., Positivism), others find that their beginning has ruled out the possibility *a priori* (e.g., Kantianism). The issue is about the way in which the limitations of human meaning and expression are to be understood; it is the grand topic of the impediments to human speech when it tries to express the sacred. The issue is, above all, about the nature of finitude. Thus, for example, for Kant, human cognition and its language turns back upon itself as upon a closed finitude; whereas for Hegel, the finite finds and eventually preserves its very being as finite in the infinite into which its self-transcendence propels it. For many contemporary thinkers, the *existential* state of so-called "modern" man (a construct taken to be normative by many authors) is closed off from any "direct" apprehension of the sacred. To define the problem and its range of answers on the basis of an existential state, however, is to risk taking the bad finite (that is, the finite as determinative) for the ground and not merely as the starting-point of the enquiry. Whatever the state of some "modern" men, there may still be an *ontological* openness to the sacred in the foundations of the human structure and the natural world. Moreover, such an ontological openness may provide a ground for a speech that,—however much it may be at odds with the existential situation of "modern" men,— is deeply in harmony with the way things truly are.

It is sometimes assumed that the ordinary secular use of language is relatively problem-free because it is a direct expression of a radically closed universe. But not even everyday language signifies its referents in a straightforward manner. There is very little of significance—I would say, nothing at all—that receives direct expression. An elementary communications system might seem to be direct, but even the simplest signs require the system and its presuppositions through which they signify. The struggle for meaning is difficult and begins in humble and obscure regions, far removed from the relative clarity of discourse. Moreover, language feeds off itself, words leech upon other words and phrases, knocking them sideways into metaphors, employing them as approximations, symbols or hints, attracted now by an analogy of meaning, now by a coincidence of sound. The very stuff of language is less syllables than it is flexibles, and its movement is by indirection. The literal meaning of what is said in Scripture, for example, is what is meant in and by the text *(littera),* but there is no literal meaning in the sense of a one to one correspondence and direct expression of what is signified. Now in this regard, the language of Scripture and of religion is not unlike everyday language. The problem of speech about the sacred, then, is not that of opening up a language that is a direct expression of a closed universe, but rather the problem of whether and how we can make intelligible the critical passage of our creaturely terms into signs of the sacred. We can never make it intelligible if we adopt the closed view of language, cognition and finitude. Since that seems unwarranted as a starting-point (in distinction from a possible conclusion) of our enquiry, I will proceed as though the possibility of human speech about the sacred is itself not impossible. It remains, however, to see if we can understand how it might be possible.

Even with such a starting-point, however, it might be objected that religious speech is only a language of invocation, and that it makes no assertions and tells us nothing at all about the one addressed. In a word, religious language does not imply any possibility of discourse at all. To address someone, however, requires an intention and a suitable expressive form; and to be addressed requires the realization of the intention. Now the intention is realized at least minimally when it is accepted in some form by the one addressed, at least by hearing or reading it. Hoping to be heard, the Psalmist cries out: "I seek Your face, Lord!" *(Ps* 26,8). To pray is not like shouting into the wind, for my shouts need not characterize the wind and may merely release me from my mood with a babble of nonsense. Such a shouting is, however, not properly an address at all, except perhaps in form. Perhaps prayers to the sacred are too often mere forms intoned out of habit, formulas that fall short of their professed aim. Still, at their best prayers do address God; or rather, the form of prayer itself proclaims the intention to speak to Him. Just before offering the reader his famous ontological proof for the existence of God, St. Anselm offers a prayer to God Himself.[2] He joins with the Psalmist:

Speak now, my whole heart, speak now to God: 'I seek Your countenance, O Lord, Your countenance I seek.' Come then, Lord my God, teach my heart where and how to seek You, where and how to find You.

Prayers take many forms: in petition, they ask of Him who can give; in despair, of Him who gives justice; in praise, of Him whose glory attracts it;

---

[2] *Proslogion,* c. 1. The translation used with very slight alterations is that by M.J. Charlesworth, ed., in *St. Anselm's Proslogion* (Oxford: Clarendon, 1965), p. 111 with the latin text of Dom F.S. Schmitt, O.S.B. on the facing page.

in love, of Him who is gracious; and in joy, of Him who is blessed. It is important to remember, however, that prayer is not the vain hope of magic; it is not meant to catch God in its net. Genuine prayer has no such assurance. Nevertheless, it may go to some lengths to catch God's "ear." St. Anselm asks further:

> Lord, if You are not present here, where, since You are absent, shall I look for You? On the other hand, if You are everywhere why then, since You are present, do I not see You? But surely You dwell in 'light inaccessible' (I *Tim* vi, 16). And where is this inaccessible light, or how can I approach it? Or who shall lead me and take me into it that I may see You in it?

Yet in calling out, even to this inaccessible light, Anselm seeks access to it:

> Again, by what signs, under what aspect shall I seek You? Never have I seen You, Lord my God, I do not know Your face. What shall he do, most high Lord, what shall this exile do, far away from You as he is? What shall Your servant do, tormented by love of You and yet cast off 'far from Your face?' (*Ps* 1, 13). He yearns to see You and Your countenance is too far away from him. He desires to come close to You, and Your dwelling place is inaccessible; he longs to find You and does not know where You are; he is eager to seek You out and he does not know Your countenance. Lord, You are my God and my Lord, and never have I seen You.

St. Anselm's prayer has both the intention and the expressive form of an address. In his search, he knows at least something about that which remains hidden, and which he has not yet found. So, too, when praise, petition or lament are addressed to someone, they are supported by an at least implicit understanding of who and what that someone is and is not. To change the example: A football fan does not call out to a line-backer about to tackle his opponent: "Softly, gently!" Nor, if the team doctor is probing a player's sensitive muscle to discover the point of injury, does the trainer urge him on with the words: "Rougher! Blitz him!" Both of these are inappropriate because they misunderstand the character of those addressed and their proper functions. And so, this is the second observation: *An address can be appropriate only if it contains within it an implied claim to recognize at least something of the nature and role of the one addressed.* If the claim is mistaken, then the address is inappropriate; but if there is no implied claim at all, the words do not form an address at all. I can, of course, call out to the sacred a proper name or title, even a unique one; but then I must go on to address the sacred with my praise, petition or complaint, and that must be based upon some putative understanding of the possibilities of my relation with the sacred. These possibilities in turn must rest in part at least upon the nature of the sacred. The claim to understand the sacred in some way, then, is always and necessarily implicit in the context of prayer, and often even in the titles that are employed. If I call upon the biblical God as Lord, Father, Judge or ever-faithful Friend, I must select appropriate terms, leaving others aside because they are irrelevant or unsuitable. The biblical Lord, after all, is not thought to be in charge of a petty fief, a transient empire, or even a cosmic region; He is the eternal creator and ruler of the universe. His benefactions include the original gift of life itself and existence, since he is addressed as Father and Maker of all.

To speak at all, of course, is to discriminate among meanings and terms; and to speak to God we must discriminate on some basis of appropriateness, by which certain terms and locutions are simply out of the question, others less inappropriate, and some positively sanctioned. Now the understanding implicit in invocation or prayer is the semantic ground for the discriminating factor at work in religious speech, and is the seed and promise of discourse about the sacred, however hidden, minimal or negative its possibility. What is at issue here is not this or that particular term or assertion, but how it is possible for us to say anything at all about the sacred. Religious speech by and to the sacred is the basis for speech about the sacred. Now religious usage already contains within itself implicit and often explicit assertions about the sacred and its relation to man and the world of nature. Discourse about religion, then, develops as a refinement of the *cognitive* possibilities *already present* in religious usage. Discourse about religion is the actualization of those possibilities in accordance with a more or less explicit theory of cognition.

It is time, perhaps, to recapitulate. The question of the possibility of the use of natural images to talk to and about the sacred led to a distinction between religious usage and discourse. The sense of inadequacy and the negative force in religious speech does not lead to an indiscriminate and total rejection of all speech, but rather to a selective use of some speech as not inappropriate. A theory of discourse that interpreted finitude, cognition and language as radically closed to the sacred would make such a discrimination among speech components unintelligible and impossible. If a closed attitude is the existential state of so-called "modern" man, his *Sitz im Leben,* then the present prospect of talk to and about God is bleak indeed. Nevertheless, the religious practice of talk to and about the sacred still goes on, and draws attention to the possibility of an ontological openness to the sacred that may lie more deeply in man than some present states of mind suggest. Still, it remains to ask, what such an openness to the sacred could be? and this requires us to indicate how it might be articulated in terms of discourse. The minimal form of talk to the sacred is that of invocation. Now an address to the sacred discloses an intention and an expressive form that contain a measure of appropriateness; and this in turn implies a pre-understanding of the sacred, its nature and role, and of man's possibilities with respect to it. In terms of discourse the initial question becomes: What conditions must hold if we are to address God and thereby to imply something about Him? More precisely, if we use natural meanings to disclose the nature of the sacred and of our relations to it, what conditions must hold if these things along with their images and sign-functions are to be used to tell us something about God?

Religious speech is not shaped exclusively by semantic forces, but it is principally so, otherwise it would be a series of accidental utterances. Now, if we return to our initial description of religious usage as speech by, to and about the sacred, we recognize a three-fold dynamic operative in religious speech, for it is constituted by a theological, an anthropological and a cosmological principle. Each of these is the expression of the three realities and ideas that make up the religious world: *theos, anthropos* and *cosmos.* The theological principle is the source of and the authority for speech sanctioned by the sacred. It is, moreover, the principle of theophany that expresses itself in non-linguistic ways as well. Insofar as individual men and groups respond to the sacred initiative, the anthropological principle is the foundation for human feelings, perceptions, conceptions and conduct; this principle, therefore, is the subjective foundation for religious thought and discourse. The cosmological principle is neither sacred initiative nor human response; instead it provides a medium and a context for much of the exchange between God and man. At one time or another, in one image or another, one of the three principles may dominate or be almost absent, but it is the interplay of them that forms the distinctive character of religious speech. And so the initial question, reformulated once again, becomes: How can the cosmological principle be appropriated by and for religious speech?

According to biblical religion, nature is not divine; and so the use of natural imagery has been under a rather cautious restraint, in contrast to the disciplined but more abundant use of it, for example, in Hindu scriptures, art and temple cult. Nevertheless,—and this is the third observation,—*natural imagery is inextricably embedded in the scripture, liturgy, piety and thought of biblical religion,* so that it is indispensable to religious life and expression. It has been used to illuminate certain traditional understandings, such as those of creation, providence and miracles, of Lordship and creaturely dependence, of sin, redemption and divine purpose. Nature has not been taken to be simply the appearance of the divine, nor the realm of pure externality. As mere appearance, it would have no integrity; and as merely external, it would have no depth or interiority. Now the biblical religions have traditionally held to an interiority in nature itself, an inside that leads to a theological presence. The cooperation of nature with God's plan is everywhere in Scripture, and is the obverse of His dominion over it. The Psalmist does not draw back from calling upon the earth to rejoice, the sea to thunder, the fields exult, the woodland trees to cry out, the rivers to clap their hands and the mountains to skip like lambs with joy at the coming presence of God (*Pss* 93:3, 96:11, 97: 1, 114: 5-8). Nor does St. Paul hesitate to speak of the whole creation eagerly waiting and groaning to be set free (*Rom* 8: 18-25); or Clement of Rome to extol the peace that has already settled upon nature with the coming of Christ.[3] The withdrawal over recent centuries of much of scientific and philosophical intelligence from the interiority of nature is not simply a particular change in philosophical position; it is the retreat of discourse from an entire spiritual domain. It is not uncommon today to withdraw all interiority from nature by a process of subjectification that heightens man's own interiority, so that nature can be given an interiority only within the human imagination and for non-discursive purposes. Many are more comfortable today with language drawn directly from human feelings, especially of the "humane" sort. If nature is appealed to, it is often only insofar as it awakens specifically religious moods and dispositions. The withdrawal of much of modern intelligence from the religious and metaphysical interiority of nature tends to reduce religion to its anthropological principle, even to the psyche. It seems to me, on the contrary, that religious speech also needs the cosmological principle and that this requires the recovery of discourse about the sacred in terms of nature.

If we look even casually at the Psalms, without any pretence, — or, for our purpose, any need, — to determine a precise typology of images, or their complex and subtle associations in the original,[4] we find a number of different uses. There is imagery drawn from the human roles of father, judge, owner, king, sleeping hero, warrior, victor, liberator, healer and saviour; from feelings of tenderness and love; and from human actions, for the Lord speaks and listens, blazes forth in anger, smiles, forgives, cures, redeems, renews, gives justice, food and liberty, restores sight, straightens the bent and protects the stranger. There is also imagery drawn from the human sphere but containing natural elements, such as the Lord's face, eyes and ears, mouth and nostrils, arm, hand and fingers. The meanings of these elements do not lie primarily in their physical structures, but in the activities expressed and performed with them. There is imagery, too, from man's association with nature, for the Lord is likened to a citadel, lamb and shepherd. The most frequent image comes from the sphere of nature itself: the Lord is rock. A consuming fire pours from His mouth when He is angry, yet He shows mercy by permitting us to shelter under the shadow of His wings. A detailed interpretation of any of these images would call for the aid of the exegetical disciplines,

---

[3] *Letter to the Corinthians.*

[4] The quotations from Scripture are, for the most part, from *The Jerusalem Bible* (Garden City, New York: Doubleday, 1966), but I have checked other translations as well, along with many commentaries and studies.

especially of form criticism. It must be remembered, therefore, that our present interest is not in particular images, nor in the particular use of an image, but in the general question: How can images communicate any meaning at all about the sacred?

The imagery sketched above shows an interplay of natural, human and divine meanings. Now, natural and human imagery differ, even when the latter includes natural elements. For imagery drawn from the human sphere is shaped by intelligence and will, feeling and emotion. These introduce considerations that transform even the natural elements, sublating them so that they serve a range of meanings wider and deeper than their own specifically natural ones. The physical fury of the storm as a natural event strikes terror in us, not least because we gather it up into all of the consequences that it scatters before and behind it. We take it up into the memory and expectation of other storms, and associate it with other displays of power. The power of the storm so frequently associated with God in the Psalms is transformed still further. The cosmological and anthropological meanings are subordinate to the theological meaning. For the power of the natural event to strike terror in us is a theophany in the Psalms. The storm comes in the wake of the warrior God; its power defends the good and punishes the wicked, so that the storm is part of a moral, or more accurately, a righteous purpose. As such it cleanses and destroys, wreaks vengeance and displays wonderful power. This sublation of natural meanings may situate them in a mythical or historical context. It is found in the New Testament also, which draws upon images from nature and from man's association with it. Thus, Christ is not only shepherd but also lamb, and in early Christian tradition, the ox. He is also bread of life, light of the world, the gate, door and way, and the true vine. C.H. Dodd[5] remarks that the gospel parables show

an inward affinity between the natural order and the spiritual order . . . The Kingdom of God is instrinsically *like* the processes of nature and the daily life of men.

Fully aware of the distinction between God and creatures, the Psalmist and the Evangelists draw from the interiority of nature a certain likeness within that difference.

Indeed, they are acutely aware of the difference. An exegete writes that "the world of El-Elohim was the world of being and power superior to man." In the Psalmist's description of God's association with nature there is a quality

---

[5] *The Parables of the Kingdom*, 3 edn., London 1961, p. 10; cited by C. Stuhlmueller, C.P. in *The Jerome Biblical Commentary*, ed. R.E. Brown, *et al* (Englewood Cliffs, N.J.: Prentice-Hall, 1968), vol. II, p. 138. The point is independent, it seems to me, from the position of "realized eschatology."

of strangeness that evokes awe: His strength holds up the mountains, He rides the clouds, bowls His enemies along like tumbleweed, raises whirlwind and tornado; He calms the sea, and strides across it (though with unseen steps), and in the Exodus parts the waves with His power, so that they withdraw at His presence, or they dry up; He visits the earth and waters the hills. In some imagery the strangeness is completely dominant, though natural and human elements remain to supply the materials: He creates the world, lays the foundations of the universe, makes man, guides and protects or uproots and punishes the nations, forms the very heavens themselves. He holds court in heaven, and indeed, beyond the heavens, for He is the Most High God. The Psalmist borrows from nature to show His glory:

Darkness would not be dark to You, night would be as light as day. (*Ps* 139:12)

Searching to articulate the divine incomprehensibility, he proclaims:

God, how hard it is to grasp Your thoughts! How impossible to count them! I could no more count them than I could the sand, and suppose I could, You would still be with me. (*Ps* 139: 17-18)

The translation is difficult, but the general meaning seems clear. We cannot comprehend God, nor compare our understanding with His. But even if we could grasp God, His mysterious presence[6] would still be with us in all His reality, power and glory. His thoughts are not our thoughts, nor His ways man's (*Is* 55:8). God would still be God and not man. And so, this is the fourth observation: *The use of imagery in biblical religion exhibits at once a relation of likeness between nature and man, on the one hand, and God, on the other; yet also a radical unlikeness.* The measure of the difference,— itself immeasurable,—is God Himself as the fullness of power, presence and glory, of life, understanding and freedom. The Psalmist catches the tension of likeness and unlikeness in an argument cast against those who say that God cannot hear the cries of the victims of injustice or see the wickedness of their persecutors:

Is the inventor of the ear unable to hear? the creator of the eye unable to see? (*Ps* 94: 8-9)

We recognize the causal ground of the argument: God is Lord of all because

---

[6] Cf. fn.1 in *The Jerusalem Bible*, p. 923: "I should still be conscious of God's presence;" or "I should still be faced with the mystery of God."

He is maker of all, but we also recognize that such a Lord is somehow like His creatures as well as unlike them.

In a similar vein, God is likened to a potter working with clay. Thus, Isaiah asks rhetorically:

Is the potter no better than the clay? Can something that was made say of its maker, "He did not make me?" Or a pot say of the potter, "He is a fool?" (*Is* 29:16, cf. 45:9-10)

And later, it is written:

We the clay, You the potter, we are all the work of Your hand. (*Is* 64: 7-8)

Jeremiah takes us to a potter's shop for the same effect: the potter can smash the pots he is displeased with (*Jer* 18: 1-17, cf. 1: 4-10). And St. Paul interprets the imagery:

The pot has no right to say to the potter: "Why did you make me in this shape?" Surely a potter can do what he likes with the clay? (*Rom* 9: 19-21)

It is important to take the imagery as a whole: God is *as* a potter, man *as* the clay. The imagery says nothing simply about man and clay or about God and potter. It does not entitle us to draw traits from the clay taken as it is outside of the relation of molding. It is not an analogy of terms considered in isolation, but rather an analogy of proportions (i.e. of relations between terms). The name, "analogy of proportionality" may be risky, however, since it may suggest a likeness between the terms themselves, so that in understanding a proportion of proportions we may think that we also understand the terms as they are in themselves and apart from their relationship.

St. Thomas says that we gain knowledge of God from creatures.[7] We do, but not directly from them alone. We cannot work out the meaning of the pottery analogy simply from them, from below. Rather, we gain knowledge of God from creatures insofar as they stand in relation to a transcendental realm and to a perfect being. For why and how and on what basis would we sift out the relevant meanings of clay, except by some pre-understanding of what was appropriate? The pre-understanding, however, is not simply an

---

[7] *Summa theologiae* I, 1c, but he adds: "and also by way of excellence and re-motion." See *Introduction to St. Thomas Aquinas,* ed., A.C. Pegis (New York: Modern Library, 1948), p. 98.

affirmative measure that separates out some ordinary meanings of pottery and clay from others. Rather, it operates as a standard for a fragile "comparison" that contains the negative character of difference. Insofar as the standard of "comparison" is that of perfect plenitude, the "comparison" rests upon a fundamental and radical diversity. But, first of all, we must look at the likeness-in-difference. Suppose that the clay were caught up in a schoolboy's fight? Its relevant features would not be those of the biblical imagery just cited. They would be instead its capacity to sting and to dirty skin and clothes without serious injury. Not its plastic formability, but rather its capacity to disintegrate on impact would be relevant in that situation. The likeness functioning in the biblical imagery, then, is not an identification of man with clay or of God with potter, for even within the ordinary senses of clay we find a difference among its characteristics. The relevant likeness in the biblical relationship is that of forming agency (molding) to formable material (clay), and of maker (potter) to made (pot). But there is a properly religious difference, too: for every beginning potter knows that in a certain sense clay does "talk back" to its human potter, and "complains" when it is being forced to provide material for an unsuitable design. Certain shapes are best made with certain kinds and consistencies of clay, and it is not entirely absurd to imagine the clay "protesting" against the shape imposed upon it by an inept potter. Not so with God: it is simply absurd for the creature to complain to the creator. So that the analogy fits God and man *better* than it fits potter and clay. The religious author has creamed off an obvious meaning: it is absurd to have the clay protest. But the meaning is reinforced in its religious use: to God not even the "back-talk" just mentioned is possible, since the religious analogy goes beyond the likeness proper to potter and clay to that moment of absolute dependence in the clay, or rather, in the man, upon which his very being depends. We might put the argument thus: If it is absurd for the clay to protest (and it is relatively absurd), then how much more absurd is it for creatures (indeed, absolutely absurd)? Whence this difference? Whence the first difference at the base of the selective appeal to some features (its formability) but not to others (its messiness)? And whence the second difference, the tightening of the fit, the increase in the absurdity of the protest? The selectivity is determined by the religious use to which the imagery is put; and the increase does not come from below, from the clay and the muddy-handed potter, but from above, from a pre-understanding of the sacred. This pre-understanding finds its source in the idea of the Most High God which has been received in biblical theophanies; but it is also available to discursive thought by means of a quite general intuition of the idea of plenitude that has been present in Greek philosophy from its beginnings. It is the theological principle.

With imagery drawn directly from nature, the Psalmist sings out that God has watered the mountain uplands (*Ps* 104:13; cf. 65:9). Now, in what sense is God said to be a hill-waterer? Biblical exegetes correctly remind us that the Israelites placed little emphasis upon creaturely activity and either ignored secondary causality or conflated it with divine causality. Of course, what seems here to be conflation may actually be a seeing of fundamentals. For the Psalmist clearly means more than that God is commander of the weather or a heavenly water supply. It may be that an older stratum of religious understanding lingers from earlier forms of the rain god. But in the attribution to the biblical God these elements are present in a purified and condensed form appropriated by the biblical meaning of God. The appropriateness of the attribution, "hill-waterer," however, must be found in a shift from the imagery of rain and growth to a more comprehensive and original ground. It is the recognition that God is hill-waterer not because He is the divinity in charge of that function but because He is Lord of the universe and all that happens in it. He is not God because He waters the hills, but rather, He waters the hills because He is God. At this point the biblical recognition has gone beyond likeness-in-difference and "comparison" to a radical diversity. Nevertheless, a relation of causal dependence points to a "likeness" that survives the infinite unlikeness between the perfect and the imperfect, the self-subsistent and the dependent, the full and the needy.

In and through the imagery we become aware of a cluster of terms that have especial import: power, presence and life, understanding, freedom and integrity, purpose, responsibility and love. They are less restricted in their import than the specific features of the imagery, more fundamental in their significance, and more central to the meaning intended by the religious use of the imagery. The specific features of the imagery are not unconditionally necessary for the meaning of these terms. This contingency is to be found not only in the specificity of the imagery but also in its very existence. *It need not be*, because the central meanings could still be expressed with other imagery. Nevertheless, the specificity is still conditionally necessary for *that* particular theophany; and so, the whole meaning intended by the religious use of the imagery demands the participation of the specific features in these central meanings. Moreover, it is the same source that grounds both the non-necessity or contingency and also the central meanings themselves. This common grounding introduces a measure of "likeness" between the specific features, the central meanings and their ground. For the particular theophany is not simply indifferent to the specific imagery. What is clear, then, is that the specific features cannot be simply cast aside, since something is meant by hill-watering that is not said by pot-making. Nor is the proliferation of different images for accumulative effect only; it is a corrective multiplicity that keeps the central terms from being imprisoned in the specific features of the images. And indeed, the imagery is over-reached by the transcendental (central) meanings and by the transcendent reality that lies beyond them. The meanings are transcendental because they are shared by creator and creature, as for example, power and presence may be said of each, though differently. The imagery is also surpassed by a transcendent reality whose ultimacy is more comprehensive and intense than the specific elements of the imagery. Something similar happens in the language of love. The lover does not measure the significance of the beloved by the specific terms that describe his or her features, but rather acknowledges them as bearers of a deeper presence. It is the whole person in his or her integrity and glory that is celebrated by the language of love. The bridegroom exults:

How beautiful you are, my love, how beautiful you are! Your eyes . . . your hair . . . your teeth . . . your lips . . . your words enchanting . . . your cheeks . . . your neck . . . your two breasts . . . You are wholly beautiful, my love, and without a blemish. (*Song of Songs* 4: 1-7)

Even more, the idea and the reality of the biblical God surpass both the specific and the transcendental meanings; but they—especially the latter—provide an access to the religious world, so that the imagery is caught up in a shift of attention to the ultimate. If a religious metaphor were permitted, the transcendentals might be called the forecourts of heaven; but in more staid language, they provide discourse with a medium in and through which the sacred may disclose itself. The fifth observation, then, is that *the specific features of the imagery are conditionally necessary for a shift to transcendental meanings that in turn offer a medium in and through which the ultimate reality may be encountered.* The root-symbolisms of the biblical religions, such as the Exodus or the Resurrection, offer such an access. In these symbolisms the natural and conventional sign-elements signify a sacred reality, the ultimate liberating power or the ultimate conquest of death. But they do not signify by their finite qualities alone or even primarily, that is, by sea and flight, or by death and body. Neither do they fail to signify, as though the natural qualities were trapped in their own finitude. They signify insofar as the specific qualities are embedded in and joined to transcendentals that give access to ultimate reality. The natural and conventional sign-elements function insofar as they are connected, immersed, transformed and grounded in the transcendental meanings and in and through them, in the transcendent reality.

Such religious symbolisms contain two kinds of elements: the positive sign-elements and the negative elements that introduce difference and diversity. Efficacious religious symbolisms, such as the Exodus or the Resurrection, are a means of *representing* the fundamental meanings of the religion, but they are also a means of *presenting* the good which the religion offers. For the main intent of such a symbolism is not to depict the sacred by a relation of likeness, or to provide thought with a basis for inference to the sacred. It does not aim at representation or inference primarily, but at transference of the faithful into the presence of the sacred itself. Even if the Psalmist were to reckon up God's thought, God would still be there before him, to be reckoned with.

The sign-elements have natural or conventional meanings. Thus, the blessed water that gives life in baptism also cleanses in ordinary life, cools and slakes thirst; bread consecrated in the eucharist satisfies hunger. There is a likeness between the ordinary uses of water and bread and their sacramental functions. The likeness points us in the direction of the religious meaning, but it does not carry us very far along the way. For the fuller sense of the imagery in the symbolism is not a simple identity between the function of the sign-elements and the thing signified, but rather a transfigured identification between sign and signified. The sign-elements are taken up into a dynamic that is at once a reference and a transference, a signification and an embodiment, a pointing to and a making present of the sacred.

For the relation between the sign-elements and the sacred signified and presented in and through them carries with it a very remote sort of "likeness." It is not the likeness of two individuals within one family, nation, culture, race or species; nor is it the likeness shared by two species within a genus, as fear is somewhat alike in animals and men; nor is it the likeness common to two genera in the same order, as the sun's rays share the common features of the physical order with the greening they bring about in plants. Nor is the likeness between sign-elements and the sacred the likeness between mind and body, spirit and matter; for however unlike they are, they still share the state of being creatures; but God is creator and not creature, ultimate not derived, uncontained in any order.[8] It seems that this "likeness" might better be called utter unlikeness and diversity. For all that, there is a certain "sameness" between creature and creator. The medieval metaphysicians spoke of a formal similitude: Every agent so acts as to produce a likeness to itself. The formula is easily misunderstood. The "likeness" between creator and creature is not a pictorial one; nor is it a likeness in any ordinary meaning of "formal." If we reconsider the greening of the plant by the sun, we will quickly discount any pictorial or even any obvious formal likeness. Nevertheless, there is a communication between them. We know this, because if we remove the sun, the plant whitens and dies. The greening disappears. If the cause fails, the effect fails. The "likeness," then, is an identification by presence, a presencing of the cause to the effect in the moment of causation or throughout it. We have, then, not an analogy of likeness in any ordinary sense of the term, but still an analogy by communication, an analogy of community, for the cause communicates something of itself to the effect. Shall the inventor of the ear not hear? In religious symbolism—and this is the sixth observation—*the imagery is given the function of pointing back to the source of its own specificity and contingency, and to its own presence to that source in a bond of community with it.* This community of presence is

---

[8] The foregoing is a free development of *Summa theologiae* I,4,2c.

the disclosure of the ground of "likeness"-in-difference and of the radical diversity upon which the co-presence depends.

Not everything has been said, of course, if we simply say "identification by presence." For the term "presence" is linguistically indeterminate, and to recover articulation about the sacred we need to discover in the transcendentals, such as power and life, understanding and purpose, the determinate medium for the communication of presence. It has been said that God is equally present to all of His creatures; but from the side of creatures there can be different degrees of presence. The richer the imagery, the more it places before us the medium through which to encounter the sacred. The specificity of the imagery, the multiplicity of the transcendentals and the degrees of presence to the sacred are the means of linguistic discrimination out of which religious speech builds itself. *Some imagery discloses one or another transcendental more clearly or deeply than another; and discrimination within religious speech is brought about by the capacity of an imagery to exhibit the transcendentals and through them to disclose the ultimate and sacred reality.*

Actual religious speech in biblical religions is co-determined by three principles. The negativity, tension, difference and diversity derive above all from the theological principle of plenitude. It is this that led medieval metaphysicians to distinguish between the manner of signifying and the sacred so signified. But the manner of signifying is especially affected by the anthropological principle, the full range of human needs appropriate to religious man within any given culture or situation. Within these two principles, however, the cosmological principle provides an important basis for linguistic discrimination. For nature exhibits features that are taken as stepping stones towards the ontological terms that open out and up towards the Most High God. Religious speech returns again and again to these indispensable carriers of the meaning and reality of the sacred.

Trinity College, University of Toronto

Notes on Contributors

1. William P. Alston, Professor and Chairman, Department of Philosophy, University of Illinois, at Urbana-Champaign. Author of *Philosophy of Language*. Editor and Contributor, *Religious Belief and Philosophical Thought* and others. Contributor to journals and books in Philosophy of Religion, Philosophy of Language, and Philosophy of Psychology.

2. Bowman Clarke, Professor and Chairman, Department of Philosophy, University of Georgia. Author of *Language and Natural Theology*. Contributor to books and journals in Philosophy of Religion and Metaphysics.

3. Frederick Crosson, Professor of Philosophy, University of Notre Dame. Editor, *Human and Artificial Intelligence, Science and Contemporary Society* and others. Contributor to books and journals in Philosophy of Religion, Phenomenology and Existentialism, and Cybernetics.

4. Frank Dilley, Professor and Chairman, Department of Philosophy, University of Delaware. Author of *Metaphysics and Religious Language*. Contributor to journals in Philosophy of Religion and Metaphysics.

5. Louis Dupré, T. Lawrason Professor of Philosophy of Religion, Yale University. Author of many books including *A Dubious Heritage, Transcendent Selfhood, The Other Dimension*. Contributor to journals and books in Philosophy of Religion, Phenomenology and Marxism.

6. Frederick Ferré, Charles A. Dana Professor of Philosophy, Dickinson College. Author of *Language, Logic and God, Exploring the Logic Faith,* and *Basic Modern Philosophy of Religion*. Contributor to books and journals in Philosophy of Religion, Philosophy of Science and Religion and the Environment.

7. Thomas Langan, Professor of Philosophy, University of Toronto. Author of *The Meaning of Heidegger, Merleau-Ponty's Critique of Reason* and co-author of *Modern Philosophy* and *Recent Philosophy*. Contributor to

177

books and journals in Philosophy of History, Philosophy of Religion and Phenomenology.

8. Hywel Lewis, Professor of the History and Philosophy of Religion, Kings College, London. Author of many books including *Our Experience of God, The Elusive Mind,* and *The Self and Immortality.* Contributor to books and journals in Philosophy of Religion and Metaphysics.

9. Eugene Thomas Long, Professor and Chairman, Department of Philosophy, University of South Carolina. Author of *Jaspers and Bultmann.* Editor and contributor, *God, Secularization and History.* Contributor to books and journals in Philosophy of Religion, Phenomenology and Existentialism.

10. John Macquarrie, Lady Margaret Professor of Divinity, Oxford University. Author of many books including *Thinking About God, God-Talk, Principles of Christian Theology,* and *Existentialism.* Contributor to books and journals in Theology, Philosophy of Religion, and Phenomenology and Existentialism.

11. James Ross, Professor of Philosophy, University of Pennsylvania. Author of *Philosophical Theology* and *An Introduction to the Philosophy of Religion.* Contributor to journals and books in the fields of Medieval Philosophy and Philosophy of Religion.

12. Kenneth Schmitz, Professor of Philosophy, University of Toronto. Contributor to many books and journals in Philosophy of Religion, Metaphysics, and Philosophical Anthropology.

13. John Smith, Clark Professor of Philosophy, Yale University. Author of many books including *Purpose and Thought, The Analogy of Experience,* and *Experience and God.* Contributor to journals and books in Philosophy of Religion, American Philosophy and Metaphysics.

INDEX OF NAMES